Rethinking Military History

Rethinking Military History is a bold new 'thought book' that re-positions military history at the beginning of the twenty-first century. Jeremy Black reveals the main trends in the practice and approach to military history and proposes a new manifesto for the subject to move forward.

This must-read study demonstrates the limitations of current approaches including common generalizations, omissions, and over-simplifications. Engaging theoretical discussions, with reference to specific conflicts, suggest how these limitations can be remedied and adapted, whilst incorporating contributions from other disciplines. Additional chapters provide a valuable and concise survey of the main themes in the study of military history from 1500 to the present day.

Rethinking Military History is essential reading for all those with an interest in military history, and all who wish to take part in moving the discipline forward.

Jeremy Black is Professor of History at the University of Exeter. He is editor of the Routledge series *Warfare and History*.

D1565424

Rethinking Military History

Jeremy Black

Routledge
Taylor & Francis Group

LONDON AND NEW YORK

First published 2004
2 Park Square, Milton Park, Abingdon, Oxfordshire, OX14 4RN

Simultaneously published in the USA and Canada
by Routledge
270 Madison Avenue, New York, NY 10016

Routledge is an imprint of the Taylor & Francis Group

© 2004 Jeremy Black

Typeset in Galliard by Steven Gardiner Ltd, Cambridge
Printed and bound in Great Britain by TJ International Ltd,
Padstow, Cornwall

British Library Cataloguing in Publication Data
A catalogue record for this book is available from the British
Library

Library of Congress Cataloging in Publication Data
Black, Jeremy.
Rethinking military history / Jeremy Black.
    p.   cm.
Includes bibliographical references and index.
ISBN 0-415-27534-2 (pbk.) – ISBN 0-415-27533-4 (hardback)
1. Military History, Modern, I. Title
D214.B575 2004
355'.0072'2 – dc22

                                                    2004004908

ISBN 0-415-27533-4 (hbk)
ISBN 0-415-27534-2 (pbk)

For
Mike and Paris Pavković

Contents

Preface

This project sets out to provide a short 'ideas book' designed to re-position military history at the beginning of the twenty-first century. That, of course, is the sort of remark guaranteed to raise every reviewer's ire, but the difficulty of the task should not lead to a slighting of the challenge. The project takes its point of departure not from any criticism of military history, most of which, especially at the operational level, is of high quality, but rather from a disquiet with the dominant emphasis within the theorization, much of it implicit, that characterizes such work. In brief, the following are the major problems, certainly with the state of military history as generally consumed by the public at large:

(a) Eurocentricity, more specifically a focus on Europe, especially Western Europe and North America, or rather, the USA.
(b) A technological bias in explaining military capability, and a fascination with technology in accounting for military developments, more specifically a 'machinization' of war.
(c) A focus on leading powers and dominant military systems, leading to a paradigm/diffusion model of military capability and change.
(d) A separation of land from sea conflict in most of the analysis.
(e) A focus on state-to-state conflict, rather than on the use of force within states. This is qualified in the case of civil wars only when these apparently correspond to state-to-state wars, as, most prominently, with the English and American Civil Wars.
(f) A lack of focus on political 'tasking' in the setting of force structures, doctrines and goals, and in the judging of military success.

This study will draw attention to the limitations of current approaches; offer theoretical discussions (informed by reference to conflict) that suggest how these can be remedied or adapted; and, in trying to deal with history historically, seek, briefly, to sketch out a different approach to military history over the last half-millennium and, more particularly, the last 250 years. There is a determined attempt to take military history up to date, not only with reference to developments in other subjects, for example the increased discussion of cultural factors by scholars of technology, but also with regard to the conflicts that have followed the end of the Cold War and the lessons they offer.

It is important to try to reconstruct military history along lines that are now well established in modern world history and in most national histories. This entails decentring the subject from its modernist, Whiggish Western preoccupations, and its concomitant primitivization of non-Western combatants, and the subject's over-emphasis on advances in military technology, and the changes that these are assumed to have brought. The public tastes and market limitations that continue to keep, at least public, military history battle-centred, and focused on the actions of Britain and the USA, are also a problem. Instead, it is necessary to see military institutions and undertakings in different settings and times, and thus present them as distinct cultures and expressions of culture in their own right.

The challenge this poses is that writers and readers of the subject become critics to the conventional practice of military history and to the public tastes it reflects and helps sustain. Changes in assumptions about 'war' and greater sensitivity to differences among the combatants would produce more profound military histories and a far more knowledgeable public.

This is a book about the practices and ideas of the military and of military force, and about the writing of military history. As such, the book seeks to draw together important work by others, as well as strands in my work, in order not only to offer an account of valuable modern advances, in addition to a statement of my own position, but also to promote further debate and research. An important theme for such research is the lowering of barriers between history and work in the social sciences on war and violence. Examples of the latter include the anthropological and ethnological approaches to war, neo-Darwinian theory,[1] studies on the relationship between violence and various, often Eurocentric, ideas of social discipline and civilization, and the importance attached by much social and political theory to the monopolization of violence as a defining characteristic of a state. Specialists in strategic studies, international relations, sociology, economics, and adminis-tration, have also contributed interesting material, although it has not been absorbed into the mainstream of historical work at present.

Nor, it has to be said, is such work generally cited by military historians. Instead, the subject suffers from the tendency among historians as a whole to compartmentalize themselves within their respective fields. The isolation of military history is part of this larger tendency, but it is matched by some scholarly military historians who are loath to study aspects of the subject other than their own. This can be seen, for example, in heavily operational accounts of wars that concentrate largely on developments at the front.

The particular strength of this 'thought book' – considering the work of others as well as advancing my own ideas – is its global approach. This is important not only for what ought to be covered but also for the way in which attitudes are analysed and relative capability considered. I do not pretend to produce a definitive statement, but I hope to encourage historiographical debate and theoretical and practical discussion, and will indeed be very interested to receive comments on the subject and on my approach. The German equivalent, *Was ist Militärgeschichte?* (Paderborn, 2000), edited by Thomas Kühne and Benjamin Ziemann, helpfully clarified the position as far as German scholars were concerned.[2] Based on a 1998 conference, it included a range of expertise I cannot match, but was Eurocentric in its approach; as was Jean Chagniot's impressive *Guerre et Société à l'Époque Moderne* (Paris, 2001) and the helpful publications of the International Commission of Military History.[3] Peter Broucek and Kurt Peball's *Geschichte der österreichischen Militärhistoriographie* (Cologne, 2000) includes a comprehensive review of the literature, but is national in its focus.[4] My book seeks to echo some of the themes in the German collection, but the selection of authors, books and topics for discussion is obviously personal. The book has had to be ruthlessly pruned to meet the contracted length, and I can only apologize to scholars who feel that their work has been slighted. That is not my intention, and many not cited have in fact provided inspiration. I also hope to write a sequel.

In organizing this book, I am mindful that, alongside those who read books in their entirety there are many, not least my students, who prefer to focus on particular chapters. As a consequence, the individual chapters are designed to link into a whole, but they are also freestanding. This is true both of the thematic chapters and of their chronological counterparts that follow, each of which includes a period overlap. The chronological chapters are designed to provide an opportunity to probe some of the key themes of the earlier section of the book, and also to serve as a reminder that there is a narrative dimension that has to be addressed. This narrative also offers a world stage that provides a standard of equal opportunity for attention, as a way to call attention to non-Western war-making and thus compensate for the normal practice of conventional military histories.

In thinking about this topic, I have benefited from many discussions over the years, and from the opportunity to visit Japan and meet Japanese scholars provided by an invitation to speak at the University of Tsukuba. In the shorter period of writing this book, I have profited from opportunities to speak at the Naval Yard in Washington and the Naval Academy at Annapolis, and to the Cambridge University Student History Society, the History Research Seminar of the University of Exeter, the New York Military Affairs Symposium, and the Virginia Historical Society, and from correspondence or discussions with David Cohen, David Graff, Geoffrey Jensen, David Killingray, John Lamphear, Stewart Lone, Peter Lorge, Frank McCann, Helen Nicholson, Doug Peers, and Bruce Vandervort. Roger Burt, Theodore Cook, Paul Fideler, John France, Jan Glete, Peter Hoffenberg, Harald Kleinschmidt, Vicky Peters, Anthony Saunders, Larry Sondhaus, Everett Wheeler, Don Yerxa, Benjamin Ziemann, and two anonymous readers made helpful comments on an earlier draft, and Kristofer Allerfeldt, Brian Bond, George Boyce, Charles Esdaile, Henry French and Richard Wylde on particular chapters. They are not responsible for any errors in my text. Peter Willis proved a most helpful production editor. I am most grateful to Mike and Paris Pavković for their hospitality on two wonderful academic trips to Hawaii in 2003. Lecturing there on military history has certainly helped to broaden my understanding of the subject.

Notes

1 R.W. Wrangham and D. Peterson, *Demonic Males: Apes and the Origins of Human Violence* (1996); D. Dawson, 'A Darwinian View of Warfare', *Historically Speaking*, III no. 5 (June 2002), pp. 21–3.
2 The volume includes contributions by non-German scholars. Jutta Nowosadtko's *Krieg, Gewalt und Ordnung. Einführung in die Militärgeschichte* (Tübingen, 2002) is a less successful work, as is E. Wolfrum, *Krieg und Frieden in der Neuzeit vom Westfälischen Frieden bis zum Zweiten Weltkrieg* (Darmstadt, 2003). See also P.H. Wilson, 'War in Early Modern German History', *German History*, 19 (2001), pp. 419–38.
3 For example, *Von Crécy bis Mohács. Kriegswesen im Späten Mittelalter, 1346–1526* (Vienna, 1997), includes a perfunctory piece on China, but the other 31 papers, including both of those on aspects of medieval warfare as a whole, are entirely devoted to war within Europe.
4 For other countries see for example G. Jensen, 'War Armies, Politics, and Culture: Historiographical Approaches to the Military in Modern Spain',

Society for Spanish and Portuguese Historical Studies Bulletin, 22, no. 1 (Winter 1997), pp. 5–13, L. Veszprémy and B.K. Király (eds), *A Millennium of Hungarian Military History* (Boulder, Colorado, 2002), and C. Paoletti, 'Writing the Official Italian Military History of the French Revolutionary and Napoleonic Wars', *Consortium on Revolutionary Europe. Selected Papers* (2004). I would like to thank Ciro Paoletti for providing me with a copy of his paper and for discussing the topic with me.

Abbreviations

BL. Add.   London, British Library, Department of Western Manuscripts, Additional Manuscripts.

LH.   London, King's College, Liddell Hart archive.

PRO. WO.   London, Public Record Office, War Office.

Unless otherwise stated, all works are published in London.

Chapter I

Introduction

[N]o field is more attuned to the present than military history, even though many of the people who are interested in it can seem nostalgic and backward-looking. Fear, especially what the current or next war may bring, concentrates the mind.

Michael Sherry, 2000[1]

Military history is arguably the last stronghold of what histori-ographers call the 'Whig interpretation' . . . [it] sees the development of warfare as progressive.

Dennis Showalter, 2002[2]

Diversity

Popular work in military history, discussed in the next chapter, tends to concentrate on an established list of topics, rather than ranging further afield; and, for such an account, it is necessary to turn to a far less extensive literature, much, but by no means all, of which is more academic in its tone and origin. With this literature, however, it is important to be wary about meta-narratives (overarching interpret-ations), and to be cautious about paradigms, mono-causal explanations and much of the explanatory culture of long-term military history. Instead, it is important to emphasize the diversity of military practice, through both time and space, and to be hesitant in adducing character-istics and explanations for military capability and change.

Linked to this, it is also important to be wary of the concept of a single Western way of war, as suggested, explicitly or implicitly, in much of the literature, unless the thesis is accompanied by due notice of the variety of contexts and 'taskings' (objectives set for the military) involved. Far from there being such a single Western way of war, there were, and still are, a variety of military cultures and practices within the West, ranging from conflict with other regular forces to counter-insurgency and policing operations. Rather than, as is usually done, treating the latter as in some ways lesser forms of warfare that, at the most, represented adaptations of existing methods, it is necessary to appreciate the pluralistic nature of warfare and then to build this into theoretical discussions about the processes of military development. Such an appreciation undermines clear rankings of capability and prowess, not least because of the range of taskings the militaries are expected to pursue, an issue discussed in Chapter five.

More troubling than the underplaying of diversity within the West, much of which stems from a misleading attempt to discern supposedly inherent characteristics, has been the tendency to simplify the non-West, an issue raised in Chapter three. Instead, in reality, in terms of military cultures and environments, the range of the non-West was immense. This, indeed, played a role in the difficulties that Western militaries experienced in seeking over the last half-millennium to exercise military dominance over much of the world's populations – although other factors, not least the very varied degree of Western commitment, were also very important. Rather than simply repeating the standard account of Western successes, beginning with Vasco da Gama and Hernán Cortes, it is worth also considering, for example, the reasons for European military failures in Africa prior to the nineteenth century, as well as the problems encountered by the Europeans in East and South Asia. While it is true that the major empires in the New World, those of the Aztecs and Incas, were rapidly conquered in the early sixteenth century, the bulk of the world's population did not live there. Further-more, although, from the late fifteenth century, European warships and merchantmen increasingly sailed the oceans, providing the means of power projection, deep-draught European ships, once on their opposite shores, found it difficult to operate in inshore, estuarine and riverine waters; and here the major changes in force projection did not occur until the nineteenth century, a change in which motivation as well as technology played a major role.

An emphasis on variety, both in the West and in the non-West, has obvious consequences for the relationship between historians' approaches to war and those of other subject specialists. If the historians' emphasis is on diversity, for example on the role of particular military cultures, this challenges generic approaches to the study of war – although the diversity can also be seen as an enabler of relative capability between powers. In addition, it is possible to seek a reconciliation between variety and theoretical models by seeing the former as arising largely from environmental adaptation. This is a question that is ripe for examination from the perspectives of history, anthropology and sociology. For example, it is possible to consider the introduction of gunpowder weaponry, to ask why this was employed differently, and with contrasting results, in particular societies. This question draws attention to issues of process when considering adaptation, an issue addressed in Chapter four: there is a somewhat crude belief that societies adapt in order to optimize their military capability and performance, but the process of change is in fact far more complex, and often unclear.

Change

More generally, there is need for a debate on how best to explain military change. Models that assume some mechanistic, if not automatic, search for efficiency, and define this in terms of a maximization of force, do violence to the complex process by which interest in new methods interacted with powerful elements of continuity. For example, the varied reaction to firearms is best understood not in terms of military progress, nor of administrative sophistication, nor of cultural superiority, but rather as a response to the different tasks and possibilities facing the armies of the period, within a context in which it was far from clear which weaponry, force structure, tactics, or operational method were better, or could be adopted most successfully. Indeed, in the case of gunpowder, like earlier the stirrup, it has been argued that 'administrative improvements preceded military change, and that military change preceded the introduction of any new military technology. . . . The age of cavalry was really the age of bad infantry, and was a political, not a technological, phenomenon'.[3]

Linked to this emphasis on different tasks and possibilities should be a measure of scepticism about the notion of a 'paradigm' power (or military culture) that others sought to emulate. This situation was indeed the case to a certain extent within particular military systems, although less so than the more common borrowing of particular techniques and weapons. The role of a paradigm power, and of the diffusion of its methods at the global level, is often exaggerated however. This is particularly the case for the situation prior to the last two centuries: the circumstances under which the USA currently fulfils the role provides scant guidance to the position with major powers several centuries ago, while the force projection sought today by the USA is exceptional, and thus lessens the applicability of the paradigm–diffusion model.

Strategic cultures

It is also necessary to consider the dynamic relationship between the problems that societies faced in determining what is optimal capability, and the contested character of what are termed the strategic cultures within which military goals were set, and thus which defined the objectives to be pursued by this apparently optimal capability. In making judgements, the perils of neglecting this contested character are significant. To take, for example, eighteenth-century India: it is fruitless to criticize Indian rulers for failing to address adequately the challenge posed by the Western-pattern militaries deployed from the 1740s by the English and French East India Companies, unless due attention is devoted to the continued assaults by cavalry forces advancing into India from the north-west: Nadir Shah of Persia in 1739, and the Afghans in the 1750s. Although the latter were to be the last iteration of a long series of attacks going back for more than two millennia, there was no reason to believe that this process was coming to a close, and that Europeans were to be a more serious military challenge. Indeed, Europeans had been active on the Indian coasts for nearly two and a half centuries before, in the 1740s, European-trained militaries started to play a key role in Indian power politics.

Similarly, to underline again the lack of agreement about strategic culture, it was far from clear in the early 1930s whether the principal challenges that Britain and France would face would be from insurrection in their colonies or from confrontation with other technologically-advanced militaries; and if the latter, there was still a considerable difference between the challenge posed by Japanese naval power in East Asian waters and what might stem from the development of the Italian or German militaries. Strategic culture as well as weaponry needs appeared to be in flux: in his *Rulers of the Indian Ocean* (1927), G.A. Ballard, a British admiral, argued that the rise in American and Japanese naval power had transformed the situation, as it was no longer sufficient for Britain to prevail over European rivals in order to win global naval dominance. He presented the British empire as particularly vulnerable in the Indian Ocean:

> As regards its present form or fabric the Empire may be roughly divided into an occidental half – including the British Isles – and an

oriental; which are held together commercially and strategically by the Imperial lines of communication across the Indian Ocean. . . . If those connections are cut, the two halves of the Empire will fall apart as surely as night follows day.

The argument about goals was directly linked to the debate about procurement in the shape of the desirability of the development of a major naval base at Singapore. In the event, prior to attack by Japan in 1941–2, Britain and its navy was to face, in 1940, the totally unexpected challenge of the German conquest of the European coastline from the Spanish frontier to the North Cape in Norway. This led to an increase in the number of German naval bases and a decrease in the capacity of the British navy to mount an effective blockade of its European rivals, a decrease that also owed much to the impact of air power. This issue serves as a reminder of the need to consider perception studies when discussing military history, particularly when addressing how strategic cultures moulded military goals.

The complexities and variations seen in the processes of military change also help break down or, at least qualify, attempts at environmental determinism. Thus, for example, rather than presenting Eurasian nomadic warfare just in terms of innate ecological advantages, stemming from the possibilities for horsemanship, it is appropriate also to consider the extent to which nomad skills and success varied and changed, alongside the limitations of nomads and the extent of inter-nomadic warfare.[4]

The intellectual context of military history

Environmental determinism is an instance of how thought about war was but part of wider intellectual currents. It is difficult to separate military history from thought about war, because the past has generally been used as the source of examples and ideas, and military history has usually been integral to military thought. This is least the case in the modern West, as, from the eighteenth century and even more the nineteenth, this has been focused on a cult of progress and thus on how best to get to the future. In such a context, military history has more clearly been a source of example, but not of wisdom – not least because of the notion that changes in war stemming from technological developments have made past war-making largely redundant.

The potency of the role of examples remains the case in modern Western public discussion. Thus, in the crisis stemming from the events of 11 September 2001, there were references to the Pearl Harbor attacks, while in the subsequent discussion of policy toward Iraq, critics of intervention were labelled appeasers and direct references were made to the failure to fight Hitler prior to 1939 (and, for the USA, 1941). It is, however, far less clear that such references add up to any coherent views on the use of force based on the application of historically tested concepts. Indeed, despite efforts to teach military history to officers, the historical memory of the American military establishment and of policy makers in the American government extends no further back in time than World War Two. Faith in technology is so strong and pervasive that earlier history is seen as irrelevant and there is a lack of interest in earlier historical parallels.

The academic study of war, including military history, cannot be abstracted from the particular contours of academic disciplines and how they have changed through time. Thus, the variable division of labour principle that interested British intellectuals such as Adam Smith, William Robertson and Edward Gibbon in the eighteenth century led them to consider cultural and historical variations in the sociology of warfare,[5] and within that context, to explain the development of professional militaries of regular troops. This approach was given a more technological emphasis in the nineteenth century, as the machine age advanced, although the theme of the power of will was also potent in this culture. The stress on technology has remained a powerful emphasis, unsurprisingly given the nature of the modern world, and the political and intellectual emphasis on programmes and practices of directed modernization. After World War Two, there was also a shift in Western attention away from combat and toward conflict and the wider resonances of military activity, specifically with the 'war and society' approach of the so-called new military history discussed in Chapter two.

Now as far as military history is concerned, the tendency to 'de-militarize' military history and to consider 'combatants' who experienced war but not fighting, seen with part, but by no means all, of the new military history, is less novel than it was – and, at least in part, has run its course. At the same time, however, new themes have been offered within this general approach, and it has been applied widely in chronological and geographical terms.[6] Furthermore, the relation between war and society continues to be very important as the broad context in which other issues are considered.

Thus, interest in the devastation and casualties caused by war, both military and civilian, which has played a prominent role in 'war and society' studies,[7] has been extended to consider the cultural impact of devastation. To illustrate the range of modern military history, recent works have looked at cultural destruction and its role in conflict. In *War Damage in Western Europe. The Destruction of Historic Monuments During the Second World War* (Edinburgh, 2001), Nicola Lambourne considered the novelty of a greatly increased extent of such destruction, which owed much to the development of bombing. She argued that definite instances of the intentional targeting of historic monuments were rare in Western Europe, but that indisputable cases of intentional avoidance of these buildings were also elusive. The physical effects of the war on historic monuments were of far more interest to propagandists exploiting the symbolism of this aspect of the war, than to those with the power to damage such buildings.

Intentional targeting, however, was more apparent in Eastern Europe. A clear account of the plunder of cultural treasures and the destruction of archival material was provided in Patricia Grimsted's *Trophies of War and Empire. The Archival Heritage of Ukraine, World War II, and the International Politics of Restitution* (Cambridge, Mass., 2001), a work that is of more general resonance as the attack on memory is increasingly seen as an aspect of conflict.[8] The attack reached its brutal apogee with the deliberate devastation of Jewish culture and learning as an integral part of the Nazi Holocaust. This genocide was anti-societal warfare, and if the absence of battles, other than the unsuccessful rising in the Warsaw Ghetto in 1943, ensures that it finds no place in conventional accounts of military history, that draws attention to the unwillingness of many authors to think 'outside the box', a point underlined by work on the complicity and at times active participation of the *Wehrmacht* in Hitler's racist policies.[9]

In the early 2000s, universities tended to establish and defend military history courses, or justify appointments, in terms of 'war and society' concerns, such as the MA in War, Experience and Memory launched by the University of Essex in 2003; but that does not necessarily amount to an either–or approach. For example, a glance at the strategies of individual publishing houses shows they can include both operational history and 'war and society'. Thus, the University of North Carolina Press published works in the former category, including *The Richmond Campaign of 1862. The Peninsula and the Seven Days* (2000), edited by Gary Gallagher, a volume in the first-rate operational series 'Military Campaigns of the Civil War', as well as Mark Bradley's *This Astounding Close. The Road to Bennett Place* (2000), on the last days of the Civil War in the East, and also dealing with a local site; and again James Marten's *The Children's Civil War* (1998), a look at how children experienced the

Civil War, that drew on diaries, memoirs and letters, as well as Alice Fahs' *The Imagined Civil War. Popular Literature of the North and South, 1861–1865* (2000), which ranged to include histories, children's stories and humorous pieces, and also considered the war's role on non-combatants. Children and popular literature are currently modish topics regardless of the period discussed, and the 'war and society' approach provides a ready way to study this material. More generally, 'war and society' is not far removed from the currently fashionable emphasis on cultural aspects of war-making. They have strong connections, not least the tendency of traditional military historians to ignore both in their work.

War-winning factors

If 'war and society', including the influential Open University course of that title from 1973, brought military history back into the academy through the back door, at least in America, there has also, outside the academy, been a continued interest in operational history, not least in its 'drums and trumpets' form (on which see Chapter two). A sophisticated operational approach, however, requires not 'drums and trumpets' but, rather, an informed consideration of what leads to operational capability.

As far as assessing capability is concerned, it is important to be cautious about explanations focused exclusively on resources and technology (on which see Chapter four). Mechanization, nevertheless, plays a major role in the modern concept of war. This is but part of a more general focus by commentators on the capabilities of particular weapons and weapons systems, and the belief that progress stems from their improvement, a belief that is central to much modern military history. This stress on the material culture of war can also be seen in discussion of earlier eras; thus, for example, in the case of the Iron Age replacing the Bronze Age, the emphasis is on how the superior cutting power of iron and the relative ease of making iron weapons led to a change in civilizations. Weaponry is certainly important, but as we know from observing modern conflicts such as the Vietnam War and the Soviet attempt to dominate Afghanistan, it is not always the most heavily armed that prevail, particularly in asymmetrical conflict. Irrespective of technological developments, there is no reason to assume that this situation will change. Looking back, this perspective from recent conflicts is an important one for the more general study of military history.

Instead, it is necessary to focus on how resources are used, with all this means in terms of issues of fighting quality, unit cohesion, morale, leadership, tactics, strategy, and other factors, as well as with reference to the organizational issues that affect the assessment and use of resources. Some of these issues, for example unit cohesion, morale and leadership, and how they are sustained, are ripe for comparative theoretical treatment. Anthropology, collective psychology and sociology have much to offer here, not least in moving beyond a largely unsystematic, if not sometimes anecdotal, approach to the 'face of battle', to a more thorough probing of the issue.

As a consequence both of changes in the experience of conflict and of wider social shifts, the pressures and requirements that mould factors such as unit cohesion, morale and leadership have been far from constant. For example, planning and command skills and, more generally, the ability to articulate and integrate different arms (such as infantry and cavalry), a long-established aspect of effectiveness, became more complex with the greater range of available technology (which increased the number of arms), and thus an aspect of the modern sociology of applied knowledge. It became necessary to aim for an enhanced level of skill and institutional effectiveness, coordinating and integrating infantry, artillery and armour successfully, as well as air and land, air and sea, and land and sea forces. In short, as technology improves, so the importance of other factors in overall capability are enhanced, not diminished.

At the same time, the focus on the intellectual challenges posed by considering how best to use new weaponry must be supplemented, as in the case of World War Two, with a consideration of the continued value of artillery and infantry, and their role in effective tactics and operations. Military historians face the same challenge, although in their case error leads not to defeat but to the profitable pastures of the conventional approach that the publishing world rewards. It is more seductive to write about the Tiger tank or the Spitfire than to discuss the continued role of infantry, let alone artillery, the forgotten arm of both World Wars but the greatest killer of soldiers in both.

To focus solely on battle for a moment, there is another problem stemming from the popular assumption that the 'face of battle', the essentials of war, are in some fashion timeless, as they involve men being willing to undergo the trial of combat. In practice, the understanding of loss and suffering, at both the level of ordinary soldiers and that of societies as a whole, is far more culturally conditioned than any emphasis on the sameness of battle might suggest. At its bluntest, the willingness to suffer losses varies greatly. Furthermore, this helps to determine differences in combat, both through time and also across the world in any one period. In addition, although to a lesser extent, this variation can play a role in military success. To contrast the willingness of the Western powers taking part in aggressive warfare (as well as those engaged in responding to aggression) to suffer heavy losses in the World Wars (not only World War One) with their reluctance to do so in the last quarter of the twentieth century, and also the different attitudes towards casualties of the Americans and the North Vietnamese in the Vietnam War, is to be aware of a situation that has a wider historical resonance, and it is likely that this was also the case for periods for which the sources are far less good or, indeed, non-existent. This may be an ahistorical reading back from the modern age, but it is more likely that there has frequently been a variation in the willingness to suffer casualties, certainly to the extent of fighting to the death and engaging in suicidal, let alone suicide, tactics. It is far from clear why variations and changes in these 'cultural' factors, factors which more generally relate to how people fought, should play a smaller role in the history of war than weaponry. What people fought with did not dictate how they fought.

Linked to this, morale, which often focuses on the willingness to suffer loss, remains the single most important factor in combat and conflict; while as a related point, war, seen as an attempt to impose will, involves more than victory in battle. This is far from new, although the extent to which past military cultures put an emphasis on battle is difficult to assess, not least if a gap is discerned between theoretical texts and reality. For example, scholars of the military history of medieval Europe debate how far commanders sought battle and how far they followed the Classical writer Vegetius in avoiding it, concentrating instead on ravaging the land.[10]

Thus, victory and defeat cease to be solely readily understood absolutes, with the defeat and capitulation of armies and the conquest of territory both measures and goals. Instead, it becomes important to appreciate that people are beaten when they understand that they have lost, and that this involves more than operational military verdicts. In the absence of such an understanding, victory in battle simply leads to the need for an onerous occupation while much of the population continues to resist, the problem that faced Napoleonic forces in Spain in 1808–13, or their German and allied counterparts in Yugoslavia in 1941–4; or with the defeated preparing to fight on, as with the Egyptians and Syrians after 1967.

In many respects, in recent decades success in war has become more difficult from this perspective due to profound social changes across much of the war. These can be summarized as democratization, but the process is far more complex: as more of the world's population has become urban, literate, and engaged in industrial and service activities, so political participation and expectations have increased and deference has declined. These social changes affect greatly the possibility of consent to defeat and occupation, although they do not prevent it.

Organizational issues – how troops were organized on the battlefield, the nature of force structures and the organization of societies for conflict – also vary greatly through time and space, not least in response to such social developments. Instead of assuming that organizational changes were driven by weaponry, specifically how best to use weapons, and maybe also how to move and supply them, it is necessary to appreciate the autonomous character of organizational factors, and their close linkage with social patterns and developments. These issues can directly influence effectiveness greatly, not least if dissension within the military is at issue.[11] Indeed, at one level, the study of Western warfare becomes an aspect of the history of systems as well as of power; and the same is true for the non-West, but with much of the scholarly groundwork simply not done.

The causes of war

A parallel case can be made with the causes of war, a topic which is at once a major sub-set of military history and a distinct field that is an aspect of international relations. These causes have an autonomous character unrelated to technology, and, again, far too little of the work has focused on the 'non-West'. Looked at differently, armies, navies and air forces are organizations with objectives or taskings (see Chapter five), and, in assessing their capability and effectiveness, it is necessary to consider how these objectives changed, and how far such changes created pressures for adaptation, including in the force structure of militaries. In short, a demand-led account of conflict has to be set alongside the more familiar supply-side assessment that presents improvements in weaponry or increases in numbers of weapons without adequately considering the wider context of their use. For example, the élites that committed Europe to war in 1914 were not motivated by developments in weaponry, nor, indeed, by economic considerations. Instead, the ruling coteries in Austria, Russia and Germany saw the July crisis as presenting imperatives that demanded a demonstration of national power: the display of force as the response to challenge. All three were willing to pay enormous costs for the sake of that aim. These costs were readily apparent to the business élites and organized labour, but the overwhelming advice of business leaders for peace was ignored, as the culture of the governing élites was very much opposed to this advice: they saw the economy as serving the requirements of higher goals of power and prestige. In Germany, among the policymakers, there was an all too common inability to think clearly, combined with a desperate euphoria.[12]

Although, as discussed in Chapter four, technological advance is far from an unproblematic concept, the analysis of tasking or the formulation of goals and policies, the subject of Chapter five, creates greater problems, especially on a comparative scale. The political context has varied greatly as an aspect of general history, although there is also a feed-back mechanism as war itself has often transformed this context and history. The experience of war, and also widespread cultural changes in attitudes towards conflict, have greatly affected tasking by altering social responses to the prospect of conflict and to the likelihood of numerous casualties; and this has become more important as major powers have been affected by the social changes of the last 150 years.

A central feature, in both democratic and authoritarian societies, has been the public character of the reporting and commemoration of war, and governments in each type of society are as one in trying to elicit support to a degree that would have surprised regimes in the eighteenth century. This drive for support during conflict, and for a public endorsement thereafter, ensures a degree of controversy over both reporting and commemoration. Uneasiness over conflict, or a particular conflict, which stems readily from the high rate of political awareness in democratized societies, is also transformed into dissent over the assessment of victory. This affects the memorialization of war, and thus influences military history in its widest definition. This history, in turn, plays its role in the validation of war as a political option.

The traumatic experience of World War One played a major role in the process by which public dissent over war developed: for what at the time was treated by Britain, France and, eventually, the USA, as a righteous struggle against German aggression became, eventually, a conflict with a far more ambivalent position in public memory. As a consequence, the victory much applauded in and after 1918 appeared, a half-century later, to be too hard-won, if not an ironic counterpoint to the horrors of trench warfare. Thus the very fact of war, and the process of conflict itself, appeared a defeat. The merits of the case were somewhat different

– any attempt to resist German aggression against Belgium and France could only have been very difficult – but the point at issue is that what became the dominant cultural trope of war in Western Europe was sufficiently anti-war to affect not only the understanding of victory but also the strategic culture of the victorious powers.

World War Two was viewed less critically, being seen by the victors as a virtuous struggle. Furthermore, the contrasting role of the USA in the two world wars – notably its far less central and less costly part in World War One – helped ensure that the commemoration of war there was less anti-war than was the case in Western Europe, although World War One led to a rejection of Europe by the USA in which the experience of conflict played a role. It was to be the Vietnam War that was the cathartic experience for Americans, and although this had a profound impact on a particular generation and on much of the American intelligentsia, it did not suffuse American public culture as a whole with anti-war attitudes. The consequent results can be seen in contrasting Western European and American responses to the use of force in the 1990s and the 2000s, although the experience of the 11 September 2001 attacks were clearly crucial to the more bellicose American attitude in the 2000s. The Vietnam War, however, did affect the methods that the Americans employed in war-making: the advent of body-bag politics affected public culture and military doctrine and tactics. Furthermore, American public culture included critical notes about war, not least through the influential lens of the cinema, as in *Cold Mountain* (2003), in which the hero, a Confederate deserter, speaks of fools 'sent off to fight with a flag and a lie'.

Cultural assumptions

The dominant American attitude in the early 2000s serves to underline the degree to which the complex interaction of public culture and strategic culture produced, at any one moment, very specific under-standings of war and victory, which in turn shaped responses to the prospect of conflict – not least as a presumption of success is the major cause of decisions for war. Thus, what can be termed cultural assumptions emerge as crucial both before and after conflict. Indeed, the combat sits between these, as part of an ongoing process of warfare, or, at least, as an accentuation of it. In the absence of a cultural presumption of victory, this accentuation is unlikely; but, in turn, a reading of other conflicts is required in order to produce or at least sustain this presumption. Thus, the recent and distant history of peoples and states is scoured to provide evidence of victory, while other wars are discussed in order to suggest that the pattern of military history is clear. This entails a conceptualization of conflict that deliberately minimizes risk, and thus denies the nature of war and of its consequences: in practice, even if victory is likely, its results are far less so. Thus, for regimes considering conflict, an understanding, or intellectual grasping, of victory, serves an important utilitarian end, however much that is also presented in terms of the social or collective psychological ends of commemoration. This utilitarianism clearly varies by age and society, but it serves as a reminder that victory has to be fought for in a double sense: both on the battlefield and subsequently.

As far as military history is concerned, however, utilitarianism is a matter not only of the politics that encourage the resort to conflict, but also, in contrast, of the wider value of an intelligent scepticism that underlines the precariousness of victory and the difficulties of translating it into lasting success. Indeed, this double sense of utilitarianism captures some of the tension in the writing about war and the practice of military history. It is not that scholarship is inherently anti-war, but rather that the process of subjecting conflict, both causes and character, to scrutiny can make it harder to elicit the automatic consent that bellicose cultures assume and require.

Modern Western militaries would accept this, and suggest that their requirement for trained soldiers and, even more, officers, who have volunteered for service, ensures that the situation has 'moved on' and that scholarly examination of war serves their purposes. While correct at one level, not least because much military training involves learning by example, there is still the question of how scholarship relates to the conditionality of military service in the modern volunteer age. The long-term consequences of the latter are controversial, especially in terms of support for expeditionary warfare. Scholarship can be seen as an aspect of this conditional social support for war.

As far as American support for expeditionary warfare is concerned, the presentation of the wars in Afghanistan in 2001 and Iraq in 2003 as a response to the terrorist attacks in New York and Washington in 2001, a form of retribution, and thus exemplary commemoration, helped overcome this problem, at least in the short term. Nevertheless, the wider issue of a rethinking within the West of the ethics and practice of war is of great importance, particularly in so far as Western states are militarily the most capable of long-range power projection. Terrorism and the spread of missile and atomic technology, however, may challenge this situation.

Culturally-specific understandings of war and victory are difficult to recover for distant times. This is even more the case with particular types of conflict, for example with counter-insurgency warfare. The understanding of victory and defeat in such contexts remains far from easy; indeed part of the strategy for both guerrilla forces and terrorist movements is to remain sufficiently active to prevent closure on any terms acceptable to the government. From the opposite perspective, despite the terrible hardships for individuals and communities, it is possible for governments to sustain high levels of disruption without accepting any sense of defeat, but the level of killing seen, for example, in Kashmir would, if repeated in modern Denmark, lead to a sense of total breakdown. This can be taken further by considering general societal levels of individual and communal violence. Where these are high, for example in Brazil or South Africa today, then the degree to which political violence represents a defeat for the state tends to be different to where they are low. In many contexts past and present, there was scant difference between banditry and rebellion, as, for example, was readily apparent in medieval Europe.

The extent to which a focus on where wars are more common leads to a re-examination of norms of conduct, including the understanding of victory, is readily apparent if the present situation is considered: there should be a geographical shift of attention to sub-Saharan Africa. This exercise needs to be undertaken for earlier periods, but, so far, such comparative work is lacking.

Political contexts therefore affected the responsibility and ethos of the military. Tasking, the choice and pursuit of goals, remains very important to force structures and military cultures. Fundamental issues of social organization are at stake in tasking, for example the degree to which internal policing is central to military purpose; or, in more anthropological terms, the dynamic character of the relation between conflict and discipline within the group, and the understanding of order and violence. The extent to which regimes have used para-militaries, and to which internal and external goals have overlapped, needs to be borne in mind. Visiting the Italian forces attacking Abyssinia (Ethiopia) in 1935, the British military thinker and former general J.F.C. Fuller found that the general to which he was attached commanded a

> group of blackshirts [a Fascist militia], a curious collection of men who looked like brigands and enjoyed looking like it. Their discipline I should say was evil. For field purpose I cannot imagine them being of much use; but I should say that they would prove

admirable in a street fight . . . a kind of Pirates of Penzance[13] business. . . . this war is not a demonstration of soldiership but of Fascism: an officer is made second in command of 4,000 men, not because he is a good soldier but a Fascist poet.[14]

If the focus is on internal conflict, and victory is seen as the maintenance of peace and order rather than the forcing of force and order on others, then we approach a position in which war understood as conflict can be set alongside the other current usage of war as a serious struggle by the state against pernicious forces, as in 'war on crime . . . drugs . . . pollution . . . poverty'. On one level, this usage reflects the centrality of bellicist images in Western culture, but, at the other, it indicates that conventional warfare has lost its special function as traumatic experience and proving ground, at least for audiences viewing conflict on television.

This linguistic usage reflects the extent to which our Western culture while, on the one hand, less bellicose than in the past (as seen not least with the end of compulsory military service and with shifts in the presentation of war[15]), has nevertheless taken the language of warfare and applied it widely. Indeed, this can be taken further by noting the extent to which the language of conflict is used to describe not simply social relationships between groups, whether in terms of class, gender, or ethnicity, but also the relationship of ideas: knowledge is widely seen as a power system, both about struggle and itself the product of struggle. Thus, the language used encompasses ideas of hegemony, spheres of contention and contested boundaries. In short, alongside the culture of war we have culture (and society, and politics) as war, and this contributes to a psychological state in which conflict is socialized as part of the human process.

'War on . . .' has become a clichéd part of the language, in the way that 'front' from the First World War was absorbed, and the language of war has been appropriated for other ends, such as treating dissent as an enemy, as well as to add weight and legitimacy to matters that have no inherent substance. This usage dilutes and even alters the original meaning of the term in question, so that to many in the West, war itself has been reduced in the eyes of the public to something akin to a playground scrap that grown men should be intelligent enough to eschew, a process aided by the feminist stance of much anti-war rhetoric that reduces bellicosity to typical male behaviour and thus antagonistic to female common sense. The consequence is that war in all its myriad forms and implications has been made 'understandable' by all and 'obviously' futile in purpose.

This is a long way from the consideration of particular victories and defeats, but it serves to underline the link between the process in which the commemoration and memorialization of individual wars shapes collective memories and that in which the use of the vocabulary and imagery of conflict helps make war a key social experience even for those who have not seen fighting. The last is not new, not simply a matter of the visualization of war on film and television. Instead, the use of bellicose language to discuss religious faith both on the individual level (the battle with Satan and sin) and collectively (religious identity as opposed to other confessional groups), ensures that this is a long-standing and continuing, albeit, around the world, very varied, process. The Iraq crisis of 2003 has suggested that the conflation of bellicosity and a sense of religious struggle is important to influential American views and experiences, although the same is also true in other cultures, while, however much a Crusader mentality might have been voiced in part of the American public debate, the military conformed to its professional goals and practices.

War, in the shape of images of violence, answers to something deep in the human psyche, at least in so far as framing identities are concerned. It helps define groups and provides them with an apparent coherence and purpose driven by need. This creates problems in advocating the alternative: the nuanced meaning and interpenetrating identities and interests that are more conducive to war-avoidance. The culture of war-avoidance indeed is a subject that has received insufficient attention, and this is a challenge for modern scholars. It is valuable to consider particular situations where wars might have happened but did not actually occur, an approach that has been taken with reference for example to crises between Britain and France in 1861, the Union side in the American Civil War and Britain over the Trent Affair, the USA and France over Mexico in the 1860s, Britain and Russia in 1877–8, and crises over Tunis (1881), Egypt, Samoa, New Guinea, Burma, West Africa, Siam, Hawaii, Fashoda (1898), and Bosnia (1908–9).[16] There is also, within Buddhist philosophy, most prominently with Vasubandhu and his school, an ethics of inaction. This theory, applied to military matters, promoted a warrior ideal according to which the warrior had the duty of preventing war by simply being around without actually fighting.[17]

The question of war-avoidance begs the question of the definition of war, an issue that requires particular care in avoiding a Eurocentric perspective. Large-scale, organized conflict is the best working definition, although as that excludes much terrorism, there may, on the part of those committed to the concept of a war on terrorism, be a preference for omitting the large-scale. In contrast to the definition in terms of large-scale, organized conflict, most commentators adopt a more restricted understanding of war as organized conflict between sovereign states, begun deliberately by a specific act of policy. A.J.P. Taylor wrote of 'the more prosaic origin of war: the precise moment when a statesman sets his name to the declaration of it'.[18]

This is too limited, not least because it is not an approach that makes sense across much of human history. For example, in pre-[European] contact warfare between Native North Americans, there was 'public warfare', in the form of conflict between tribes, but also 'private warfare', raids with no particular sanction, often designed to prove manhood; while in North America, as in other areas, there also appears to have been no sharp distinction between raiding and hunting, an economic necessity, in part possibly because non-tribal members were not viewed as human beings, or at least as full persons. A similar situation was noted by John Speke in his *Journal of the Discovery of the Source of the Nile* (1863). In the eighteenth century, in Senegambia in West Africa, there were conflicts dominated by a quest for slaves, while in India military operations were related to revenue collections, often dictated by the need to seize or protect revenue. Ignoring these and similar conflicts, and focusing instead on struggles between European-style powers, risks offering a very partial account of warfare.[19]

Whatever the geographical area, there is an important difference between wars of defence and those of aggression and conquest, although there can also be a significant overlap. Resisting an aggressor entails goals, doctrine and practice that are different to those involved in attempts to overwhelm and subjugate an enemy, and outcomes are also likely to be different. At the same time, too much of the literature on the causes of conflicts present them in terms of planned policy, which under-rates the role of the cultural parameters within which decisions are made and responses formulated. Thus, it is necessary to emphasize bellicist factors (which vary in their intensity), and their impact on both strategic cultures and particular decisions.[20]

Such an emphasis has to be alert to the particular character of specific states and periods. For example, in considering the strategy of Imperial Rome, it is necessary to note the extent to which the existence of a Roman grand strategy remains a debated topic. Alongside a presentation in terms of modern concepts of defence[21] has come a stress on factors such as honour and revenge.[22] In considering the complex reasons why states go to war, however, it is also valid to note that honour and revenge were not diametrically opposed concepts to strategy in antiquity any more than they have been subsequently. In short, what is summarized as culture, in this case the culture of decision-making, has to be handled with care.

Irrespective of the particular goal in conflict, the maintenance of order and discipline within states, policing at the larger scale, tends to be underrated in conventional military history. In this context, there is a need for a systematic consideration of how ideological assumptions affected counter-insurrectionary and policing policies, in short, to employ the currently fashionable term, the cultural dimension of the use of force for control. This was (and is) a dynamic process within countries, and also at the level of empires, and one that is linked to the nature of political and social authority. In this respect, military history is close to sociology, as well as to political history.[23]

In the case of states and, even more, empires, the willingness on the part of subject peoples to accommodate, and, indeed, to acculturate to, the more powerful, especially conquerors, has been far from constant across history. This can be seen as adding another cultural dimension to conflict, its pursuance and resolution. In general, the availability of syncretic options, for example the assimilation of local religious cults by the conqueror's religion, and the co-option of local élites by the conquerors, or at least the winning of co-operation,[24] have been the most important means of success. In short, military history becomes an aspect of total history; not in order to 'demilitarize' it, but because the operational aspect of war is best studied in terms of the multiple political, social and cultural contexts that gave, and give, it meaning.

Despite the volume of work appearing on military history, the subject is far from exhausted. Instead, there is a need to encourage research in a number of fields that have been relatively under-studied, particularly regionally, for example the military history of South-East Asia and the 'Horn' of Africa (modern Ethiopia and Somalia). It is also necessary to address the problem of how best to develop analytical concepts that do not treat the world as an isotropic (uniform) surface, but instead make sense of different military goals and traditions, and assess their impact. Imposing our concepts on purpose and conflict, and abstracting, organizing and analysing the evidence in Western analytical terms, risk leading us to failures of judgement, which have policy as well as scholarly implications. Yet, it is unclear how far it is possible to consider all aspects of the non-Western past on their own terms, and what a global military history would look like from a multifaceted methodological stance is uncertain.

This issue has policy implications, which are readily apparent in the case of expeditionary warfare. Whatever the state in question and the area of its operations, there will remain military and political limits to effective force projection; skilful policy-making on the part of great, as well as lesser, powers will continue to require a shrewd understanding of capability and limits. Great powers have always found it necessary to learn and adjust to their capabilities and limits. Thus, China under the Mongols could not conquer Japan or Java, while the Ming could not dominate the steppes and the Manchu failed in Burma. Successive Chinese regimes tried to keep news of failures out of their history. Similarly, between 1775 and 1842, Britain was defeated in America (but maintained Canada), and also intervened unsuccessfully in Argentina, Egypt and Afghanistan. The process by which military limits are learned and understood, or, instead, not grasped, is one that would benefit from comparative examination, and would in turn benefit military planners.

To look at recent years, too much of the literature of war is devoted to the ongoing 'revolution in military affairs' that is discerned in American advances in information warfare and precision weaponry, and this in turn is treated by many as the current terminus of military history. The marked contrast between the speed with which the Americans won their definition of war in Iraq in 2003, and their subsequent difficulties in ensuring the outcome they sought (which was more than a contrast between operational success and strategic problems) underlined, however, how even for the most modern military, the combination of different forms of conflict had unexpected results.

More generally, the modern Western cultural restraint on anti-societal war (at the extreme, the use of nuclear weaponry, and the criminalization of biological and chemical warfare, but also, for example, the retributory slaughter of prisoners or civilians) ensured that there is scant remedy when a professionalized military meets opposition or non-compliance from portions of a society refusing to accept the consequences of the overthrow of their state's formal military, other than the slow and patient process of armed policing, one that relies for its eventual success on political outcomes and requires a long time-scale. The British military developed a doctrine accordingly, in large part as a result of experience in anti-insurgency conflict in the colonies and in Northern Ireland, but this did not conform to American assumptions, particularly the political direction of American war-making. The resulting confusion in the USA led, in 2003, to criticism of such Iraqi practices as appearing to surrender and then attacking, or indeed to suicide bombing; but however repellent, these were effective in challenging a sense of control, as well as affecting military morale, and serve as a reminder of the very varied cultures of warfare.

The USA is, as the strongest, the exceptional, military power, and thus, in some respects, eccentric to the analysis of modern warfare, particularly if the paradigm–diffusion model is challenged. Furthermore, the emphasis on technology in the American style of war helps make it distinctive.[25] Its interest in large-scale expeditionary warfare also ensures that the objectives facing the US military are exceptional, while the lack of any need within the USA for militarized policing by regular forces contributes to the same situation. It is equally pertinent, when considering modern conflict, to look elsewhere: at the problems faced by 'advanced' militaries in ending violent opposition, for example in Kashmir or the West Bank, or at the efforts by would-be local hegemons, such as Brazil, India, Nigeria, and South Africa, to develop forces to give effect to their regional aspirations, or to consider the practice of violence in unstable regions, such as the Caucasus and Central Africa.

Partly as a result of such ambitions and conflict, it is likely that one of the most important future developments will not be the use of new military technologies (which tend to dominate predictions of future war), but the spread of established technologies to states that had not hitherto possessed them. This will lead to pressures for adaptation in organization and, in turn, the moulding of the use of such technology by existing force structures, doctrine, and strategic and sociological cultures. To stress the strength and continuity of such cultures, and the resulting variety in military practice and thought, is not a 'cop out', but rather a reminder of the flaws of schematic interpretations and an attempt to recreate the uncertainty and confusion within which choices and changes occur.

Whatever the technology, the problem, in pursuit of both external and internal goals, of eliciting consent to the consequences of military capability will remain a central issue. This is not so much a matter of securing agreement about the definition of capability, as a question about the impact of military strength, especially in the face of political resilience.

The uncertainty within which war and the prospect of war occurs has always been challenged in military thought. Indeed, planning represents a way to confront, if not manage, the risk of war, and this is true at all levels. The resulting level of abstraction, particularly at the strategic and operational levels, is not a problem as long as the degree of abstraction is appreciated. This was an aspect of the critique of conventional military history by the advocates of 'face of battle' studies; but, while this critique has considerable force, the very pursuit of strategic and operational planning ensure that their abstractions require consideration. Furthermore, war is an organized process, not a random series of individual acts, and the understanding of this organized character requires a degree of engagement with abstraction. Many members of the military may experience, or, rather, recall their experience not in terms of war's organized facets but as a series of individual acts and emotions. While important and understandable, that series is, however, less than a full account of conflict and of the military, and provides only scant guidance to capability and outcomes.

The naval dimension

As another level of variety, it is important, at every stage, to appreciate the difference between armies and navies, and between land and sea operations and conflict, a range accentuated from the early twentieth century by the addition of air warfare. The unnatural character of fighting at sea, and the need for specialized facilities in the form of ships, provide a very different context from that of conflict on land. Naval history is different, but it is not helpful to study it without the comparative context provided by conflict on land and in the air. Nevertheless, a distinct institutional context, in the shape of naval academies, has helped to underline difference, as has the practice of naval history, and the sense among publishers that there is a distinctive and important market.[26] The valuable work surveying the content and process of naval history that has appeared in recent years[27] tends, unfortunately, to offer little by way of comparison with armies and air forces.

As serious as the failure to consider naval alongside land conflict has been a definition of naval history in terms of the Western paradigm. Thus, the inshore and riverine fleets of peoples across much of the world are usually neglected, and to ask a naval historian about Hawaiian, Malagasy or Yoruban[28] war canoes is to risk being treated as if one is talking about men on the moon. The valuable conferences held in Newport, Rhode Island, demonstrate the problem by describing 'the essential nature of navies' in the following terms: 'all will agree that navies are instruments of government and operate as highly technological organisations'.[29] This narrow definition ensures that the naval history of much of the world is primitivized, not least because government and technology are generally conceived of in modern Western terms, and with an assumption that the military and mercantile functions of maritime activity should have been separated, as they were increasingly in Europe from the seventeenth century. There has recently been welcome attention to earlier periods of naval history, although most of the work tends to be on conflict in European waters. Considering these periods makes it more readily apparent that the dominant ideas of naval power, those advanced in the nineteenth and twentieth centuries and associated in particular with Alfred Thayer Mahan (1840–1914, see pp. 194–5), need to be complemented by other concepts that are more appropriate to a very different interaction of maritime potential, naval goals, ship technology, and financial and organizational resources.[30]

From the medieval period, European expansion was heavily (although far from exclusively) dependent on its maritime achievement.[31] Europe was not alone in this relationship, although no other area matched the scale of European maritime power projection. Yet, it would be mistaken to regard this as an obvious naval goal far superior, for example, to that of using maritime power to control coastal provinces and trade. The latter was certainly important in China, but Asian naval history is understudied compared to its European counterpart. There was great variety in the naval history of South and East Asia, not only within particular areas, with considerable variations in the extent of Chinese state-directed naval policy, but also between them, with the Indian states generally lacking such a commitment.[32]

Conclusion

Variety and uncertainty are not the themes sought by many who read about war; but they are the dominant conclusions that emerge from this study. As such, they serve as a challenge to the desire for synthesis, meaningful integration and overarching interpretation, and an ironic contrast to the immutable laws of war so often discussed in popular texts. The continued popularity of the latter, when their equivalents in other fields were generally dismissed decades ago, indicates the continued strength of popular presuppositions about the subject.

Notes

1 M. Sherry, 'Probing the Memory of War', *The Chronicle of Higher Education*, 7 Jan. 2000, p. B6.
2 D. Showalter, 'Europe's Way of War, 1815–64', in J.M. Black (ed.), *European Warfare 1815–2000* (2002), p. 27.
3 S. Morillo, 'The "Age of Cavalry" Revisited', in D.J. Kagay and L.J.A. Villalon (eds), *The Circle of War in the Middle Ages* (Woodbridge, 1999), pp. 57–8.

4 N. Di Cosmo (ed.), *Warfare in Inner Asian History, 500–1800* (Leiden, 2002).
5 W. Robertson, *The History of the Reign of the Emperor Charles V. With a view of the progress of society in Europe, from the subversion of the Roman Empire, to the beginning of the sixteenth century* (1769; 3 vols, 1782 edn) I, 5–6; A. Smith, *An Inquiry into the Nature and Causes of the Wealth of Nations* (1776) edited by R.H. Campbell and A.S. Skinner (2 vols, Oxford, 1979, cont. pag.), pp. 687–708; E. Gibbon, *The History of the Decline and Fall of the Roman Empire* (1776–88), edited by J.B. Bury (7 vols, 1897–1901), I, p. 93, V, pp. 358–9, VII, p. 2.
6 K. Raaflaub and N. Rosenstein, *War and Society in the Ancient and Medieval Worlds* (Cambridge, Mass., 1999).
7 And not only in the English-speaking world, e.g. J.-P. Rorive, *Les misères de la guerre sous le Roi-Soleil. Les populations de Huy, de Hesbaye et du Condroz dans la tourmente du siècle de malheur* (Liège, 2000).
8 R. Bevan, *The Destruction of Memory. Architecture and Cultural Warfare* (2004).
9 O. Bartov, *Hitler's Army: Soldiers, Nazis, and War in the Third Reich* (Oxford, 1991); M. Herr and K. Naumann (eds), *War of Extermination. The German Military in World War II. 1914–1944* (2000); A.B. Rossino, *Hitler Strikes Poland: Blitzkrieg, Ideology, and Atrocity* (Lawrence, Kansas, 2003); B. Shepherd, '*Wehrmacht* Security Regiments in the Soviet Partisan War, 1943', *European History Quarterly*, 33 (2003), pp. 493–529.
10 J. France, 'Recent writing on Medieval Warfare: From the Fall of Rome to *c.*1300', *Journal of Military History*, 65 (2001), p. 462.
11 W.E. Kaegi, *Byzantine Military Unrest 471–843: An Interpretation* (Amsterdam, 1981).
12 R.F. Hamilton and H.H. Herwig (eds), *The Origins of World War I* (Cambridge, 2003).
13 A reference to a Gilbert and Sullivan comic operetta that featured a plodding police force and an unbattleworthy general.
14 New Brunswick, New Jersey, Rutgers University Library, Fuller papers, Box 4, Italy–Abyssinian War Diary, pp. 16–17.
15 M. Paris, *Warrior Nation. Images of War in British Popular Culture 1850–2000* (2002).
16 J. Dülffer, M. Kröger and R.-H. Wippich, *Vermiedene Kriege. Deeskalation von Konflikten der Grossmächte zwischen Krimkrieg und Erstem Weltkrieg* (Munich, 1997).
17 K.F. Friday, 'Beyond Valor and Bloodshed: The Arts of War as a Path to Serenity', in R. Deist and H. Kleinschmidt (eds), *Knight and Samurai. Actions and Images of Elite Warriors in Europe and East Asia* (Göppingen, 2003), pp. 1–13.
18 A.J.P. Taylor, *How Wars Begin* (1980), p. 14.
19 G.E. Dowd, *A Spirited Resistance: The North American Struggle for Unity, 1745–1815* (Baltimore, 1992), pp. 11–12; P. Curtin, *Economic Change in Precolonial Africa: Senegambia in the Era of the Slave Trade* (2 vols, Madison, 1975), I, 153–68; P. Spear, *Twilight of the Mughuls: Studies in Late Mughul Delhi* (Cambridge, 1951), p. 9.
20 J.M. Black, *Why Wars Happen* (1998).

21 E.N. Luttwak, *The Grand Strategy of the Roman Empire from the First Century AD to the Third* (Baltimore, 1976).

22 S.P. Mattern, *Rome and Enemy. Imperial Strategy in the Principate* (Berkeley, 1999).

23 M.S. Drake, *Problematics of Military Power. Discipline, Government and the Subject of Violence, from Ancient Rome to Early Modernity* (2001).

24 For seventeenth-century New England, M.L. Oberg, *Uncas: First of the Mohegans* (Ithaca, New York, 2003).

25 C.S. Gray, 'National Styles in Strategy: The American Experience', *International Security*, 6, no. 2 (1981), p. 22.

26 There are also publishers that specialize in naval history, e.g. Conway (UK) and the Naval Institute Press (USA), although they also publish in other fields of military history.

27 J.B. Hattendorf (ed.), *Ubi Sumus?: The State of Naval and Maritime History* (Newport, 1994) and *Doing Naval History. Essays Toward Improvement* (Newport, 1995).

28 Many other societies of course employed similar vessels: on the sea or in deltaic, estuarine, riverine, and lacustrine environments.

29 Hattendorf, 'Introduction', to Hattendorf (ed.), *Doing Naval History*, p. 2.

30 Hattendorf and R.W. Unger (eds), *War at Sea in the Middle Ages and Renaissance* (Woodbridge, 2003).

31 J. Pryor, *Geography, Technology and War. Studies in the Maritime History of the Mediterranean 649–1571* (Cambridge, 1987).

32 S. Chandra (ed.), *The Indian Ocean: Explorations in History, Commerce and Politics* (New Delhi, 1987).

Chapter 2

The sound of guns: military history today

Deeply hostile to, and, indeed, prejudiced against, military history, the academic community has on the whole surrendered its study to writers who lack the sources, languages, institutional support and intellectual formation necessary to see beyond the smoke and dust of battle.

Charles Esdaile, *The Peninsular War* (2003), p. x

The signs are very different. On one hand, 'drums and trumpets' history flourishes; indeed, the British journal *Publishing News*, in its issue of 24 January 2003, referred to 'the rapidly growing market for military history'. The situation is no different in the USA, Spain or in Japan, where, if it is defined to include biographies of famous samurai, it accounts for a large percentage of the history sections of bookstores. Elsewhere, the situation is the same. *Le Figaro littéraire* of 16 November 2000 noted the growth in interest in France in operational military history.

Yet military historians frequently complain about the state of the subject in academe,[1] indeed about being in the 'ghetto' that, in 2000, Maurice Vaisse, a central figure in the subject in France, declared French military history had recently escaped from.[2] The conversation of academic military historians is frequently about how subject specialists are not replaced and how interest from students is not matched by support from colleagues, the whole contributing to an impression that the subject has been the victim, particularly in the USA, of what the Americans term culture wars. A certain indication of marginal status is provided by the neglect of military history in general surveys of historical work,[3] while in the USA, from the 1970s, the Society of Military History as well as non-organizational panels struggled to gain admittance to the programme for the annual conference of the American Historical Association. Military historians were angry that, although the 2004 meeting of the American Historical Association included military history panels, there were many panels and papers proposed that were rejected – though in fact all fields had rejections. Furthermore, although it is a very different issue, in the educational structures of certain militaries, there is concern about threats to the role of military history in training and preparation.

At one level, the problems may not seem particularly significant, given both the strength of non-academic writing for the popular market and the interest shown in war by other subject specialists, such as political scientists and anthropologists. But there is a particular historical insight that is worth noting. In contrast to other specialists, among historians there is more of a sense of the specific character of past periods, and thus a reluctance to treat history as if it was an isotropic surface and an unvarying data-set: this gives historical work on subjects such as the causes of war a different quality to social science approaches.[4] However, the degree to which many historians are reluctant to address the extent to which military developments were of general importance is a factor, and hostility to military history has done much damage to academic writing. Thus, in the USA, there is a penchant for historians in other, allegedly more relevant, fields to dismiss much military history as irrelevant both to courses dealing with the broader development of Western or World civilization, and to their particular fields of expertise.

The world of print

A different issue arises as a consequence of the contrast between much (but by no means all) popular military history and the more academic approach, which constitute the two subjects of this chapter. At the baldest, this contrast was expressed in comments in the *Reader's Guide to Military History* on Antony Beevor's *Stalingrad* (1998), the best-selling history book in Britain in 1998: 'offers nothing in the way of new insights or analysis. . . . It presents many of the main themes of the battle in accessible form'.[5] The same comments could be made about many other commercially successful works. Well-written operational histories not based on the scholarly scrutiny of archival sources, published by trade houses both major and minor, for example John Bierman and Colin Smith's *Alamein. War Without Hate* (2003), are all too common.

As much of this type of work does not seek to offer new insights, a point driven home by the far too frequent reprint of works without any attempt to take note of more recent relevant scholarship,[6] it is unclear that such criticism is helpful. Indeed, as academics benefit from public interest in military history, with, for some, consequent possibilities of publication of their own work, they need to be prepared to understand the conventions and constraints of current publishing for this market. In many respects, this publishing is an echo of the traditional practice of military history, with its focus on celebratory tales and exemplary narrative. Indeed, military history has been moulded by the exigencies of the world of print. The same was true of war literature, whether it considered contemporary or recent conflict, or earlier wars: in the former case, certainly in some states, institutional constraints were also an important aspect of the context.[7]

Understanding the pressures of the popular market, however, does not mean the lack of a critical faculty. The principal problems that emerge are that the market-driven approach leads to a (Western) Eurocentric emphasis (Western Europe, with the important addition of the USA), and to an operational and tactical focus. War becomes a matter of campaigns and battles, more particularly battle and biography; and this is as true of the visual mediums of film and television as of the written word. Indeed, film and television increasingly help set the normative standards for written work. Much of the popular work is repetitive and responds to the market opportunities of the familiar topic, or, to take a more favourable tone, this literature is a matter of making established knowledge accessible anew. Whichever approach is taken, there is a lack of originality in content and analysis. Not only does most military history written for the popular market lack perceptive insights, new material or judicious reflection; there is often also a style of writing that is novelistic, if not partisan. Thus, Robert Asprey's *The Rise and Fall of Napoleon. Vol I. The Rise* (2000) suits those who like their scimitars 'gleaming' and the French 'smelling Piedmontese blood'.

There is also a widespread practice in many popular (and some academic) works of claiming far more than is delivered. Titles and blurbs can be actively misleading. For example, John Winton's *An Illustrated History of the Royal Navy* (2000) claimed to be 'a comprehensive and authoritative history of the Royal Navy from its earliest times to the present day', but was, instead, a heavily illustrated work designed for a popular market. Allowing for this, there were still important problems with the book, which are all too typical of the genre. The early history of the British navy, for which there is a lack of illustrative material, was rushed through, there was no real understanding of developments in other states, which ensured that relative capability cannot be assessed, and there was a great focus on the sinkings of ships, which made for interesting tales, but could not be said to offer new insights. As another all too typical instance of the misleading character of titles, Russell Miller's *Behind the Lines. The Oral History of Special Operations in World War II* (2002) dealt with the British and Americans, therefore omitting most of the combatants.

For commercial reasons, many other works are also presented in a surprising fashion. In 2001, Osprey, a leading British publisher of popular military history, began a series described thus by the editor Robert O'Neill: 'Study them and gain a deeper understanding of war and a stronger basis for thinking about peace'. In fact, far from being as claimed 'a unique exploration of the history of human conflict . . . groundbreaking', or 'comprehensive', books like Todd Fisher's *The Napoleonic Wars: The Rise of the Emperor 1805–1807* (2001) and John Sweetman's *The Crimean War* (2001) were handsomely illustrated operational accounts. This is the usual type of work, but one that the drive for market share leads to mistaken claims for enhanced significance.

Statements made about novelty can also be misleading. The press release for Gordon Corrigan's *Mud, Blood and Poppycock. Britain and the First World War*, published in 2003 by Weidenfeld and Nicolson, a major London trade house, claimed that this 'groundbreaking new book shatters our preconceptions about the First World War' and 'will overturn everything you thought you knew about Britain and the First World War', when in practice it was introducing some readers to the insights freely available in works such as Paddy Griffith's *Battle Tactics of the Western Front. The British Army's Art of Attack, 1916–1918* (New Haven, 1994). Similarly, what is often covered in what claim to be general histories of war is limited. As another aspect of familiarity, too many of the photographs and other material employed in illustrated works are from established picture libraries, and, in addition, insufficient material is taken from foreign sources.[8] Aside from commercial factors, other motives play a major role in popular military history. In Germany, for example, it appeals to right-wing audiences, the elderly, neo-Nazis, and collectors of *militaria*.

Another aspect of novelty is provided by the argument that whatever is being written about is important to the development of warfare, as with the emphasis on manoeuvre in Robert Lyman's *Slim: Master of War. Burma and the Birth of Modern Warfare* (2004). That particular claim underplays the role of the Soviet campaigns of 1944–5, but, more seriously, there is the problem of assuming that there is a clear pattern of development.

Problems with the sources

Given the nature of what is published it may be wondered at times whether the entire operational dimension of war has not already been thoroughly covered, but this is not in fact the case. Even frequently recounted battles benefit from re-examination, as was brilliantly shown in *Salamanca 1812* (New Haven, 2001), by Rory Muir. The ethos of his book made it instructive for the entire subject. Taking a valuable reflective approach, Muir explained that it was difficult to provide a detailed account of what happened:

> while the sources are plentiful, they do not always fit neatly together; indeed, they are riddled with contradictions, incon-
> sistencies, gaps and uncertainty. . . . Normally the historian deals
> privately with these problems. . . . This method is inescapable in
> addressing a large, sweeping subject if the narrative is not to lose its
> momentum and the reader to miss the thread of the argument.
> However, it can also mislead the reader by suggesting that our
> understanding is far more securely based than is the case.

Throughout, unlike the vast majority of writers on military history, particularly on operational military history, Muir probed the sources. For example, of the British cavalry charge on the French left, he wrote, 'How can an account written more than twenty years after the event be so clear, comprehensible and detailed, when letters written within days are generally confused and fragmentary?'[9] Muir's ability to question and probe the sources, and to reconcile different accounts, reflected the value of a scholarly training, and his book is an able comment on much of the available and current work on battle, with its preference for repetition over scholarship. *Salamanca*, therefore, highlights how much still remains to be done on war in the West, even for the familiar topic of battles.

Problems with the sources are not restricted to warfare in the nineteenth and earlier centuries. The records of the Centre for Military Archives in King's College, London, launched in 1963 and formally inaugurated in May 1964, reveal that many generals who were approached replied that they had not kept records.[10] In 1963, J.F.C. Fuller wrote, 'The only time I kept a real diary was when at the War Office at the end of and after World War One. It ran to some 6 or 7 foolscap volumes, and was destroyed in the Blitz' [bombing of London, 1940–1]. Sir Ernest Swinton's secretary added, 'Ernest used to indulge in orgies of tearing up', while a progress report noted that Air Marshal Harris and Field Marshal Slim had kept no papers, and that General Sir David Campbell 'kept no diary, and letters written to his wife were burnt at her death in accordance with her wish'.[11]

In addition, the official histories faced problems in trying to assess numbers. In the case of the British histories of World War Two, Brian Melland referred to 'Axis sources which are unfortunately not so complete as we would wish, particularly in the latter stages of the war', while a British paper on the tank strength of German armoured divisions in 1942–3, which argued that casualties and fluctuating replenishment priorities were important factors in variations, commented:

> It shows how misleading formal establishments can be compared with the actual – and fluctuating – establishment of a division, and illustrates the importance of keeping this factor in mind. It doubtless applies to all armies at one time or another in their war careers.[12]

The prominent military writer Basil Liddell Hart, who sought information for his own historical work from those working on the official histories, himself complained 'The longer I have explored history the less satisfied I become about anything'.[13] As far as Axis personnel strengths and casualties were concerned, Melland delivered an answer that scarcely matches the requirements of popular history:

> the captured records, rich as they are in many ways, do present us all along the road with tiresome gaps, and it is only possible to state what they state. This means that the nice, tidy answer is often regrettably elusive.[14]

Brigadier C.J.C. Molony added: 'I am apt to turn a rather jaundiced eye on strength returns – perhaps because of vague memories of conjuring rabbits out of hats, as an adjutant a long time ago!'[15] Tank strength was a particular issue, because as Liddell Hart pointed out, 'To deduce correct lessons it is necessary, above all, to determine the tank strengths on either side in any important operations'. Reconciling sources involved addressing issues such as how best to distinguish those tanks that were fit for action, and also the treatment of light tanks that were only appropriate for reconnaissance duties.[16]

Muir was not alone in challenging conventional accounts of a battle. Niall Barr tried to do the same on the battle of Flodden (1512), and his book similarly illustrates the possibilities for revisionism, although less adroitly than Muir. Barr's focus on success in adopting innovations as a guide to capability is more generally valuable.[17] Interest in Flodden also exemplifies the way in which 'proto-nations' search for a particular military history; in this case Peter Reese's *Flodden: A Scottish Tragedy* (Edinburgh, 2003) argues that catastrophic defeat played a role in the eventual unification of Scotland and England.

The need to reconcile different sources also suggests the problems (of omission) facing scholars when they have only one source to rely on. Indeed, when it is possible to move from a single source, such as William of Tyre on Christian campaigning in twelfth-century Palestine, for example the siege of Ascalon in 1153, to consider several, there is a welcome deepening of understanding.[18] This underlines the drawback of work that seeks to rely on a limited range of material, a point made by Hans Delbrück (1848–1929), a key figure in the development of German military history, who emphasized the value of the critical examination of sources. More sources do not necessarily equate with more understanding, but they overcome the problem of having only one source.

At the operational level, another recent instance of the value of a scholarly re-examination of a much-trodden field is Christopher Duffy's *The '45. Bonnie Prince Charlie and the Untold Story of the Jacobite Rising* (2003), which argued that the turning points in the rebellion against Hanoverian rule in Britain were not the battles in themselves, the usual topics of popular writing, but, rather, the successive closing down of the options that were open to the Jacobites. More specifically, Duffy avoided the customary fault in discussion of the 1746 campaign of focusing on the battle of Culloden and neglecting the more general flow of operations, especially William, Duke of Cumberland's skill in gaining the initiative. As far as Culloden is concerned, Duffy, in line with scholars across the range of military history, emphasized the importance of discipline, in this case that of Cumberland's infantry, which blunted what would otherwise have been sensible, preliminary Jacobite lunges, and of the careful deployment and use of troops, a non-heroic approach to the discussion of victory. Whereas in earlier battles, at Prestonpans (1745), Clifton (1745) and Falkirk (1746), the government cavalry had plunged, or been plunged, into the fray regardless, and the control of the engagement had passed to the Jacobites, at Culloden the cavalry was fed around the two flanks, ready to intervene when the favourable opportunity offered, and, for the first time, the action on the side of the government forces was initially left to the artillery.

Weapons and battlefields

Conflict in the Western world has engaged most writers, often in a very predictable fashion. Thus, as an aspect of the focus on battle, there has been a mass of work on the weapons used in conflict, with far less attention devoted to machinery and other systems important in logistics, communications and other aspects of war. This can be seen for example with publications under popular imprints, such as, in the case of Britain, the Arms and Armour imprint, for example Roger Freeman's *The B-17 Flying Fortress Story* (2000), Alfred Price's *The Spitfire Story* (2000), and Y.E. Tarrant's *King George V Battleships* (2000), as well as with Osprey's New Vanguard series, such as Chris Bishop's *Bell UH-1 Huey 'Slicks' 1962–75* (2003), with works published by Cassell, for instance Tim Laming's *The Vulcan Story, 1952–2002* (2002), and with books such as Taylor Downing and Andrew Johnston's *Battle Stations. Decisive Weapons of the Second World War* (Barnsley, 2000). Such titles need citing as they are apt to be forgotten by academics who consider military history in terms of the work of major scholars, but as this book seeks to argue, that is an approach that is flawed by its partial character.

In many respects, the popular fascination with machines is a continuation of the schoolboy interest in making replicas that was vastly enhanced by the development of plastic technology and was exploited by Airfix. Indeed, one of Osprey's series, Osprey Modelling, responds to the range of model kits and the continued popularity of modelling, publishing works such as Geoff Coughlin and Neil Ashby's *Modelling the M3/M5 Stuart Light Tank* (2003). It is indicative that most of the weapons covered, if not British, are as in this case American. Chris Smith's bestseller *The Lord of the Rings: Weapons and Warfare* (2003) provided an instructive variant on the popularity of this genre, while the three films in the *Lord of the Rings* sequence (2001–3) depicted war very much in terms of battle, with the contrasting capabilities of different species – for example elephant-borne troops against cavalry, and Nazgûl against eagles in *The Return of the King* (2003) – enhancing those of particular weapons. Computer games reflect these interests.

Weaponry also plays a crucial role in popular works on the general history of war. Thus, John Keegan's series guidelines for the *History of Warfare*, for which he acted as general-editor for the London trade house Cassell, included 'As to themes: the technical determinants will always be important, particularly in the volumes devoted to naval and air warfare, but must form a major element in all volumes'.[19] This linked in with the series' need for a large number of illustrations for all the volumes, even when less appropriate, as in Martin Van Creveld's *The Art of War. War and Military Thought* (2000).

Another variant of popular military history is the battlefield guide, which has enjoyed considerable popularity in recent decades, first as a result of mass car ownership in the West, and then as a consequence of inexpensive foreign travel for Westerners. Thus, large numbers have been able to visit not only domestic battlefields, especially Civil War ones in the USA,[20] which were also much visited in the earlier age of rail travel, but also foreign battlefields. As an instance of the demand, *Major and Mrs Holt's Battlefield Guide to the Somme* (Barnsley, 1996) appeared in a fourth edition in 2003, while the Holts have also produced battlefield guides for Ypres, the Normandy beaches, and Gallipoli. Some battlefield accounts offer a new glimpse of very familiar terrain, as with Clive Harris' *Walking the London Blitz* (Barnsley, 2003), and the brief walking tour in Barnet Schecter's *The Battle for New York. The City at the Heart of the American Revolution* (2002), but much is far further afield, and the declining real cost of air travel has seen battlefield tourism expand to include, for example, the sites of the Peninsular, Crimean and Zulu wars. Battefield tour guides also sell well in Spain.

Television and film

Again, there has been a significant link with television, as the specific character of the battlefield has provided setting and subject for television treatments, for example with Richard Holmes' popular 'War Walks' series on BBC, which in turn have served as the basis for books published in 1996 and 1997. Similarly, as an instance of the television–book linkage in military history, David Mearns and Rob White's *'Hood' and 'Bismarck'. The Deep-Sea Discovery of an Epic Battle* (2001) was a book that accompanied two television documentaries, and made good use of visual material – state-of-the-art underwater photography, computer graphics and sonar scans – in order to recreate the 1941 clash, and show why the *Hood* went down.

One of the major flaws in much television history, however, is the poor choice of imagery together with frequently inaccurate commentary. Events, devices and even people in contemporary footage are used indiscriminately because the image is appealing rather than accurate. Programmes about the Battle of Britain, for example, can include footage of aircraft from later in World War Two, or even the wrong aircraft. The same problem occurs, although to a lesser extent, with photographs in books, and is often due to a lack of knowledge on the part of the picture researcher/obtainer, who is unlikely to be an historian. In addition, there is sometimes a lack of professionalism, whereby anything will do provided it looks exciting.

The perception of television is also an issue. Its 'reality' has persuaded many viewers that what they see and hear is real, rather than fictionalized life or at least only a partial view of real life. This was seen with the much-aired footage of the shooting of a captured Viet Cong by a South Vietnamese chief of police during the Tet Offensive in 1968, usually without an explanation of the background, namely that the Viet Cong had just been captured in the vicinity of the police chief's house, and that the police chief thought that his family had been killed: the shooting was an emotional, not a political, social or military reaction. Conversely, and here again the limited amount that can be conveyed by an image is apparent, the shooting was not a premeditated act, but it can be seen as a predisposed one.

Television and film tend to take things out of their original context and label them in simplistic terms, then jump to simplistic conclusions. The process by which any programme is produced is overlooked: the blurring of the reality is as much a dramatic technique as it is deliberate deception. Film-makers are apt to argue that they are portraying a deeper 'truth', although the search for profit, and thus impact, tend to be the dominant factors.[21] The accuracy of historical films is frequently a matter of controversy. In early 2004 British and French historians of the Crusades criticized *Kingdom of Heaven*, a film based on the battle of Hattin, as deeply flawed.

Face of battle

The engagement with conflict is the case with a very fashionable approach to military history, that termed 'face of battle' in reference to John Keegan's 1976 book of that name, although his stance was scarcely novel. A *Guardian* profile on 25 October 1967 of Barrie Pitt, the editor of Purnell's part-work histories of the two World Wars, noted that he was against asking writers who had not seen action to produce battle or campaign accounts: 'when we get down to the details, what happens to companies and platoons, there appears a lack of reality, a certain hollowness'. Keegan's much-applauded (although also ably criticized[22]) attempt to recreate what actually happened in battle concentrated on three famous engagements, all in a small section of Western Europe: Agincourt (1415), Waterloo (1815), and the Somme (1916). It was an attempt to set a standard for the genre of battlefield accounts, and, in an accessible revisionism, raised the question of the accuracy of established descriptions, not least those written from the perspective of the Staff College mind, with its understandable tendency to reduce the chaos of war to order so that movements can be readily explained.

This top–down approach, with its stress on command decisions, and the ready response of troops organized as units, conformed, however, neither to the democratic interests of modern readers concerned with the individual experience and contribution, nor to the role of confusion, the 'fog of war', at the tactical and operational level. Furthermore, the subordination in explanation of an army's fighting quality to its leaders' command skills appeared questionable. Aside from encouraging the scholarly 'face of battle' riposte, the top–down approach also, in reply, led veterans to offer accounts that recovered their experience, and thus served as an appropriate memorialization.[23]

Important books that recreated the 'face of battle' included Peter Englund's *The Battle of Poltava* (1992; Swedish original 1988), although it was all too typical of the genre in focusing on the experience of one side: the Swedes, in this case unsuccessful against Russia in 1709. The 'face of battle' process continues as new insights are gained, as when Ann Hyland employed arguments from an equestrian point of view to query whether chariots charged *en masse*.[24] Given the need to understand what happened in battle in order to assess relative capability, a topic of particular concern to scholars, it is worth noting a successful recent book-length extension of the 'face of battle' approach to the Classical world: Gregory Daly's analysis of the battle of Cannae (216 BCE). Daly could not match the detail of Muir's *Salamanca*, and his was indeed a shorter book, but he fulfilled his goal of

> a full-scale analysis . . . along the lines pioneered by John Keegan . . . while not neglecting traditional methods of analysing battles in terms of Grand Tactical manoeuvres. . . . One of the major tasks of this book has been to penetrate in some sense beyond Polybius' account, in order to recover the experience of battle.[25]

Like Muir (see pp. 30–2), Daly showed that the 'face of battle' and battlefield approaches were far from incompatible with scholarly progress. An increase in archaeological and geological evidence makes it possible to try to do the same for certain other battles of the Classical period, such as that between the Spartans and the Persian invaders of Greece at Thermopylae (480 BCE).

A focus on battle is also particularly apparent with popular naval history. There is important scholarly work on naval power, especially its administrative aspects, but the sound of guns is what readers prefer to hear. Thus, the battle of Jutland in 1916 between Britain and Germany, the largest-scale engagement in the age of dreadnought battleships, is frequently revisited, and the appearance of excellent works, such as Andrew Gordon's *The Rules of the Game: Jutland and British Naval Command* (1996), does not encourage others to turn to other topics. Instead, the respective merits of Jellicoe and Beatty are revisited yet again, for example in Nigel Steel and Peter Hart's *Jutland 1916. Death in the Grey Waters* (2003), and, less originally, in Robert Massie's *Castles of Steel: Britain, Germany, and the Winning of the Great War at Sea* (New York, 2003). The British press release for the latter claims that Massie brings 'unparalleled' knowledge to the subject, which a reading of the text and of other books suggests is a surprising verdict. The American equivalent to Jutland is the sound of carrier-borne planes, and the coverage of Midway in particular has been exhaustive. Reminiscences played a major role in the most successful recent popular naval history, Ronald Spector's *At War at Sea: Sailors and Naval Combat in the Twentieth Century* (New York, 2001), a work that, in a reflection of the concerns of the period, also devoted considerable attention to the living conditions of sailors.

Biography

Military biography has provided another way to make operational military history commercially successful. It taps into a wider popular market for biography, but does so in a way that provides something particular for male readers. Indeed, the commercial success in Britain of *Field Marshal Alanbrooke's War Diaries 1939–1945* (2001) owed much to its widespread purchase as a Christmas present for ageing fathers. Similar books have included *Churchill's Generals* (1991) edited by John Keegan, Nigel Hamilton's *The Full Monty I: Montgomery of Alamein, 1887–1942* (2001), and their American equivalents. Generals with powerful personalities (or, rather, those whose personalities can be readily seen as powerful, such as Patton) have also benefited from film treatment, and this in turn helps ensure interest in books about them. Much of the writing is laudatory. Thus, John Pollock's *Kitchener* (2001) presented him as a man of mission, with an admirable sense of purpose and persistence in the face of adversity.

The fascination with biography has much to do with the 'great man' approach to (military) history and with battle as theatre,[26] one that begins, chronologically, with Alexander the Great, and that has frequently overlapped with the literary genre of the epic and with the style of the romance. In modern times, this approach is generally accompanied, as in the discussion of Allied generalship in France in 1944, by a partisanship that is related to the need to find heroes, and then to make them the key figures in not only the narrative but also the accompanying explanation.[27] The latter, indeed, poses particular problems for popular military history, as the need to provide a degree of explanation tests the genre even more than the narrative. To make this explanation readily explicable, it is comforting to turn to leadership, not least to an almost mystical reading of generalship, as in many of the accounts of Napoleon's war-making. These accounts have been questioned by Owen Connelly in his *Blundering to Glory. Napoleon's Military Campaigns* (1987; second edition, 1999), with its stress on Napoleon's skill as an improviser, but this has had scant impact at the popular level. Instead, there is a preference for almost mechanistic, and certainly uncomplicated, explanations of success, rather than for appreciating the complexities of command. The focus on great men has ensured that second-rank commanders, or simply those overshadowed by the more flamboyant or apparently noteworthy, are generally neglected, which makes it harder to evaluate command skills.[28]

The popular market

Battlefield accounts continue to be very popular in all major national military history markets, and large numbers of them appear. Some publishers specialize in such works. Thus, Pen and Sword, one of the leading British publishers of military history, produced Julian Paget and Derek Saunders' *Hougoumont. Waterloo* (Barnsley, 2001), Carl Shilleto's *Utah Beach* (Barnsley, 2002), and Michael Tolhurst's *Bastogne. Battle of the Bulge* (Barnsley, 2002). These works tend to be very specific, so that Tolhurst, for example, does not offer a comparison with the German offensives on the Western Front in 1918, nor with others mounted by German forces on the Eastern Front in the last stages of World War Two, and there is often no attempt to search for wider significance.[29] In addition, some of the writing jars, not least due to a degree of partisanship. For example, in his treatment of the battle of Asiago, in the Battleground Europe series, Francis Mackay provides useful material on the conflict in northern Italy in 1918 at the tactical level, but uses phrases such as 'The bag of k.u.k. [Austrian] men and material was impressive'.[30] Many battlefield accounts include tour itineraries, such as Tim Saunders' *Hill 112. Battles of the Odon* (Barnsley, 2001), a work in the Battleground Europe series dealing with part of the 1944 Normandy campaign.

Work of this type is validated through structures, largely, if not exclusively, commercial in character, that are outside those of the academic profession, but that does not make it less important. With the 'academy' in large part closed, authors who focus on operational military history are obliged to live by their pens, and this encourages publication in a style that further marginalizes the subject in terms of the academy. These writers receive publishers' advances and have no teaching, but they do not benefit from sabbaticals or research grants, and have to construct their projects in the likelihood that none will ever be provided. This lessens the feasibility of archival research and, definitely, the chances of work in foreign archives, without which it is impossible properly to understand the multiple interests that led to conflict or to compare military capability and effectiveness. Just as, before judging a book, one should consider for whom it is intended, so in assessing an author it is necessary to understand his position. For example, the fact that Ian Fletcher, one of the leading British writers on the Peninsular War of 1808–14, is a freelance writer who runs Ian Fletcher Battlefield Tours, does not lessen the value of his books, such as *In Hell Before Daylight. The Siege and Storming of the Fortress of Badajoz, 1812* (Staplehurst, 1983) and *Fortresses of the Peninsular War 1808–14* (2003), but it helps explain his operational focus.

The consequences of a lack of resources on the part of many, if not most, authors writing for the popular market affects their response to new archival possibilities, although as many know what they want to say beforehand they are not greatly interested in archival research, analysis or reflection. Language skills remain an issue, but now that the Soviet archives are far more open than they were before the fall of the Iron Curtain, there is far less need than before for discussion of the Eastern Front in World War Two that relied on the German perspective alone. This has accentuated the contrast between scholarly and popular accounts, as the latter do not tend to integrate Soviet material adequately.

Furthermore, commercial possibilities ensure that the Eastern Front receives less attention than conflict directly involving Britain and the USA, leading to the comment: 'we can only reflect on the flood of articles and television shows doubtless being planned for the sixtieth anniversary of D Day next year with some misgivings – if one considers the almost non-existent coverage in the West on the Red Army's greatest triumph. Such blind historical ethno-centricity does us little credit'.[31] Japanese advances in China in 1944 were even more flagrantly neglected. Continuing restrictions on access to Soviet material affects research for the espionage aspects of war, hot and cold. This is a commercially successful area of publication, and one that deserves far more scholarly attention, but hitherto there has been only a limited integration of this field with other aspects of military activity.[32]

It would be misleading to suggest that work for the popular market is necessarily weak, and sometimes the approach is refreshingly original. Thus, in *The Hutchinson Atlas of World War Two Battle Plans: Before and After* (Oxford, 2000), battle plans were usefully contrasted by Stephen Badsey with what actually happened, a focused form of counterfactual study. The lack of a conclusion evaluating the general reasons for failure to achieve operational objectives, and the lack of any inclusion of Japanese ground-offensives were the sole disappointments, but in the treatment of World War Two in the East, there is a general preference for discussing battles at sea and conflict involving the Americans, and certainly not Japanese campaigns in China, while Japanese plans are rarely as neat and well-preserved as those usually studied. Badsey's book was more grounded than the bulk of the counterfactual literature on war. This literature became popular in the 1990s, reflecting not only the continued popularity of military history, but also, more specifically, both academic disquiet with structuralist interpretations of history and publishers' sense of market opportunity. Thus, the tenth anniversary issue of *MHQ: The Quarterly Journal of Military History* led to *What If? Military Historians Imagine What Might Have Been* (2000) edited by Robert Cowley, and that, in turn, had two sequels.

As another instance of successful work for the popular market, the route of a joint biography was employed with considerable originality by Andrew Roberts when, in *Napoleon and Wellington* (2001), he showed how their views of each other's generalship changed greatly. Napoleon was initially very arrogant about Wellington, and, in 1810, was so certain that Wellington's army in the Peninsula would be defeated that he included it in a list for a proposed exchange of prisoners of war. Wellington himself was offended to be referred to that year as 'the sepoy general', a reference to his earlier command in India and a fascinating indication of Napoleon's lack of respect for experience of conflict outside Europe, but by 1815, his victories over Napoleon's marshals in the Peninsular War had made Napoleon anxious about him. In turn,

Wellington, who admired Napoleon the soldier in 1814–15, came increasingly to criticize his former opponent, enabling the Duke to present himself as the equal, if not the better, of his former rival. This device, which can be employed for other pairs of generals,[33] is particularly valuable if it focuses on the changing character of military reputations and on how reputations are created and contested.

Similarly, history written for a general readership can make available material that is not well known. Thus, in Tempus' Battles and Campaigns series, Tim Travers' *Gallipoli 1915* (Stroud, 2001), making effective use of the Ottoman General Staff archives in Ankara, argued that Allied failure resulted in part from a much stronger Turkish defence, greater Turkish numbers and firmer Turkish motivation than had been anticipated. In *Bismarck. The Story Behind the Destruction of the Pride of Hitler's Navy* (2001), David Bercuson and Holger Herwig provided not only an able operational account, but also linked the struggle to wider strategic issues, not least the development of the Anglo-American relationship and tensions within German naval policy: the breakout by the *Bismarck* in 1941 was seen as a threat to Roosevelt's direction of American naval policy.

Both these instances, however, in some way prove the point about the weakness of popular military historians, as these popular-style books benefited from academic authors trained in source evaluation. The same was true of Richard Overy's *The Battle* (2001), an account of the Battle of Britain that drew on a command of German strategy. Even when authors base themselves on published primary sources, rather than the full range of archival material, it is still possible to write effective popular history if the scholarly values of a judicious evaluation of material are deployed. Thus, in *Redcoat. The British Soldier in the Age of Horse and Musket* (2002), Richard Holmes pointed out that military executions were rarer than letters and diaries might suggest; although the intensely pro-British army position of the author affected the character of the work.

In Japan, the line between academic and popular history is much less distinct than in the USA or Europe. There is a fairly large number of amateur historians – mostly journalists – without formal graduate-level training in history, who produce a vast corpus of work on famous battles, weapons and armour, illustrated books on castles, and similar publications. Much of this, however, is well-balanced work, often based, at least in part, on primary source research. In addition, many Japanese academic historians do not publish exclusively through scholarly journals and presses. Instead, they also write books for popular consumption, and contribute to magazines and special series commissioned by newspapers and popular presses. A number of major Japanese writers, such as Hata Ikuhiko, while dipping into the popular media for both infusions of cash and mass-distribution, still produce fine work.[34] There is a Society for Military History (*Gunji-shi Gakkai*) that produces its own academic journal and has several hundred members, many working in academe, while the National Defense Academy has a history department that is quite active. Several Japanese specialists in modern East Asian history focus on military matters, and there is a number of foreigners who work as japanologists in Japan and specialize in military history.

Across the world, popular military history faces the problem of being expected to fit into general assumptions. Thus, a foreword to a book on the battle at Glorietta in New Mexico in March 1862 notes that the campaign 'still struggles to find its place within the larger context of the war. Robert E. Lee and Ulysses S. Grant were not involved, and its combatants genuinely fretted over missing the spotlight'.[35] There is also an emphasis on battle in popular military history, when, in fact, other aspects of conflict, such as sieges, are more important.[36] Authors writing on subjects for which there is no general market face grave difficulties.

Memoirs and oral history

'Face of battle' work was prescient, in that the mass readership of the last quarter of the twentieth century and into the 2000s was particularly interested in the experience of individuals; this led to the extensive use of oral evidence, both in books and on television. Indeed, war memoirs constitute an important part of military history publishing, overlapping with (fictional) war literature, which, in the modern form, developed from the early nineteenth century and helped to mould what was expected from memoirs – although the process was also two-way. Fictional memoirs provide an interesting variation: most were serious, although George Macdonald Fraser's comic *Flashman* series, which began in 1969, with its protagonist a much-decorated Victorian scoundrel, offered a perspective that reflected the anti-heroic mood of many British (and other) readers in the late twentieth century and was particularly interesting because the author himself was a veteran.

To return from the world of fiction, individual memoirs appear more pertinent than unit histories, or, rather, they are increasingly, the best way to make the latter more attractive, although unit histories continue to be a rich vein for publishers. For example, the French publisher

Lavauzelle produces a series of well-illustrated histories of units of the French military: 2000 saw the publication of *Cavalerie Légion, 1er Régiment d'infanterie de Marine* and *43e Bataillon d'infanterie de Marine*. In some countries, memoirs are the most accessible form of recent military history. This is the case in Spain with the Civil War of 1936–9, which has been a sensitive subject for historians in that country, a situation accentuated by the extent to which Spanish historians traditionally have not covered military history.

Memoirs are not without value, especially in describing the role of individuals and drawing attention to neglected conflicts,[37] although they need to be handled with care. Thus, for example, while the emphasis on the dangers of U-boat (submarine) operations in Werner Fürbringer's *Flips. Legendary U-Boat Commander 1915–1918* (Barnsley, 2000) is reasonable, the argument that the U-boats would have been more effective had there been no restrictions on their choice of targets prior to 1917 has to be handled with care and requires a different level of scholarly discussion. For the same war, the autobiographical records of British sailors provide interesting insights on the quality of patriotism. Henry Welch of HMS *Kent* reported vividly on the sinking of the German *Nürnberg* in the battle of the Falkland Islands in 1914:

> we have avenged the *Monmouth*. I really believe it was in the *Nürnberg*'s power to have saved many of the *Monmouth*'s crew. Instead, she simply shelled her until the last part was visible above water. Noble work of which the German nation should feel proud. Thank God I am British.[38]

The paucity of reference to such sources certainly weakens Robert Massie's *Castles of Steel*. Several of the widely-cited memoirs of World War One, including Robert Graves's autobiography *Goodbye to All That* (1929), are highly structured for dramatic effect, and have to be treated with caution. This is an instance of the 'problem' of much military history – the application of a structure of the author's choosing where a pattern did not exist. In practice, all patterns are illusory and why a particular pattern is chosen ought to be treated with scepticism.

Memoirs and biographies are frequently uncritical, if not downright eulogies. Thus, Charles Messenger's *Hitler's Gladiator. The Life and Military Career of Sepp Dietrich* (2001), produced by one of the major commercial publishers in the field, Brasseys, displayed the worrying failure of judgement, seen in too much work on the SS, with regard to the argument that Dietrich, a willing participator in the SS, was a child of his time, ignoring the extent to which many Germans did not become Nazis or join the SS. Scholarly work on Wehrmacht atrocities that had appeared since Messenger first published his book in 1988 was neglected. The 'top–down' character of such works is countered by others, such as Henry Metelmann's *Through Hell for Hitler. A Dramatic First-hand Account of Fighting on the Eastern Front with the Wehrmacht* (2001), paperbacked in 2003, which presented a decline in morale and discipline from 1943. Metelmann wrote from the perspective of an ordinary soldier.

Memoirs and biographies are frequently reprinted, and are presented as worthy of attention because of their personal view and novelistic quality. Thus, James Goodson's *Tumult in the Clouds* (1983), published in new editions in 1986 and 2003, was described on the front cover of the 2003 edition as 'The Classic Story of War in the Air. . . . An utterly compelling and intensely personal account of war in all of its horror and excitement'.

The wider applicability of this method was less clear, and the same problem affects the oral history of combatants, a method developed for the American army in World War Two by S.L.A. Marshall, a journalist who had become an officer. He used his research, in *Men Against Fire: The Problem of Battle Command in Future War* (New York, 1947), to throw light on the peer-group character of combat motivation; a valuable perspective, but one limited by the chronological constraints of oral history,[39] while, more specifically, the accuracy of Marshall's research about the percentage of American conscripts not firing at the enemy in combat was challenged.[40]

There is also a geographical factor largely driven by commercial rationale: readers want to hear accounts of the experiences of earlier generations, and this leads to a focus on the most popular markets: Britain and the USA. Thus, British readers are particularly interested in the two world wars, so in 2003 Pimlico could think it appropriate to publish a paperback version of Peter Vansittart's *Voices from the Great War* (1981). The same year, Allen Lane, a major British imprint, published *Storm of Steel*, a new translation of Ernst Jünger's Western Front classic *In Stahlgewittern* (1920). A large number of memoirs of World War One are also published for French readers.

American publishers focus far more on World War Two than on World War One, while the most controversial exhibition of recent years, the *Enola Gay* display at the Smithsonian in 1995, reflected debate about the war, in this case the dropping of the first atomic bomb. American publishers emphasize biographical and autobiographical approaches.

For example the Aberjona Press, which prides itself on having a 'publishing division overwhelmingly comprised of retired and other former soldiers, sailors, and airmen', publishes American and German accounts of the war, based heavily on interviews and memoirs.[41]

The personal element is popular with American readers. James Bradley's *Flags of Our Fathers* (2000) became an American bestseller with its account of the conquest of Iwo Jima in 1945 based on the records of the author's father, who had been one of the flagraisers portrayed in Joe Rosenthal's famous photograph. Bradley followed this with *Flyboys* (New York, 2003), an account of eight American airmen shot down and captured by the Japanese in World War Two, which rose high in the American bestseller lists. Personal letters also played a major role in McKay Jenkins' *The Last Ridge. The Epic Story of the U.S. Army's 10th Mountain Division and the Assault in Hitler's Europe* (New York, 2003), while that topic also indicated the sense of commercial opportunity provided by America's conduct in World War Two, as Jenkins' book, published by Random House, was matched by Peter Shelton's *Climb to Conquer. The Untold Story of World War II's 10th Mountain Division Ski Troops*, published by another leading New York publisher, Scribner. The same year saw the publication of *Ours To Fight For: American Jewish Voices from the Second World War* (New York).

The experiences of common soldiers are given particular force when written by veterans, as in Eugene Sledge's *With the Old Breed at Peleliu and Okinawa* (Novato, 1981) and Paul Fussell's *The Boys' Crusade: The American Infantry in Northwestern Europe, 1944–1945* (New York, 2003), neither of which minimize the horror. In *Wartime: Understanding and Behavior in the Second World War* (Oxford, 1989), Fussell presented an account of the experience of American ordinary soldiers that emphasized the problems of maintaining morale. This offered a harsher account of the army than that presented by Stephen Ambrose in *Band of Brothers: E Company, 506th Regiment, 101st Airborne from Normandy to Hitler's Eagle's Nest* (New York, 1992) and *Citizen Soldiers: The U.S. Army from the Normandy Beaches to the Bulge to the Surrender of Germany* (New York, 1997). Other wars are similarly covered with similar ends. Allan Millett's preface to his *The War for Korea. American, Asian and European Combatants and Civilians, 1945–53* (Washington, 2002) notes 'this book attempts to find the meaning of the Korean War through the experience of individual and small groups of people'. Greenwood/Praeger has launched a new series on American Soldiers' Lives, designed to come out in 2006 or thereabouts.

Oral history and memoirs also testify to the public and commercial appeal of the 'war and society' approach, as they are open to civilians as well as combatants. Indeed, this has proved particularly important over the last decade. In 2003 in Britain, the BBC (British Broadcasting Corporation) launched 'The World War Two People's War website', urging people to 'Write your story directly on to the BBC website. Do your bit: pass on your family story for future generations', a stress on memorialization that was at once individual and collective, and was certainly democratic. Many books tackle the experience of ancestors. Thus, in 2003, Simon and Schuster, a leading New York publisher, produced in *Testament: A Soldier's Story of the Civil War*, Benson Bobrick's account of the war service of one of his grandfather's based on the latter's letters. Re-enactments are another aspect of coming to grips with the past. They are particularly popular in the USA and Britain. In the USA, aside from the very popular Civil War re-enactments, others also drew considerable numbers: the annual re-enactment of the Battle of the Bulge drew about 5,000 re-enacters in the early 2000s.

In able hands, the recollections of soldiers serve to help recover the experience of conflict,[42] but there is a potential clash between this approach to informing our understanding of events and the require-ments of scholarship. More specifically, there is the problem with oral history, as with personal memoirs, of the process of construction[43] and thus of validating accounts, an issue that led to controversy in 2003 over a book that rose to the top of the *New York Times* bestseller list, Rick Bragg's *I Am a Soldier, Too: The Jessica Lynch Story* (New York, 2003). The following year the National Endowment for the Arts announced a programme called Operation Homecoming, in which American troops returning from duty would be encouraged to write about their wartime experiences. Of the initial budget of $300,000, $250,000 was provided by Boeing, a major defence contractor, and there is a possible tension between the granting of money without restrictions and attitudes such as that of the Boeing executive Jim Albaugh: 'Their wartime experiences . . . will be a powerful portrayal of commitment, sacrifice and patriotism.'

This is scarcely new. John Frederick Maurice, the author of *Military History of the Campaign of 1882 in Egypt* (1888), a campaign in which he had served, had to reconcile clashing views from participants about the crucial battle of Tel-el-Kebir,[44] the battle that led to the British conquest of Egypt. When Maurice came to write the *History of the War in South Africa* (1906–10), the official history of the Boer War of 1899–1902, he was allowed to go through the correspondence with General Redvers Buller, had lunch with Earl Roberts, who had masterminded British success in 1900, and was offered advice by key politicians – Chamberlain and Milner. But Maurice also received notes from General Pole Carew, who explained why his views differed from those of Roberts.[45] George Howe's *Northwest Africa: Seizing the Initiative in the West* (Washington, 1957), the official American account of the Torch and Tunisia Campaign of 1943–4, was criticized for his use of memoirs:

> It is evident that he has made considerable use of post-war writings as well as of contemporary documentation and a tendency to stitch the two together should be borne in mind in view of the large number of 'pieces' written after the war for the Americans by senior German officers connected with Africa. These accounts were largely written from memory and inevitably tend to be coloured by hindsight or personal prejudice. They are, of course, useful but should, in our view, be handled with care.[46]

Major-General Ian Playfair, who was responsible for two of the volumes in the British official history of World War Two, noted 'The fun really begins when individuals trying with the best intentions to amplify and clarify the documents by personal recollection, disagree among themselves'.[47] Reviewing the process of writing military history, Arthur Swinson noted in 1967 that generals offered clashing advice in interviews with authors, and because he emphasized the role of personality and human failings in war, Swinson saw this factor as important.[48]

Liddell Hart, the leading British writer on military topics in the interwar period, had already drawn attention to the deficiencies of the individual voice:

> Any man's personal experience, however long and however highly placed, can cover no more than a fragment of any one war. It suffers still worse limitations in comparison with the general experience of warfare in its different conditions and times, so that personal experience of one type of war may be more misleading than helpful in preparing for another. But in history we have bottled experience, from all the best growths, only waiting to be uncorked.[49]

At the level of a former junior officer engaged in combat in Italy during World War Two, the British military historian Michael Howard responded to Liddell Hart's comments on minor errors in the diaries and letters he had written then: 'The errors which you pointed out in them show how little eye-witnesses are to be trusted'. In their

correspondence, Liddell Hart drew valuable attention to differences in
the records left from particular conflicts:

> I much admire the courageous frankness with which you wrote
> about your experiences and impressions – a frankness more
> characteristic of the fighting soldiers' accounts of World War I than
> most of those which have been written about World War II.[50]

There is also a tendency to mine memoirs and oral histories for support
for preconceptions, despite the clear intention of the writers to offer far
more nuanced stories. This can be seen with the focus on combat, as
opposed to other experiences of war, and also with the emphasis on
atrocities.

Possibly, however, the process of validation is less important for the
many readers who are concerned with experiencing the vicarious
excitement of war and seeking to understand it in terms of individual
experience.[51] Indeed, the overlap of fact and fiction is seen in the
fictionalization of television and film accounts, the style and tone of
books for the popular market,[52] and part of the sales language used to
recommend books. The Osprey *New Books October–December 2003*
catalogue included on the front cover ' "The best military history series
published today – indispensable" – Bernard Cornwell, author of the
best-selling *Sharpe* novels'. The 2003 History Channel series on the
Peninsular War was narrated by Cornwell and subtitled 'The War Sharpe
Fought'. From the period covered by his novels came works such as Eric
Hunt's *Charging Against Napoleon. Diaries and Letters of three Hussars*
(Barnsley, 2001), a skilful interweaving of diaries and letters.

Novels themselves led to interest in the period they depicted. The
success in 2003 of the film *Master and Commander: The Far Side of the
World*, based on Patrick O'Brian's novel of that name but with the
enemy significantly the French rather than the Americans, encouraged
the reading of works about the British navy in the period, especially
about Nelson, himself a character often presented in a novelistic fashion.
The novelistic character of military history was not restricted to the
coverage of early-nineteenth century Britain. In the 1960s, the editorial
policy of Purnell's histories of the Second and then First, World War
was 'to present the hard facts of history in the prose of highly-skilled
novelists'.[53] The press release for John Nichol and Tony Rennell's *The
Last Escape. The Untold Story of Allied Prisoners of War in Germany
1944–5* (2003) includes the description 'Packed with first-hand
testimony and impressive scholarship but with all the pace of a novel'.

This of course is not a new process. Polyaenus' *Strategemata*, a work of military strategy focused on stratagems written by a Greek in about 162 CE and dedicated to the joint Roman Emperors Marcus Aurelius and Lucius Verus as an aid to conducting the Parthian War (161–6) then in progress, included stories of brave gods and heroes.[54] Later, epic and romance literature were important in medieval Europe, and 'despite the fact that writers of chronicles, annals and histories claimed to be writing objective truth, their works were also intended to be read and enjoyed' and should not be accepted at face value.[55] Similarly, in medieval and early-modern Japan (to employ Western chronological classifications), history was largely indivisible from literature. Most historical narratives were epics, meant to serve dual–didactic and entertainment – purposes, usually cast in clearly Buddhist and later also Confucian tones, emphasizing the effects of fate and/or divine intervention, and the wages of good or evil. This pattern can also be seen in European Dark Age oral tradition and mythology, and in that of the Middle East. For early medieval Japan, the romanticization of conflict by later fourteenth- and fifteenth-century producers of court literature has been very misleading.[56]

In recent years in the West, alongside the stress on memoirs, diaries and letters,[57] oral history has found much favour, being seen as an aspect of recollection that provides a key guide to what war is like,[58] and these sources are pushed hard in press releases.[59] Oral history has also amplified the archival basis of the subject. Thus, the impressive Imperial War Museum Sound Archive in London has been used in works such as Max Arthur's *Forgotten Voices of the Great War* (2003), and in the books of the (British) Regimental Actions series, for example Peter Hart's *The Heat of Battle: The Italian Campaign. 16th Battalion, Durham Light Infantry, 1943–45* (1999), to produce evocative accounts, although they offer very one-sided accounts of campaigns. The same is true of the use of interviews in books such as Robin Neillands, *Eighth Army: From the Western Desert to the Alps 1939–1945* (2004).

War and society

'Face of battle' and battlefield approaches were distinct from the dominant approach in the scholarly literature in recent decades. This has been summarized as 'war and society' or 'new military history', both of which are acceptable definitions as long as it is appreciated that this approach is far from static. Instead, 'war and society' has proved capable of registering developments in other branches of history and, indeed, more generally in the social sciences, not least changing understandings of society itself.[60] War and society pursues the relationship between war and social class, gender, etc. at one level and at another asks how far war mirrors society: in what way the military and the exercise of military might reflect social constructs and images. There is now an extensive literature on such varied subjects as conscription, memorializing war,[61] the appearance of the military, not least the purpose of uniform, the military and health, the environmental consequences of war, the gender aspects of military history, and war as a form of disciplining bodies and applying violence to the body.[62] Each of these perspectives offers much, although they share the Eurocentricity that characterizes so much of military history. This is less the case with the literature on war and the military as explanations for state-building, which is, however, rather a political-science approach than an aspect of the 'war and society' literature. 'War and society' is a very varied field, although one important theme is the extent to which wartime social activities represent an extension of peacetime practices or an aberration from them.

The social dimension of the military as a subject for study is particularly valuable due to the emphasis, in much recent work, on comradeship as a key to understanding the thoughts, ethics, and actions of soldiers and sailors. Thus, for example, in the first half of the twentieth century, comradeship greatly influenced the type of British warship in which ratings preferred to serve. Given a choice, most sailors said they preferred to serve in ships with small complements, although they offered less off-duty entertainment and privacy than big vessels.[63] The links between fighting effectiveness, morale and unit cohesion, and their importance as opposed to tactical sophistication,[64] underline the value of the study of comradeship, and this bridges 'war and society' and 'face of battle'.[65]

Recruitment of both soldiers and officers, the internal dynamics of officer corps and the life of soldiers are other fields in which the 'war and society' approach has much to offer, not least because they provide a way to study the nature and impact of change. Thus, in *The French Army 1750–1820. Careers, Talents, Merit* (Manchester, 2002), Rafe Blaufarb used interesting sources, such as letters of application and recommendation sent to the War Ministry, to indicate how professionalism clashed with the social politics of revolution. It is fair to say that such works can tell us more about the social history of the period than its military counterpart, but the two are related.[66]

In many cases, the 'war and society' approach throws scant light on military capability, let alone operational effectiveness, but in others there are much more explicit links. Thus, Elizabeth Venn's study of the smallpox epidemic in North America during the War of American Independence *Pox Americana: The Great Smallpox Epidemic of 1775* (New York, 2001) showed not only how the virus was speeded by the movement of troops but also how it affected the war's progress, including the devastation that the virus visited on Lord Dunmore's 'Ethiopian Legion' of escaped African-Americans in the Chesapeake, as well as on the American army in Canada in 1776, helping to blunt the effectiveness of the latter in response to the British offensive of that year. Due to a well-developed system of inoculation, British forces suffered less than their opponents, but, thanks to George Washington's decision to inoculate the Continental Army, one of his most prescient decisions of the war, it acquired an immunity that helped it greatly in the campaigns of 1780–1.

Other approaches and prominent studies offer less for the issue of military capability. In *A War of Nerves. Soldiers and Psychiatrists 1914–1994* (2000), Ben Shephard skilfully moved between psychiatry and war in the USA and Europe, showing how World War Two produced a new confidence in the effects of psychiatry and a new sense of the social role of the psychiatrist; but the study is essentially of value for the history of psychiatry, rather than of war. It also reflected a wider interest in battlefield stress as an aspect of combat experience. A similar Eurocentricity can be seen in the scope and assumptions of Joshua Goldstein's *War and Gender. How Gender Shapes the War System and Vice Versa* (Cambridge, 2001). As an instance of what military studies could then include, Goldstein discussed the feminization of enemies as a form of symbolic domination, the role of male sexuality as a cause of aggression, wartime female labour, the phallic symbolism of weapons, gendered massacre, sweethearts, nurses, mothers, prostitutes, and the relationship between hunting and war.[67] To critics, however, ascribing sexual connotations to the nature of conflict and the shape of weapons is spurious and polarizes ideas according to an artificial and simplistic right or wrong, female or male. Women in warfare in China and Japan have been largely ignored,[68] except for the issue of 'military comfort women': enforced prostitution.[69]

Work on the military and race is less bounded geographically than that on gender usually is, although an important topic is racial relations within individual militaries, which tends to mean Western militaries.[70] The experience of racial minority groups in these militarities has also attracted those interested in memoirs and oral history.[71] The military and race also offers a way to approach Western policies toward the non-West and, in particular, to consider how far racial stereotyping affected military conduct, for example the treatment of prisoners. The latter led to an instructive debate about the conduct of the US Marines in the Pacific in World War Two, instructive because it has offered the possibility of discussing methodology. It has recently been claimed that the mutual blood-shedding during the conflict was a product of the dynamics of the battlefield, rather than a consequence of outside social influences, and that an appreciation of this dynamic depends on an understanding of the process and context of surrender on the battlefield. In particular, the reluctance of the Japanese to surrender and their willingness to employ ruses helped mould American responses. In short, the issue of practicality is pushed to the fore, rather than the indoctrination underlined in the 'war and society' perspective.[72]

Racialism can be differently presented as a form of societal conflict, and this is an instance of the extent to which the 'war and society' approach can be related to the problem of defining warfare, an issue that has been accentuated by the large-scale role of civil conflict in recent years, particularly in sub-Saharan Africa. As an aspect of this question, there is the problem of how far it is appropriate to distinguish large-scale uses of force, such as massacres, from war, and also how best to approach high levels of societal violence, as in modern South Africa.[73] To distinguish these too readily from war, especially civil war, is to adopt a definition that has only limited value across much of the world; it also risks taking the nineteenth-century Western state and states system as the model for judging conflict.

Furthermore, force was (and is) employed as a means of state power, not simply in order to protect governments, but also in order to push through policies of social, economic and ethnic transformation, most obviously by Communist regimes and by the Nazis. They presented their policies in terms of war: waged with enemies of the state, the people, or the race. In this context, civil war was seen as a continuous process; and this also underlines the degree to which the 'players' in the history of war are not only the regular military and insurrectionary forces, but also secret police forces, para-militaries, and intelligence agencies.

Civil war is both the denial of, and an aspect of, the process by which warfare created states and moulded societies, which is an issue not only for the 'war as state formation' approach but also for the 'war and society' literature. For both these approaches, wars are important in bringing a degree of association between people and cause, in creating the sense of 'us' and 'them' that was, and is, so important to the idea of statehood, as opposed to the earlier *natio* in its original meaning of people of a common descent. The territorialization of authority in terms of its organization and extension spatially rested in large part on the availability or use of force. This territorialization was also related to the development of a sense of political community separate from the ruler: in parts of Europe in the late Middle Ages, but later, more generally, both in Europe and elsewhere. As a result, the construction and territorialization of identity was not restricted to the political élite, and this helped to integrate heterogeneous groups into the gradually emergent 'states'. In terms of military capability, this process of integration could also aid recruitment and support for conflict. There is in this approach an implicit teleology, but it captures a long-term contrast that was of importance to the development of backing for war.

Another aspect of 'war and society' studies, remembered conflict, the memoralization of war in the shape of drawing lessons, is particularly interesting for the light it throws on the imaginative experience of conflict. This provides a way to probe the understanding of conflict by different groups, and thus to construct the social memory of war.[74] World War One has been particularly important for studies in this field,[75] although it is far from alone.

Another aspect of a different form of moralization is provided by the recent stress on the environmental consequences of war. Although these consequences are as old as war itself, most of the work has focused on very recent conflicts, such as the Gulf War of 1990–1, and the Kosovo War of 1999.[76] A more wide-ranging chronological account was offered by Edmund Russell in *War and Nature. Fighting Humans and Insects with Chemicals from World War I to 'Silent Spring'* (Cambridge, 2001), a stimulating work that linked the American interest in chemical warfare with the presentation of pest control as warfare in a skilful study that related culture, technology and institutional (in the shape of the Army's Chemical Warfare Service) aspects of war. There was also an instructive parallel to a more general shift against bellicosity:

> Confident of the technology they had gained during and after World War II, chemical officers and federal entomologists promoted eradication of human and insect enemies to the American public in the latter 1950s. The strategy backfired as scientists and the public protested against chemical warfare and large pest eradication projects.[77]

The 'war and society' approach risks demilitarizing the subject, in that the approach responded at least partly to those who disliked war,[78] and, in moving away from the perspective on battles and campaigns, and focusing, for example, on commemoration,[79] it can be too easy to forget that fighting was a prime concern of the military, its special function, and should therefore play a central role in military history.[80] Nevertheless, many militaries fight or prepare for war only occasionally, while, irrespective of this point, the 'war and society' approach still has much to offer. Thus, in contrast to the operational focus and chronological structure of standard treatments of World War One, such as Spencer Tucker's *The Great War, 1914–18* (1998), Ian Beckett, in a 2001 work of the same title, devoted considerable attention to 'nations in arms', 'war and the state', 'war and society', and 'war, politics and revolution'.

More generally, 'war and society' suffers from a Western bias and from a lack of comparative studies. For most wars, we do not know the social composition of the soldiery among all the combatant powers: who they were, from what social background and what motivated them to join, if they were not coerced. Much is assumed about these elements, but the reliability of what is known is limited, especially for non-Western states. Similarly, comparative studies of societies in war are few and focused on the West: what it meant to lose so many young men, how the societies adjusted, and what happened in reverse when they returned from conflict. The patchwork nature of the studies of the effects of war on societies, country by country, war by war, are very useful; but the systematic nature of the corpus is limited. Thus, alongside the problem that 'war and society' risks demilitarizing the subject, is a different but unfortunate practice of studying war, with society rather coming after and, certainly, with a lack of systematic attention to such topics as the effect of war on class, racial relations, women, the economy, and political institutions, other than on a limited scale.

'War and society' studies sometimes include valuable comparative elements, but there is also a danger that the focus is very much on one of the combatants, often for reasons of source availability and linguistic skill. Thus, Ian Ousby's *The Road to Verdun. France, Nationalism and the First World War* (2002) put the struggle in the wider context of French nationalism, but failed to consider German war-making adequately. Ousby argued that the Third Republic encouraged the idea that the battle reaffirmed a strength and greatness not seen during the Franco–Prussian War of 1870–1 and that it displayed the soul of France uniting soldiers and civilians, but that the meaning that the battle of Verdun (1916) held remained equivocal, as alongside celebrating successful resistance, it could also be used to emphasize France's suffering and her need not to suffer again.

The 'war and society' approach has also lent itself very readily to the popular market. Thus the experience of war is re-created, or, at least, its memorialization fostered by memoirs as well as by television pro-grammes,[81] such as the 2002 British re-creation of a family's experience of World War Two life on the Home Front. This was also true of fictional television series, for example *Foyle's War* (2002–3), a detective series set in south coast England in 1940, and of films, such as *Hope and Glory* and *Yanks*.

Cultural dimensions

The 'war and society' approach does have the virtue of directing atten-tion to cultural aspects of war and the military, as a way to understand the 'war and society' relationship. The variety of issues and concepts summarized as the cultural aspects of war is a subject that has recently attracted considerable attention, offering a different way of assessing capability to that focused on weaponry. While some scholars have argued in favour of the need to consider particular cultural elements, especially the way in which understandings of appropriate military conduct, victory, defeat, and casualty are culturally conditioned,[82] others have sought to employ cultural issues as explanatory factors in synoptic theories. Thus, for example, in an eloquent, if somewhat simplistic, account of Western military success that reflects the misleading looseness of cultural definitions, Victor Davis Hanson has argued that Western civic culture is particularly efficacious.[83] Aside from serious criticisms of Hanson's accuracy in particulars,[84] his general approach, however, suffers from a lack of due attention to process, and, linked to this, from a tendency to reify cultural factors and too readily give them explanatory force. This is a problem whether a grand schema is offered or whether there are attempts to define and focus on more specific cultural environ-ments. Any discussion of Western military culture, for example, has to consider the extent to which the nature of military glory in the Western context was distinctive, as well as the specific role and impact of chivalry and its relationship with other Western developments, such as the particular character of professionalism.[85]

Culture is a much employed term for, aside from the culture of society as a whole, including why people fought, there is the organiz-ational culture of particular militaries,[86] a topic that overlaps with sociology. There is also the concept of strategic culture, employed to discuss the context within which military tasks were 'shaped',[87] a concept that overlaps with that of strategic landscapes, and a topic that overlaps with international relations.[88] This use of culture approximates to earlier discussion of distinctive ways of war, in particular the notion of American exceptionalism.[89] The concept of strategic culture, however, does have to address the issue of the contested character of national interests, as well as the issue of consistency. Thus, Liddell Hart noted of the draft of a volume on pre-war 'Grand Strategy' in the British official history of World War Two:

> A minor point of a general kind is that the names of ministers who held particular offices at particular times might be mentioned more frequently – otherwise the reader may not realize that the occupant of the office had changed. That is important because defence policy, and the discussion of it in government quarters had less continuity and was more spasmodic than present-day students may realise.[90]

In addition, there is the question of the strategic culture of individual military services, which in part are shaped by their assessment of their domestic role. For example, the emphasis in the organizational culture of the Russian army on a reluctance to intervene against the political leadership[91] in turn affected the understanding of goals in its strategic culture. Both for states and for services, there is also the issue of the consequences of the extent to which strategic thinking is a process mediated primarily through language. This refers to the question of how, and why, military and political organizations give meaning to language.

As a related issue, there has been considerable scholarly interest in symbolic aspects of the military and of war – although, by their nature, it is difficult to assess their relative importance. A failure to give due weight to the cultural contexts of past warfare has ensured that much military history has devoted insufficient weight to these symbolic aspects. At present military display, not least in uniforms[92] and music, is an up-and-coming subject. The symbolic dimension is clearly part of the subject of 'war and society', but gives a new focus within that subject. There is, however, a danger that symbolic aspects will be overstated. To take the example of castles in medieval England: a recent study by Rickard has suggested that

> there was undoubtedly a symbolic element to much castle building, particularly in areas without any realistic threat. Even buildings of

undeniable military intent such as Caernarvon castle could contain such symbolism, in its resemblance to the walls of Constantinople, and a whole series of imperial connections. Indeed Coulson has suggested that very few castles had anything but a symbolic nature. However, one must not overplay this element. Even excluding towers, the northern border still saw more building work than any other area, and it is clear that a constant military threat was a more significant factor than any desire for ostentatious display for its own sake.[93]

It would be mistaken, however, to class as symbolic everything that is not recognizable as pertaining to the military sphere. The value of the word is lessened if the opposite of the symbolic is the military.

An understanding of the role of castles is linked to an issue of more general importance: the understanding of frontiers, a topic in which 'realist' interpretations vie with others. This is an instance in which modern Western-derived concepts, in this case of clear linear frontiers separating defined sovereign territories, are actively misleading – and not simply for the non-West, but also for most of Western history. Instead, the sense of frontiers as a zone, sometimes of shared power if not authority, is important to an assessment of strategy, and can also be significant for that of causes of war.[94] More generally, it is possible to present wars in a 'cultural' context different from the more 'realist' conventional war of the rivalry of states, not least in emphasizing the psychological element in warfare, for example the role of punishment and revenge in Roman policy.[95]

Cultural imperatives and weaponry have also been linked for much more recent times, as in the argument that the B-17 bomber embodied the dreams of glory of American air power enthusiasts, or Rachel Holloway's account of President Reagan's 'reinvigoration of the technological sublime'.[96] Indeed, the role of cultural assumptions in the response to the whole idea of air power, and the extent to which these assumptions varied within the organizational cultures of particular militaries, are clearly important;[97] there is no reason why this approach should not be more generally applied.

'Culture' is a term so widely and loosely used as to have its analytical value at least in part compromised. Furthermore, the idea has been politicized in that the notion of a specifically Western way of war has become an aspect of the American culture wars. For some commentators, the notion is a response to political correctness and multiculturalism in American education. There is also a contemporary political aspect to this, as belief in the effectiveness of such a war-making provides encouragement to those encouraging American interventionism. The notion of a specifically Western way of war, nevertheless, ignores diversity within the West, including what has been a frequent reluctance to engage in pitched battle, and also simplifies the non-West. Thus, the dichotomy of a Western preference for open battle versus Oriental trickery that is offered is doubly flawed.

The looseness, and therefore flexibility and extendability, of the cultural interpretation, however, can in itself be instructive, as it encourages a focus on the impact and role of ideas and assumptions. For example, the study of combat styles has been seen as indicating the possibilities that a borrowing from other disciplines offers military history,[98] while views on promotion reflect cultural factors. Thus, in World War Two, the British army showed a tendency to value personal recommendation over specialist expertise or operational experience.[99]

Furthermore, the varied nature of assumptions affecting military capability and its assessment encourages a departure from the more structured ranking of militaries that arises when the focus is on weaponry and organization, ones that more readily lend themselves to notions of proficiency. In practice, these issues are not separate, as cultural factors help to explain why particular weapons, such as firearms, or organizational systems, for example conscription, are adopted or discarded with very different readiness and success.[100] These factors do not, however, readily lend themselves to the clear-cut assessment, let alone quantification, required by some social science theorists; although, in practice, neither, completely, do such more apparently simple factors as army size.[101]

Conclusion

To move from sketching major developments to considering the position at present is to pretend, even more misleadingly, to a panoptic gaze, oracular knowledge and Olympian judgement that no scholar or group of scholars possesses. More than perspective is at issue, for at any one time, much of the important work is in process – being considered, researched and written, or at least not yet in print. The genesis of some projects is such that the immediacy suggested by a snap judgement, for example the situation in early 2004, is only so helpful, as important books being researched then may not appear for several years. Perspective is also affected by the myriad of factors that set the parameters for judgement. Aside from such obvious issues as access to publications or linguistic expertise, there are particular but varying boundaries. For example, in Britain, there are distinctions in terms of separate structures for Classical or area studies, whereas, in the USA, such specialists are more usually present in history departments. The disciplinary divide between history and the social sciences is also important. For both, however, the challenge of how best to confront Eurocentricism is central.

Notes

1 For two American views, J. Lynn, 'The Embattled Future of Academic Military History', *Journal of Military History*, 61 (1997), pp. 775, 777–89; V. Hanson, 'The Dilemma of the Contemporary Military Historian', in E. Fox-Genovese and E. Lasch-Quinn (eds), *Reconstructing History* (1999), pp. 189–201, esp. 190, 196–7; K. Raaflaub and N. Rosenstein, 'Introduction' to their (eds) *War and Society in the Ancient and Medieval Worlds* (Berkeley, 1999), p. 1, but, more optimistically, p. 4.

2 M. Vaisse, editorial, *La Lettre* [newsletter of the Centre d'études d'histoire de la Défense], no. 12 (Dec. 2000), p. 1.

3 D. Cannadine (ed.), *What is History Now?* (2002); P. Burke (ed.), *History and Historians in the Twentieth Century* (2002).

4 For a more wide-ranging consideration of the relationship between history and the social sciences, J.L. Gaddis, *The Landscape of History. How Historians Map the Past* (Oxford, 2003).

5 J.F. Gentsch, 'World War II: Eastern Front, Stalingrad, 1942', in C. Messenger (ed.), *Reader's Guide to Military History* (2001), p. 767.

6 For example Barrie Pitt's *1918. The Last Act* (Pen and Sword, 2003) is a reprint of a 1962 work that suffers from a failure to take note of a mass of important work. See also, David Chandler's *Campaigns of Napoleon* (1966) in 1995, Martin Middlebrook's *the Battle of Hamburg* (1980) and *The Schweinfurt–Regensburg Mission* (1983) and *Napoleon's Marshals* (1987) edited by Chandler, reprinted in 2000, Chandler's *Napoleon* (1973) and John Prebble's *Mutiny. Highland Regiments in Revolt* (1975) in 2001, Robin Reilly's *The British at the Gates. The New Orleans Campaign in the War of 1812* (1974), M.J. Whitley's *Destroyers of World War Two* (1988), and Bevin Alexander's *How Great Generals Win* (1993) in 2002, and Philip Ziegler's *Omdurman* (1973), and Pierre Berton's *Vimy* (1986) in 2003.

7 W.G. Natter, *Literature at War, 1914–1940: Representing the 'Time of Greatness' in Germany* (New Haven, 1999).

8 For example J. Keegan, *The First World War. An Illustrated History* (2002).

9 R. Muir, *Salamanca 1812* (New Haven, 2001), pp. xi, 141. A good grasp of the archival sources is also shown by Richard Hopton in *The Battle of Maida 1806. Fifteen Minutes of Glory* (Barnsley, 2002). For an earlier historian of the Peninsula War walking the battlefields, Charles Oman to Major General John Frederick Maurice, 13 Aug. 1903, LH, Maurice papers, 2/3/82.

10 Correspondence of Liddell Hart and Colonel Kenneth Garside, Librarian of King's, LH, Liddell Hart papers, 4/27.

11 Fuller to Liddell Hart, 22 Aug., Betty Vaucour to Liddell Hart, 23 Aug., Progress Report, 28 Oct. 1963, Tedder to Liddell Hart, 8 Jan. 1964, LH, Liddell Hart papers, 4/27.

12 Brian Melland to Liddell Hart, 23 Mar., 17 May 1961, LH, Liddell Hart papers, 4/31.

13 Liddell Hart to Major General Ian Playfair, 8 Feb. 1954, LH, Liddell Hart papers, 4/32.

14 Melland to Liddell Hart, 2 June 1961, LH, Liddell Hart papers, 4/31.

15 Molony to Liddell Hart, 7 Oct. 1958, LH, Liddell Hart papers, 4/32.

16 Liddell Hart to Playfair, 23 Jan. 1954, 27 Oct., 12, 19 Nov., 4 Dec. 1956, reply 28 Nov. 1956, LH, Liddell Hart papers, 4/32.

17 N. Barr, *Flodden 1513: The Scottish Invasion of Henry VIII's England* (Stroud, 2001).

18 H. Nicholson, 'Before William of Tyre: European Reports on the Military Orders' Deeds in the East, 1150–1185', in Nicholson (ed.), *The Military Orders II. Welfare and Warfare* (Aldershot, 1998), pp. 111–18. For a comparable emphasis on the need to consider all sources, in this case for the ninth century BCE, S. Yamada, *The Construction of the Assyrian Empire. A Historical Study of the Inscriptions of Shalmaneser III Relating to His Campaigns in the West* (Leiden, 2000).

19 Keegan, series guidelines for *A History of Warfare*, 19 Apr. 1997, pp. 1–2.

20 J. Weeks, *Gettysburg, Memory, Market and an American Shrine* (Princeton, 2003).

21 L.H. Suid, *Sailing on the Silver Screen: Hollywood and the U.S. Navy* (Annapolis, 1996) and *Guts and Glory. The Making of the American Military Image in Film* (Lawrence, Kentucky, 2002). For a defence of historical film making that appears in a perceptive collection, see K.M. Coleman, 'The Pedant Goes to Hollywood: The Role of the Academic Consultant', in M.M. Winkler (ed.), *'Gladiator'. Film and History* (Oxford, 2004), pp. 45–52.

22 E.L. Wheeler, 'Firepower: Missile Weapons and the "Face of Battle"', *Electrum*, 5 (2001), pp. 170–4. Wheeler sees J.G. Gray's *The Warriors: Reflections on Men in Battle* (New York, 1959) as more valuable.

23 S.L. Falk, 'Burma Memoirs and the Reality of War', *Army History*, no. 57 (Winter 2003), pp. 4–13.

24 A. Hyland, *The Horse in the Ancient World* (Stroud, 2003), pp. 75–7.

25 G. Daly, *Cannae. The Experience of Battle in the Second Punic War* (2002), pp. 203–4.

26 P. Lenihan, *1690. Battle of the Boyne* (Stroud, 2003), pp. 272–4.

27 For example S. Reid, *Wolfe. The Career of General James Wolfe from Culloden to Quebec* (2001).

28 Though see R.F. Weigley, *Eisenhower's Lieutenants: The Campaigns of France and Germany, 1944–1945* (Bloomington, Indiana, 1981).

29 For example R. Westlake, *British Battalions on the Western Front. January–June 1915* (Barnsley, 2001).

30 F. Mackay, *Asiago 15/16 June 1918. Battle in the Woods and Clouds* (Barnsley, 2001), p. 69.

31 J. Hughes-Wilson, 'Kursk – Sixty Years On', *RUSI Journal*, Vol. 148, no. 5 (Oct. 2003), p. 78.

32 J. Prados, *Lost Crusader: The Secret Wars of CIA Director William Colby* (New York, 2003).

33 For example P. Aleshire, *The Fox and the Whirlwind. General George Crook and Geronimo. A Paired Biography* (Chichester, 2001).

34 I would like to thank Theodore Cook for his advice.

35 D.S. Frazier, Foreword to D.E. Alberts, *The Battle of Glorietta. Union Victory in the West* (College Station, Texas, 1998), p. xii.

36 S. Duffy, *Robert the Bruce's Irish Wars. The Invasions of Ireland 1306–1329* (Stroud, 2002).

37 A. Hezlet, *HMS Trenchant at War. From Chatham to the Banka Strait* (Barnsley, 2001), the submarine *Trenchant* operated in the Far East in 1944–5; J. Holland, *Fortress Malta. An Island Under Siege 1940–1943* (2003).

38 C. McKee, *Sober Men and True. Sailor Lives in the Royal Navy 1900–1945* (Cambridge, Mass., 2002), p. 113.

39 S.L.A. Marshall, *Bringing Up the Rear: A Memoir* (San Rafael, California, 1975).

40 R.J. Spiller, 'S.L.A. Marshall and the Ratio of Fire', *RUSI Journal*, 133 (Winter 1988), pp. 63–71.

41 Catalogue for the Aberjona Press [Bedford, Pennsylvania, 2002], p. 1.

42 P. Ziegler, *Soldiers. Fighting Men's Lives, 1901–2001* (2001).

43 J.R. Freedman, *Whistling in the Dark: Memory and Culture in Wartime London* (Lexington, Kentucky, 1999).

44 LH, Maurice papers, 2/3/5, 10–23, 52–3.

45 LH, Maurice papers, 2/3/79–80, 83–4, 86, 92, 94–99, 101.

46 Nan Taylor, 'Assessment of the American History of the Tunisian Campaign', in Brian Melland to Liddell Hart, 17 May 1961, LH, Liddell Hart papers, 4/31.

47 Playfair to Liddell Hart, 16 Feb. 1954, LH, Liddell Hart papers, 4/32.

48 A. Swinson, 'The War Mongers', *Books and Bookmen*, Jan. 1967, pp. 58–9.

49 B. Liddell Hart, *The Ghost of Napoleon* (1933), pp. 180–1.

50 Howard to Liddell Hart, 22 Aug., and reply 24 Aug. 1961, LH, Liddell Hart papers, 4/31.

51 A. Beevor, 'The New History', *Waterstone's Books Quarterly*, 4 (2002), p. 36.

52 For example W.B. Brewer, *Daring Missions of World War Two* (Chichester, 2001); S.T. Smith, *The Rescue* (Chichester, 2001).

53 Undated memo on *History of the First World War*, LH, Liddell Hart papers, 3/184.

54 P. Krentz and E.L. Wheeler (eds), *Polyaenus, Strategems of War* (Chicago, 1994).

55 H. Nicholson, *Medieval Warfare. Theory and Practice of War in Europe 300–1500* (Basingstoke, 2004), p. 8. See also C. Saunders, F. Le Saux and N. Thomas (eds), *Writing War. Medieval Literary Responses to Warfare* (Woodbridge, 2004).

56 K.F. Friday, *Samurai, Warfare and the State in Early Medieval Japan* (2004), e.g. pp. 137, 162.

57 R. Muir, *Tactics and the Experience of Battle in the Age of Napoleon* (1998).
58 S. Hynes, *The Soldiers' Tale: Bearing Witness to Modern War* (New York, 1997), p. xii.
59 For example the press release for N. Steel and P. Hart, *Jutland, 1916. Death in the Grey Wastes* (2003).
60 B. Ziemann, 'Sozialgeschichte, Geschlechtergeschichte, Gesellschafts-geschichte', in R. van Dülmen (ed.), *Fischer-Lexikon Geschichte* (Frankfurt, 2003), pp. 84–105, and 'Überlegungen zur Form der Gesellschafts-geschichte angesichts des "cultural turn"', *Archiv für Sozialgeschichte*, 43 (2003), pp. 600–16.
61 For example D.W. Lloyd, *Battlefield Tourism: Pilgrimage and the Com-memoration of the Great War in Britain, Australia, and Canada, 1919–1939* (1998).
62 For example, J. Bourke, *An Intimate History of Killing: Killing in Twentieth-Century Warfare* (1999).
63 C. McKee, *Sober Men and True. Sailor Lives in the Royal Navy 1900–1945* (Cambridge, Mass., 2002).
64 For this as the conclusion from a detailed study of the Battle of the White Mountain of 1620, O. Chaline, *La bataille de la Montagne Blanche: Un mystique chez les guerriers* (Paris, 2000).
65 S. Fritz, *Frontsoldaten: The German Soldier in World War II* (Lexington, Kentucky, 1995).
66 See, for example, E. Weber, *Peasants into Frenchmen: The Modernisation of Rural France, 1870–1914* (Palo Alto, 1976); J. Bushnell, *Mutiny Amid Repression: Russian Soldiers in the Revolution of 1905–1906* (Bloomington, 1985); R. Cobb, *The Peoples' Armies* (New Haven, 1987); O. Roynette, *'Bons pour le Service'. L'Expérience de la Caserne en France à la fin du XIXe siècle* (Paris, 2000).
67 A stress on the Western experience is also a problem with L.G. De Pauw, *Battle Cries and Lullabies: Women in War from Prehistory to the Present* (Norman, Oklahoma, 1998).
68 Though see J.S. Mostow (ed.), *Gender and Power in the Japanese Visual Field* (Honolulu, 2003) and R. Zölner, 'Husbands and Wives in Japanese Feudalism', in R. Deist and H. Kleinschmidt (eds), *Knight and Samurai. Actions and Images of Elite Warriors in Europe and East Asia* (Göppingen, 2003), pp. 119–37.
69 G. Hicks, *The Comfort Women: Japan's Brutal Regime of Enforced Prostitution in the Second World War* (1994).
70 S. Mershon and S. Schlossman, *Foxholes and Color Lines: Desegregating the U.S. Armed Forces* (Baltimore, Maryland, 1998).
71 F.N. Schubert, *Voices of the Buffalo Soldier: Records, Reports, and Recollec-tions of Military Life and Service in the West* (Albuquerque, 2003); S.L. Harris, *Harlem's Hell Fighters: The African-American 369th Infantry in World War I* (Washington, 2003).
72 J.W. Dower, *War without Mercy: Race and Power in the Pacific War* (1986); C.M. Cameron, *American Samurai: Myth, Imagination, and the Conduct of Battle in the First Marine Division, 1941–1951* (Cambridge, 1994); E. Bergerud, 'No Quarter: The Pacific Battlefield', *Historically Speaking*, III, 5 (June 2002), pp. 8–10.

73 M. Levene and P. Roberts (eds), *The Massacre in History* (Oxford, 1989); M. Bellesiles (ed.), *Lethal Imagination. Violence and Brutality in American History* (New York, 1989).

74 W. Schivelbusch, *The Culture of Defeat: On National Trauma, Mourning and Recovery* (New York, 2003).

75 P. Fussell, *The Great War and Modern Memory* (New York, 1975); S. Hynes, *A War Imagined: The First World War and English Culture* (1990); G.L. Mosse, *Fallen Soldiers: Reshaping the Memory of the World Wars* (New York, 1991); J. Winter, *Sites of Memory, Sites of Mourning: The Great War in European Cultural History* (New York, 1995); P.H. Hoffenberg, 'Landscape, Memory and the Australian War Experience', *Journal of Contemporary History*, 36 (2001), pp. 111–31.

76 See, for example, C.E. Bruch and J.E. Austin, 'The Kosovo Conflict: A Case Study of Unresolved Issues', in Austin and Bruch (eds), *The Environmental Consequences of War. Legal, Economic, and Scientific Perspectives* (Cambridge, 2000), pp. 647–64.

77 E. Russell, *War and Nature. Fighting Humans and Insects with Chemicals from World War I to 'Silent Spring'* (Cambridge, 2001), p. 15.

78 G. Best, Preface to J.R. Hale, *War and Society in Renaissance Europe, 1450–1620* (second edn, Stroud, 1998), p. 6.

79 L.V. Smith, S. Audoin-Rouzeau and A. Becker, *France and the Great War 1914–1918* (Cambridge, 2003).

80 M. Howard, 'Military History and the History of War', in *Contemporary Essays* (The Strategic and Combat Studies Institute, Occasional Paper no. 27, 2004), p. 55.

81 T. Clayton and P. Craig, *Finest Hour* (1999) and *End of the Beginning* (2002).

82 J. Black, *War. Past, Present and Future* (Stroud, 2000).

83 J. Keegan, *A History of Warfare* (1993); V.D. Hanson, *The Western Way of War: Infantry Battle in Classical Greece* (New York, 1989) and *Carnage and Culture: Landmark Battles in the Rise of Western Power* (New York, 2001); published in London as *Why the West Has Won*.

84 S.J. Willett, 'History from the Clouds', *Arion*, 3rd series, vol. 10, no. 1 (Spring/Summer 2002), pp. 157–78, and, more briefly, by E. Wheeler in *Journal of Interdisciplinary History*, 21 (1990), pp. 122–5.

85 D.J.B. Trim (ed.), *The Chivalric Ethos and the Development of Military Professionalism* (Leiden, 2003).

86 For a controversial approach, C.M. Cameron, *American Samurai: Myth, Imagination, and the Conduct of Battle in the First Marine Division, 1941–1951* (Cambridge, 1994). See also, J.L. Legro, *Cooperation Under Fire: Anglo-German Restraint During World War II* (Ithaca, 1995); E. Kier, *Imagining War: French and British Military Doctrine Between the Wars* (Princeton, 1997); T. Farrell, 'Culture and Military Power', *Review of International Studies*, 24 (1998), pp. 405–14; and J. Lynn, *Battle. A History of Combat and Culture. From Ancient Greece to Modern America* (Boulder, Colorado, 2003).

87 R. Jervis, *Perception and Misperception in International Politics* (Princeton, 1976); K. Booth, *Strategy and Ethnocentrism* (1979); C.G. Reynolds, 'Reconsidering American Strategic History and Doctrines', in his *History of*

the Sea: Essays on Maritime Strategies (Columbia, South Carolina, 1989); A.I. Johnston, *Cultural Realism: Strategic Culture and Grand Strategy in Chinese History* (Princeton, 1995); C.S. Gray, 'Strategic Culture as Context: The First Generation of Theory Strikes Back', *Review of International Studies*, 25 (1999), pp. 49–70; L. Sondhaus, 'The Strategic Culture of the Habsburg Army', *Austrian History Yearbook*, 32 (2001), pp. 225–34; W. Murray, 'Does Military Culture Matter', in J.F. Lehman and H. Sicherman (eds), *America the Vulnerable. Our Military Problems and How To Fix Them* (Philadelphia, 2002), pp. 134–51. For valuable applications, E. Ringmar, *Identity, Interest and Action: A Cultural Explanation of Sweden's Intervention in the Thirty Years War* (Cambridge, 1996) and G. Parker, *The Grand Strategy of Philip II* (New Haven, Connecticut, 1998).

88 P. Kennedy and W.I. Hitchcock (eds), *From War to Peace. Altered Strategic Landscapes in the Twentieth Century* (New Haven, 2001); S. Morewood, *The British Defence of Egypt, 1935–1940. Conflict and Crisis in the Eastern Mediterranean* (2001).

89 R.F. Weigley, *The American Way of War: A History of US Military Strategy and Policy* (Bloomington, 1973); M.D. Pearlman, *Warmaking and American Democracy: The Struggle over Military Strategy, 1700 to the Present* (Lawrence, Kansas, 1999); B.M. Linn, 'The American Way of War Revisited', *Journal of Military History*, 66 (2002), pp. 501–33.

90 Liddell Hart to Norman Gibbs, 7 Dec. 1959, LH, Liddell Hart papers, 4/29.

91 B.D. Taylor, *Politics and the Russian Army. Civil–Military Relations, 1689–2000* (Cambridge, 2003), esp. pp. 320–30.

92 S.H. Myerly, *British Military Spectacle: From the Napoleonic Wars through the Crimea* (Cambridge, Mass., 1996), and 'Political Aesthetics: British Army Fashion, 1815–55', in M.H. Shirley and T.E.A. Larson (eds), *Splendidly Victorian. Essays in Nineteenth- and Twentieth-Century British History in Honour of Walter L. Arnstein* (Aldershot, 2001), pp. 45–68.

93 J. Rickard, *The Castle Community. The Personnel of English and Welsh Castles, 1272–1422* (Woodbridge, 2002), p. 25.

94 T.J. Barfield, *The Perilous Frontier: Nomadic Empires and China, 221 BC to AD 1757* (Oxford, 1989); R. Bartlett and A. Mackay, *Medieval Frontier Societies* (Oxford, 1990); C.R. Whittaker, *Frontiers of the Roman Empire* (Baltimore, 1994); T. Winichakul, *Siam Mapped: A History of the Geo-Body of a Nation* (Honolulu, 1994).

95 E. Wheeler, 'Why the Romans Can't Defeat the Parthians: Julius Africanus and the Strategy of Magic', in W. Groenman-van Waateringe *et al.* (eds), *Roman Frontier Studies 1995: Proceedings of the XVIth International Congress of Roman Frontier Studies* (Oxford, 1997), pp. 575–9; S.P. Mattern, *Rome and the Enemy. Imperial Strategy in the Principate* (Berkeley, 1999), esp. pp. 162–210, 221–2.

96 S. Weinberg, 'What Price Glory?', *The New York Review of Books*, 6 Nov. 2003, p. 59; R. Holloway, 'The Strategic Defense Initiative and the Technological Sublime: Fear, Science, and the Cold War', in M. Medhurst and H.W. Brands (eds), *Critical Reflections on the Cold War: Linking Rhetoric and History* (College Station, Texas, 2000), p. 225.

97 For air force and army differences, D.I. Hall, *The Birth of the Tactical Air Force. British Theory and Practice of Air Support in the West, 1939–1943* (Oxford, D.Phil. 1996), esp. pp. 165, 177, 287.

98 Lynn, 'Embattled Future', pp. 787–9.

99 W.F. Buckingham, *Arnhem 1944, A Reappraisal* (Stroud, 2002).

100 E.J. Zürcher (ed.), *Arming the State. Military Conscription in the Middle East and Central Asia, 1775–1925* (1999).

101 K.A. Rasler and W.R. Thompson, *The Great Powers and Global Struggle 1490–1990* (Lexington, Kentucky, 1994), pp. 193–5.

Chapter 3

Redressing Eurocentricism

> Most records are from antiquity's successful monarchs, and are accordingly biased, boasting of their military prowess.
> Ann Hyland, *The Horse in the Ancient World* (Stroud, 2003), p. 7

If the cultural turn discussed in the last chapter is one of the major developments in the study of war, whether the emphasis is on strategic, organizational, social, or other cultures, then this turn has largely affected only academic military history. The results of the emphasis on cultural factors are far less prominent in the popular market, other than through a simplistic stress on supposed cultural attributes contributing to a Western way of war. The major impact in academe has been a questioning of what can now be seen as an early cultural stress on machines, and an emphasis instead not only on the different types of culture mentioned above, but also on the need to consider the variety of cultures within the world. This consideration has been linked to a critique of Eurocentricity, specifically the focus on European militaries and, to a lesser extent, analytical concepts. The use of this term, however, should be sharpened as the focus in fact is on Western Europe and the USA, and even then, as discussed later in this chapter, the presentation of medieval European military history has been in part as one with that of the non-European world.

There have been interesting anticipations of the contemporary call to devote more attention to non-Western military history. One of the most instructive occurred in the early years of the twentieth century when Japan defeated Russia on land and sea, challenging established interpretations of the primacy of Western war-making. This was the subject of a collection *The Russo–Japanese War in Cultural Perspective, 1904–5* (Basingstoke, 1999), edited by David Wells and Sandra Wilson, which deserves wider attention because of its skilful probing of the issue of symbolic memory and how it encodes the process of war-learning. The variable readings of the war made possible its presentation by contemporaries in terms of a wider Westernization, with Japan allegedly successful because it had adopted Western weapons and norms, but, in contrast, it was also possible to present Japanese victory in terms of the triumph of spirit and as a victory for a non-Western power.[1]

Eurocentricism, understood as a focus on Europe and the USA, involves a number of problems. There is the emphasis on the military history of, and involving, the West, with the latter ensuring that other states and societies appear primarily in order to be defeated – so that the 'non-West' is misunderstood when it is not ignored.[2] Thus, in *The Oxford History of Modern War* (Oxford, 2000), there was a heavy slant towards Europe and the USA, and away from other parts of the world, in particular East and South Asia. The Chinese Civil War received one short mention, and the military history of China was on the whole neglected. Similar problems affected Azar Gat's *A History of Military Thought. From the Enlightenment to the Cold War* (Oxford, 2001), which the preface reveals in successive sentences was intended to tackle 'the evolution of modern military thought' by offering a 'view of the wider conceptions of war, strategy, and military theory which have dominated Europe and the West'. The challenging question of thought elsewhere was not addressed.

Furthermore, the appearance of the 'non-West' in many works only when in conflict with the West ensures that the military cultures of the former are neglected. This was clear in the discussion of conflict in Afghanistan in 2001. The country was presented as difficult because of its terrain, and with little understanding of the contrast between mounting interventions there from abroad and the subsequent problems of maintaining control.[3]

There is also the more insidious and long-standing[4] use of Western analytical concepts to describe global military history, a usage that in part stems from the nature of language and from a general failure to probe the wider possibilities of analytical concepts, but that also helps to rank achievement. For example, notions such as decisiveness are generally applied from a Western perspective. This was seen with the Gulf War of 2003, which was proclaimed as a decisive Western triumph because the campaign conformed to Western notions of victory, with the defeat and dissolution of the opposing field army and the overthrow of Saddam Hussein's government. The difficulty, however, of managing an 'exit strategy' (a Western concept) in Western terms from Iraq indicated the problems of applying that model without qualification.

It is useful to turn to modern examples in order to understand the problem, but the use of Western concepts is not restricted to recent conflicts; it can also be seen in the more general primitivization of the non-West both now and in the past. Note, for example, the assumptions about definitions offered in the following:

> Ritualized, anarchic, and transient, primitive warfare is best classed with feuding, brawling, and other forms of physically expressed hostility between individuals or small groups, more akin to the antagonistic behaviour of nonhuman species than the civilized war of organized states.[5]

This argument, in fact, underrated the complex character of producing a globally valid statement about the relationship between warfare and civilization.

Definitions are also embedded in the use of language. In an important essay that drew attention to the misleading character of linguistic images for the medieval European military, Stephen Morillo extended his scope to consider the position in Japan, noting that the terminology there 'warns us against an automatic association of function with organisation and of social status with either, associations built into the words infantry and cavalry'. He concluded, 'The pitfalls of European military terminology are just as real . . . they are simply less obvious because the words are misleadingly familiar to us';[6] and this point is valid in all comparative projects of research. Indeed, as language is an aspect of the bounded nature of cultures, so an attempt to offer a global perspective automatically faces a major conceptual hurdle.

The case of cavalry

The problems of comparative research emerge, for example, in the need to put due weight on cavalry, a subject that tends to be neglected for warfare over the last half-millennium. The devastating character of cavalry is generally primitivized by being located in the Middle Ages (a European concept for the organization of history), with the implicit or explicit assumption that subsequent usage of cavalry reflected a failure to modernize or, at best, an environmental adaptation that entailed redundancy as soon as more modern forces intervened. This is misleading, not least because it exaggerates the role of cavalry in medieval warfare,[7] and also underrates the earlier triumphs of cavalry forces, for example the Parthian victory at Carrhae over the Romans (53 BCE). The early sixteenth century is generally presented as a transition from the medieval past and seen in terms of the triumph of gunpowder forces, most obviously with Spanish victory over the Aztecs and Incas, the role of firepower in defeating Swiss pikemen and French cavalry during the Italian Wars (1494–1559), and, indicating that not only European power was at stake, with the series of spectacular Ottoman victories over the Safavids of Persia, the Mamlukes of Egypt, and the Jagiellons of Hungary in 1514–26.

But far from becoming redundant, cavalry forces could also still be devastating, not least because they could make the transition to firearms, as shown by the Moroccans to victorious effect at the expense of the Portuguese at Alcazarquivir in 1578, and also, within Europe, by pistoleers in the mid sixteenth century. The transition to firearms, however, was not necessary to the continued effectiveness of cavalry. Aside from the value of cavalry as a shock force, the use of mounted archers had for long combined firepower with the mobility of cavalry, providing a means to force the pace of battle that infantry lacked and were to continue to lack until they were mechanized in the twentieth century. The earlier failure of infantry forces to exploit victory, repeatedly for example in the American Civil War (1861–5), was an important instance of the extent to which, although the mass firepower of infantry brought some advantages, it lacked others that cavalry possessed, particularly mobility.

Furthermore, although horse-archers are generally seen as a medieval force, as with the defeats of European heavy cavalry, for example by Saladin at Hattin in 1187 and by the Mongols at Liegnitz in 1241, they continued to be important in the 'early modern period'. Ming Chinese advances against the Manchus were defeated by the mobile mounted archers of their opponents, while the Mughals made successful use of mounted archers in India in the sixteenth century. Furthermore, in considering military capability in terms of the objectives arising from strategic culture, it is also important to note the extent to which the ends and means of steppe warfare favoured raids, not battles.[8] The traditional tactics of steppe warfare, such as feints, continued to be valuable, playing a major role in battles between the Safavids (Persians) and the Uzbeks in the sixteenth century. In addition, the bow remained more accurate than the musket until the nineteenth century. The slow rate of fire of the latter was also a problem. The continued vitality of cavalry helps counter claims that Eastern European states were backward because they did not adopt the emphasis on infantry firepower seen in Western Europe.[9]

Even in symmetrical warfare within the Western context, the potential of cavalry continued to be an issue into the twentieth century[10] (while the use of horses and mules as draught animals was large-scale in World War Two), which raises questions about how best to assess the continued employment of cavalry by non-Western powers and people. Part of the problem is the isolation of a given arm for purposes of analysis, and the widespread failure to consider its tactical integration with other arms, as well, irrespective of this, as the simultaneity of different arms, when assessing effectiveness. Thus, Lieutenant Hugh Pearce Pearson of the British 84th Foot wrote in 1857 to his parents from Cawnpore where he was taking part in the suppression of the Indian Mutiny. He noted that the rebels did not dare 'charge our little squares with their clouds of cavalry', a description that apparently paints a clear picture of the superiority of Western fighting methods, but continued 'They had most magnificent gunners'.[11] As this indicates, selective quotation from this letter can be patronizing and would create very different impressions of respective capability, and the same is more generally true. Despite the variety of factors that in fact comprise the fighting effectiveness of individual units, different accounts or models of the same events are not often allowed to co-exist in writing about war. Furthermore, what a horse means has varied greatly, not least in terms of height and bone mass.

While the importance of the battlefield role of cavalry is considered, even if generally minimized, by Western scholars, there is insufficient work on the organizational dimensions of cavalry, especially the supply of horses and the provision of fodder, both of which were crucial. Jos Gommans clarified the importance of the former for South Asian warfare in the eighteenth century,[12] but his work needs to be matched for other periods. For example, the emphasis on firepower in the discussion of South Asia in the sixteenth century should be focused not only to note the continued major role of mounted archers, especially in the early decades, but also to appreciate that the widespread dispersal of firearms ensured that the key to success, for both Mughals and Safavids, was not the possession of firearms, as others matched this, but rather organization: among those who fought, as well as in terms of exploiting agricultural resources and sustaining effective tribal alliances.[13]

Like the cult of the machine in the twentieth and twenty-first centuries, the role of cavalry brings up cultural issues. Indeed it is argued that the importance of the horse to the Spanish conquest of much of the Americas was exaggerated by Spanish contemporaries, in large part because of the cultural context, specifically the association of cavalry with honour and social status.[14] Fascination with cavalry also played a role in the genesis of the twentieth-century cult of the machine. There was a common emphasis on movement, and this left some surprising legacies. Liddell Hart explained that his bookplate included not only the 'Globe – to represent a global view and subject', but also Mongol horsemen 'because my theory of future mechanised warfare was evolved originally from my study of the campaigns of Genghis-Khan's all-mobile army of Mongols'.[15]

Governmental effectiveness

At the sociological level, if cavalry is not seen as necessarily anachronistic in the early-modern period (which itself would be a powerful check to implicit or explicit Eurocentric views), then this has consequences for assumptions about whether particular governmental–social systems were best, or at least better, suited to military success. This is an approach that is generally conceptualized in Western terms. There is a tendency to see the Western state, a defined body with unlimited sovereignty, as the model for governmental development, to present the military potency of Western powers as product and, in part, cause of this development, and to claim that Western expansion, especially at the expense of governmental systems that were not suited to the maintenance of substantial standing forces, demonstrated the validity of this analysis.

The contingent nature of this approach to the governmental context, or even motor, of military history requires examination. It can be challenged chronologically from two directions. The first is from the present, with the argument that this model does not adequately explain the varied nature of governmental structures and political developments in the present day at the global scale, nor, indeed, the complex relationship between these developments and military capability. Second, there is the issue of the foreshortening of the past. It is problematic to read back from the later failure of governmental systems that were not suited to the maintenance of substantial standing forces, such as societies in Africa or Amazonia in which political processes took place largely within and between kin groups; or many of the peoples between the Caspian and China: the long history of tribal confederations in Central Asia, of which Attila's Hun empire and the medieval Mongols were the most prominent, and the Dzungars the last powerful example. To read back in this fashion entails repeating the nineteenth-century Western perception of the relationship between disciplined, drilled, well-armed, and adequately supplied permanent firepower forces and those that were not so armed, with the governmental dimension presented in terms of the superiority of states able to mobilize and direct resources to that end. This approach draws on the cultural, ethnic and geographical structuring of value that Western military history inherited from its Classical roots, not least in accepting the propaganda element in Greek historians, for example Herodotus and the presentation of non-Greek forces, especially those of the Persians.

The comparison of governmental sources of military power discussed above suffers from presupposing a common goal against which different states can be judged. But the degree of organization required to create and support a large, permanent long-range navy, or large, permanent armies, was, across most of the world, not necessary to maintain military forces fit for purpose. Furthermore, the cost and value of such an invest-ment also need to be considered. In addition, there is a problematic empirical dimension. In the early modern period, administrative sophis-tication did not suffice for victory, as the Chinese discovered with their defeats at Mongol and, more completely, Manchu hands in the mid-fifteenth and mid-seventeenth century respectively.

More generally, the central conceptual problem with military history is how to acknowledge, appreciate and analyse its diversity, but the conventional approach ignores this problem. Thus, for example, the focus in discussion on military revolutions is the West, the definitions are Western, and, in so far as non-Western powers feature, it is in order to record the success of their Western counterparts.[16] There is, indeed, a circular quality in this analysis, which is a serious methodological limitation and one that is shared by an empirical failure to note develop-ments in other cultures.

The clash of civilizations? The case of Islam

It might be thought that the discussion of other cultures in terms of conflict with the West addresses this issue, but this is not the case. Instead, there is a linked empirical and methodological problem, in that there is a tendency to treat what is frequently marginal as if it was central. Thus, for China, Japan and Persia, conflict with the West prior to the mid-nineteenth century was episodic and relatively minor, while the Ottoman Turks focused for much of the period 1514–1743 on Persia, rather than against Christendom. There has been a tendency to exaggerate the centrality of relations with the Western world in Islamic history, and to focus on conflict in these relations.[17] This is at the expense of three different tendencies, first the need for Islam to confront other societies, second the importance of divisions within the Islamic world itself (with the equivalent obviously being true for the Western world), and third, the variety of links between Islam and the West. The last point can be related, more generally, to modern revisionism on the multiple character of Western imperialism.

Throughout its history, Islam has interacted not only with Christendom but also with other cultural areas. Our own concerns on the relationship between Christendom and Islam appear to be underlined by the standard map with its depiction of an Islamic world stretching into the Balkans and the Western Mediterranean. However, if the conventional map – an equal-area cartogram – is replaced by an equal-population cartogram, then a very different perception of Islam emerges. It becomes a religion not primarily of the Arab world but of South and Southeast Asia: Iran, Pakistan, India, Bangladesh, Malaysia, and Indonesia. In some respects, there is a parallel with the diversity and range of Christendom, which is now more prominent in the Americas and (increasingly) Africa, than in Europe.

The range of Islam in South and Southeast Asia reflects the extent to which the Muslim advance helped to mould the modern world. It was a cultural as much as a military advance, and, in that, can be compared to Classical Rome's conquest of much (but by no means all) of its empire. Some Muslim lands would pass under non-Muslim control, especially under that of European colonial rulers from the mid-nineteenth century, but Islamicization was reversed in relatively few areas, principally Iberia, Sicily, Israel, and the Volga valley. Instead, as the post-Soviet history of Central Asia from the 1990s indicated, the extent of control won for Islam by the Arabs in the seventh and eighth centuries established an important and lasting cultural realm.

Reconceptualizing the geography of Islam is linked to a focus on different challenges than those from Christianity. In particular, the clash between Islam and Hinduism has proved a major aspect of political tension in South Asia, and this became more pronounced after the end of British imperial rule in 1947. Thus, Kashmir is a major fault-line for many Moslems, and there is considerable concern about increasing Hindu militancy in India after the difficulties the Congress Party that ruled for half a century encountered in maintaining a secular approach: the Hindu nationalist Bharatiya Janata Party came to power in India in 1996 and led the National Democratic Alliance that governed from 1999 until 2004.

In part of Central Asia, the historical challenge to Islam came as much from Chinese as from Russian expansion. In 751, near Atlakh on the Talas river by Lake Balkhash, an Arab army defeated the Chinese, helping to ensure that the expansion of the Tang dynasty into western Turkestan was halted and, instead, driving forward a process of Islamicization in Central Asia. But this was contested by non-Islamic powers, including the expansion of Manchu China into Xinkiang in 1755–7 and into what became Chinese Turkestan, where Kashgar fell in 1759. Tension over the position of Islam in Xinkiang has continued to this day. Furthermore, like the Christians for example in Amazonia, Islam competes with (and has to adapt to) tribal beliefs, particularly in Indonesia. The importance of the eastern world of Islam is such that areas of conflict with the 'West', at least in the shape of Christendom, include the Philippines and Timor.

To turn back to Islamic history is to be reminded of the persistence of conflict with non-Christian peoples and, indeed, its prominence for much of Islamic history. It is, for example, all too easy to present the medieval period in terms of the Christian Crusades,[18] a theme that has recently been pushed back into prominence, and to suggest, as some Islamic polemicists have done, that modern Western pressures sit in this tradition. The Crusades, however, were also directed against 'heathens' (in Eastern Europe, for example Lithuanians), heretical Christians (such as Albigensians and Hussites), and opponents of the Papacy. Furthermore when, in early 2003 Saddam Hussein wished to emphasize the idea of a terrible foreign threat to Baghdad, he referred not to earlier Christian attacks on Islam (nor to the British, who seized the city in both World Wars, in 1917 and 1941), but to the Mongols. Indeed, when Baghdad fell in 1258 to a Mongol army under Hülegü, reputedly hundreds of thousands were slaughtered. The Mongols were far more important to the history of the thirteenth-century Islamic world than conflict with Crusaders: Persia and Anatolia had already been overrun by the Mongols and, in 1260, Hülegü captured Damascus, as the Crusaders had failed to do in 1148. Thereafter, however, the Mongols were to be stopped in the Near East by the Islamic, Egyptian-based Mamluks.

The sweeping initial successes of the Mongols demonstrated another point that is important to bear in mind when considering military relations between Christendom and the West, namely the danger of assuming that a Western model of warfare in the shape of Western forces, later especially infantry focused on volley firepower, was dominant. In many respects, this is an anachronistic reading-back of more modern conflict. South Asia provides a good example of this. The emphasis, in Western works, is on how Europeans sailed round Africa, arrived in Indian waters at the close of the fifteenth century, and then used infantry firepower to subjugate opponents (both Muslim and non-Muslim), with the British victory under Robert Clive over a far larger force under Siraj-ud-daula, the Nawab of Bengal, at Plassey in 1757 taking pride of place.

The arrival of first the Portuguese and then other Europeans in the Indian Ocean and linked waters, especially the Red Sea and the Persian Gulf, did indeed greatly expand the extent of contact between Christendom and Islam, but the extent of the challenge should not be exaggerated. The Islamic world was able to mount a robust response: the Portuguese were repelled from the Red Sea and Aden in the early sixteenth century, and driven from Muscat (1650) and Mombasa (1698) by the Omani Arabs. In India itself, assaults by non-Europeans from across Afghanistan – particularly the Mughal conquest of the Sultanate of Delhi in the 1520s, the Persian invasion in 1739–40 at the expense of the Mughal empire, and that of the Afghans in the 1750s, culminating in the victory over the (Hindu) Marathas at the Third Battle of Panipat (1761) – were, for long, more important to military history and political developments than European moves.

The Third Battle of Panipat looked back to a long series of conflicts between cavalry armies that had a crucial impact on the Islamic world, for example the campaigns of Timur the Lame, which included the capture of Delhi (1398), Damascus (1401) and Baghdad (1401), and his defeat of the Ottoman Turks at Ankara (1402). This was a politics of force: Timur was brutal towards those who resisted, most vividly by erecting pyramids from the skulls of the slaughtered: possibly 70,000 when a rising at Isfahan was suppressed in 1388. Again, in the sixteenth and seventeenth centuries, the crucial fault-lines in the Islamic world divided the Ottomans from the Safavids of Persia, and the latter from the Mughals of India. Their struggles were more important than those with Christendom. Thus, the Safavids were more concerned about Ottomans, Mughals and Uzbeks than about the Portuguese, who were driven from Hormuz in 1622, and the Safavid empire finally succumbed in 1722 to Afghan attack. Even along the traditional frontier with Christendom, there was little sign of Islamic failure until the loss of Hungary to the Austrian Habsburgs in the 1680s and 1690s. Thus, the Portuguese challenge in Morocco was crushed at Alcazarquivir in 1578, and European pressure there did not subsequently become serious again until the French advanced in 1844 from their new base in Algeria.

The view of an historical clash of civilizations, and of military tasking accordingly, fails to account for the complexity of events, and should be revised. It tells us more about rhetoric, past and present, than about the range of relationships that played a role in the Western encounter with Islam. In addition, notions of relationship constructed largely in terms of either conflict or non-conflict are in some ways rather simplistic. The relations between any two cultures extend along a continuum that encompasses conflict and the opposite. In the case of the latter, it is important not to underrate the extent of syncretism.

In every century of Islamic history, more people have been killed in the Islamic world in conflict among Islamic powers than have been killed in conflicts between Islam and the West. From an extraordinarily early stage, Islam fractured between a large number of polities, some of which were linked to religious and/or ethnic divides. These divisions were much more important in many senses than what took place on the margins. To take the sixteenth century, most commentators looking at world history and writing about Islam might refer to the advance of the Ottoman Turks in Europe under Suleyman the Magnificent, ruler from 1520 to 1566. In 1521, indeed, the Ottomans seized Belgrade, in 1526 smashed the Hungarians at the battle of Mohacs, and in 1529 besieged Vienna. In 1565, the Ottomans attacked Malta, and in 1570 Cyprus. In 1571, there was a dramatic naval battle at Lepanto. To look at the discussion of the sixteenth-century Islamic world in most Western or world civilization books in the USA or UK, will be to read about the Ottoman impact on Europe, but, in fact, the Ottomans spent much of their time fighting non-Christian powers, and their capability and effectiveness need to be assessed accordingly.

The usual map of Europe concentrates on Ottoman expansion, but a different map, focusing on the sweep of Eurasia, will provide other insights. There were two other very important areas for Ottoman expansion in the early sixteenth century. One was into Syria, Lebanon, Palestine, what became Israel, and Egypt; the second one was east, against Persia. Suleyman the Magnificent's father, Selim I (Selim the Grim), who ruled from 1512–1520 and was one of the most successful military figures of the sixteenth century, overcame the Mamluk Empire. He first conquered Syria and Palestine as a result of victory at Marj Dabiq in 1516, while victory number two, at al-Rayda in 1517, led to the conquest of Egypt. Earlier, in 1514 Selim had turned east against Persia, as the new dynasty there, the Safavids, were pressing on the power of the Ottoman Turks in Anatolia and challenging their influence there. Selim won the battle of Chaldiran, a victory followed by the capture of the Safavids' capital, Tabriz.

War, however, is not about beating an opponent: war, in the sixteenth century as also today, is about enforcing one's will on an opponent – and, although the Safavids were beaten in battle, they simply would not give in, but continued resisting. Thereafter, for most of the sixteenth century and the early seventeenth century, conflict between the Ottomans and the Safavids was at a much higher, more intense and more continual level than conflict on the European margin. In the 1530s, major operations by Suleyman the Magnificent led to the conquest of Iraq, which, particularly the major bases at Mosul and Baghdad, became as it were the front line between these two rival empires. And this rivalry continued: in the early eighteenth century, the Safavids and the Ottomans competed in the Caucasus, while, after the Safavid empire collapsed in the 1720s, the successor regimes also competed with the Ottomans, right through into the nineteenth century: thus there were wars between the two powers in 1774–9 and in 1820–3.

This competition between Islamic states is just one example of a much wider process. The Safavid dynasty of Persia did not fall to a Western power. The Westerners had a presence in the region: there were Western commercial interests and military bases in the Persian Gulf area from the early sixteenth century on, while the Portuguese established bases at Hormuz and Muscat. There was to be no parallel, however, to the way the Spaniards brought down the Incas and the Aztecs in the New World in the early sixteenth century. Instead, in military terms the European impact on the Asiatic world was pretty minimal through the sixteenth, seventeenth, and early eighteenth centuries (see Chapter six). The people who brought down the Safavids were Afghan invaders. Similarly, in the late sixteenth century, the only other major opponent of the Safavids, other than the Turks, were Uzbeks, who were defeated by Abbas I at Pul-i Salar in 1598.

Indeed, there was one major military clash between the Portuguese (the crown of Portugal was then in a personal union with that of Spain) and the Persians: this was when the Persians under Abbas I besieged and captured Hormuz in 1622. Similarly, Muscat, now the capital of Oman, had been a Portuguese commercial base from 1550. In 1650, the Sultan of Muscat took it, again an artillery fortress falling; it was never regained by the Europeans. From Muscat, the Omani Arabs became an important naval force in this area, principally operating and prevailing against other Islamic powers.

In short, for the majority of Muslim powers, fighting Europeans was of limited importance. This is instructive because, until the beginning of the sixteenth century, the actual fault-lines between Islam and the Christian West had been much more geographically limited than they were to become. In the twelfth–fifteenth centuries, the fault-lines between Islam and the Christian West ran, in terms of geography, across only a small part of the world. The major one essentially passed right through the Mediterranean, and depending on the advance of the Ottoman Turks, through the Balkans and then to the north of the Black Sea along the frontier between Islamic khanates and, on the other hand, Lithuania and the Grand Duchy of Muscovy.

In the sixteenth century, in contrast, the front lines, or the contact zones, between Christendom and Islam dramatically increased, with Europeans sailing around southern Africa and arriving in the Indian Ocean, at the cusp of the fifteenth and sixteenth century: the first European ships showed up off Calicut in 1498. As a result of the Europeans' arrival in the Indian Ocean, suddenly there were many more contact zones between Islam and Christendom, including in India, southeast Asia and Indonesia, where there was a major Islamic sultanate at Aceh in Sumatra. In addition, the already existing contact zone in what we would call the Horn of Africa became more violent, as Ottoman power and influence came to play a role, while in support of the Christian kingdom of Abyssinia the Portuguese fought the sultanate of Adal in the 1540s. In other words, compared to the Middle Ages, there was a far greater range of contact zones between Christendom and Islam, across which all sorts of relationships occurred: sometimes conflicts, sometimes trade. We are still in this period of contact between Islam and the West across a major range of the Islamic presence, as opposed to only a portion of Islamic activity.

Yet even in the sixteenth century, the majority of international relationships involving Islamic peoples in conflict actually involved each other. Furthermore, to consider only external commitments, the Christians were only one of a number of external forces that had to be confronted. For example, for the early sixteenth century, it is a very Eurocentric view of the world that argues that the major expansion of Islam is the one that takes the Ottoman Turks a bit further forward in the Balkans. They had already advanced there in the fourteenth and fifteenth centuries, overrunning Constantinople (1453), Greece, Bulgaria, Macedonia, and Serbia; to go forward to Vienna was dramatic in terms of European history, but not crucial to the rest of the world.

In contrast, in South Asia there was a major eruption of the Mughals, first into northern India, where the Lodi Sultanate of Delhi, another Muslim polity, was destroyed in 1526 at the First Battle of Panipat, and then a spread of Mughal power in India into areas that had been under the political dominance of Hindus. In many senses, that was a much more dramatic example of the bringing of non-Muslims under non-Muslim authority than developments in Europe. In addition, the preference for expansion into the Deccan, rather than regaining their Central Asian heartland, that characterized Mughal policy is a reminder of the role of policy choice. Increasingly for Islam, India was one of the crucial contact zones with the non-Islamic world, and, again, one that involved a range of relations, not simply conflict.

There were Europeans on the coast of India, but they did not worry the Mughals greatly, for they were foreigners who were there bringing them goods. The Europeans had a few fortified coastal positions by permission, such as Goa, the main Portuguese base. Every so often the Mughals got irritated, as with the English East India Company in 1686, when the Emperor Aurangazeb besieged Bombay, one of the major British settlements, and the East India Company sued for peace. They were not reading out of some script which talked about the triumph of the West. By the 1680s, and even more the 1690s, when Peter the Great captured Azov, Russian pressure was a major factor to the north of the Black Sea, but further south and east there was no comparable challenge to Muslim powers from any Christian force.

To turn to the western extreme of contact between the Europeans and Islam, the Moors had penetrated up to just below the Loire, fighting (and losing) the battle of Poitiers in 732. Most of Iberia below Cantabria (northwest Spain) had been Moorish from that period, and the Moors maintained a presence until they were pushed out of the kingdom of Granada in southern Spain in 1492 (they had essentially been confined to Granada from the late thirteenth century: Cordova had fallen to Castile in 1236, Seville in 1248, and Cadiz in 1262). This appears an indication of Western dominance, but that was not true in the early modern period. Spain and Portugal had tried to expand Western power into northwest Africa, and they had considerable success, capturing a whole series of bases along the Atlantic and Mediterranean coasts in the fifteenth and early sixteenth century. However, it all went totally and utterly wrong in 1578, when King Sebastian of Portugal invaded Morocco. His army was destroyed by the Moroccans at Alcazarquivir, one of those many battles that, because it is not a Western triumph, tends to be ignored. The Portuguese army was crushed, the king was killed and most Portuguese bases were captured. No other European military force successfully operated in Morocco until 1844, when there was a French invasion from Algeria.

Far from it being the central concern to fight the Christians, in 1590 the Moroccans set out to do something that in its own way was as dramatic and bold as anything the Europeans did sailing across the oceans. An army crossed the Sahara (only about half of the 5,000 men sent across the desert survived), captured Timbuktu, smashed the Songhay empire at the battle of Tondibi in 1591, and set up a state based on Timbuktu. Furthermore, in 1684 Moroccan pressure forced the English to abandon Tangier: English colonists and forces could defeat Native Americas and, eventually, the French in North America, but they could not hold Tangier against the Moroccans.

For the eighteenth and nineteenth century, it is possible to point to major Christian advances at the expense of Islam, especially by the Russians in the Balkans and Central Asia, but it is necessary not to anticipate these. The Russians under Peter the Great took advantage of Persian weaknesses to establish a presence on the southwestern and southern shores of the Caspian, but with their garrisons badly affected by disease, the Russians returned their gains to Persia in 1732 and 1735, while Peter had been defeated by the Ottomans at the Battle of the Pruth in 1711. In contrast, Nadir Shah, who came to power in Persia in 1729, overcoming the Afghans, was able to defeat the Ottomans in a long war, and to campaign widely – from Khiva (captured in 1740) to Muscat, and Daghestan to Delhi, which he took in 1739, only for the empire to split apart after Nadir was assassinated in 1747 by Persian officers concerned about his favour to Afghans and Uzbeks.

If the French conquered Algeria from 1830, the Spaniards had failed at Algiers in 1775 and 1784. If the British conquered Egypt in 1882, they had failed there in 1807, and in the meanwhile Egypt had been a dynamic power, expanding into Arabia, the Near East, Sudan, and the Horn of Africa. As a reminder of the variety of Islamic military history, Mehmet Ali, Viceroy of Egypt from 1805 to 1848, organized an impressive military system. This included a staff college, established in 1825, and the introduction of conscription in the 1820s, which enabled him to create an army 130,000 strong. A ministry of war was the first permanent department of state that Mehmet Ali instituted. In 1813, Mecca and Medina were retaken from the Wahhabis, an orthodox Muslim sect that energized much of Arabia, after an Egyptian expedition launched in 1811 had been ambushed. A fresh rebellion, however, led to initial disaster for the Egyptians until, in 1814, the Wahhabi forces were defeated. In 1816, the Egyptians resumed the offensive into the deserts of Arabia, seizing the Wahhabi strongholds, culminating in the capture of their capital, Dar'iyya, in 1818 after a six-month siege. The resilience of the Wahhabis, however, was shown by their continued opposition, and in 1824 the second Sau'di-Wahhabi state was founded in the interior. This demonstrated that the regular forces of settled societies could achieve only so much, prefiguring Egyptian problems when they intervened in the civil war in Yemen in 1962–7 and, to a far lesser extent, the difficulties that faced the Americans in Iraq in 2003–4.[19]

Massawa and Suakin on the Red Sea were occupied by the Egyptians in 1818 and Nubia (northern Sudan) in 1820. In Yemen, the Egyptians made major gains over the Asir tribes in 1833–8, and when Mehmet Ali turned on his Ottoman overlord, he won major victories at Koniya in 1832 and Nezib in 1839. Egyptian forces also took Equatoria (southern Sudan) in 1871, and three years later both Darfur (western Sudan) and Harrar (later British Somaliland).

These dates are a reminder of the brevity of the period of Western dominance and the relatively recent period in which it began. Aden was occupied by the British in 1839 and abandoned in 1967; Egypt was conquered in 1882, but the last British military presence there, in the Suez Canal Zone, ended in 1954; while Sudan was only conquered by the British in the late 1890s, with the crucial battle being fought at Omdurman in 1898, and independence was granted in 1956. The continued importance of Ottoman–Persian rivalry into the nineteenth century also requires attention. In short, the notion of modernity as in some way arriving in the early sixteenth century, with a world dominated by the Western powers in which their pressure on Islam is an aspect of their greater world presence, is inappropriate. It is true only in parts of the world. Just as, for the Chinese, European pressure became acute only in the nineteenth century, with the Opium War of 1839–42, so also for the Islamic world. The modern world in terms of international relations did not really begin until then, and, partly because of this, the attempt to internationalize Western norms of state sovereignty and intra-state conduct have only limited purchase elsewhere.

The political, as much as the religious, tensions within the Islamic world can therefore be discussed as much more historically significant to Muslims themselves than the relatively recent Western ascendancy. Even in the heyday of Western imperialism, this ascendancy had serious limits. In the inter-war period (1918–39), the British were able to suppress the Arab rising in Palestine, but their ambitions and commitments in Persia,

Egypt and Iraq all had to be abandoned, while the French position in Syria and Lebanon rested in large part on force, surveillance and an ability to respond to divisions among the subject population. In the post-colonial world, divisions between Islamic rulers have reasserted themselves and, in many respects, been as, or even more, important than Western power-projection: the war over the last half-century in which the most Muslims died, the Iran–Iraq war of 1980–88, was waged between Muslim powers, albeit powers armed by the West and others.

Alongside rivalries between Islamic and Western powers, there have frequently been alliances across confessional divides, prefiguring the present situation wherein Muslims as well as Westerners are threatened by extremist Islamic terrorism and it is appropriate for them to co-operate against the challenge. Suleyman the Magnificent co-operated with the French against the Habsburgs in the 1530s, while, when the Portuguese were driven from Hormuz, Abbas I of Persia benefited from English co-operation. As imperialists, both the British in India and Nigeria, and the Russians, in Central Asia, co-operated with some Muslim rulers and interests at the same time as they fought others, and this co-operation was vital not only to the process of conquest but also in the subsequent stabilization of imperial rule – a situation that repeated earlier episodes of conquest.

This is part of a more general process by which links – political, economic and cultural – co-existed with rivalry, or at least tension,[20] a situation whose military dimension, however, currently includes an important strategic divergence between the USA and some Gulf State partners over regional threats and security requirements.[21] Co-operation has very different meanings and, as a term for analysis, should not be depoliticized. There is no reason why the co-existence of links with tensions, which co-operation often entails, should cease in the case of the West and Islam, although the nature of many Islamic societies, with rapidly growing, youthful populations centred on volatile urban communities, poses particular problems.[22] Past experience suggests the need for political engagement in responding to the challenges likely to arise; this is an aspect of the 'tasking' discussed in Chapter five.

Such an understanding is important in the shaping of strategic cultures. To be effective, they need to respond to political and other changes. The changing character of Turkey in the twentieth century and its relationship with Western strategic planning provides a good example of this process. Turkey moved from political rivalry to co-operation with the West. It refused to accept a peace settlement after World War One that included Greek rule over the Aegean coast and European troops in Constantinople. Under Kemal Ataturk, the Turks were able to impose their will after defeating the Greeks in 1922 and facing down the British the same year in the Chanak Crisis. This, however, was the background to a long-term improvement in relations with the Western world, which also helped to contain continued Greek–Turkish animosity, albeit with both Armenians and Kurds understandably feeling dissatisfied.

In shaping goals, it is necessary to note the mutability of alignments and the extent to which military objectives have to be located in a sound political analysis. Today, a robust and pro-active approach to radical Islamic terrorism is necessary, but destroying al-Qaeda, while necessary, will only profit its opponents so much if other radical, anti-Western Islamic organizations in turn arise and flourish. To understand the challenge, it is necessary to offer informed judgement of the Islamic worlds and to avoid simplistic claims of immutable cultural clashes with the West. As a defining organizational principle in history, such claims rest on a structuralist account, presenting identity and power in terms of clear-cut blocks – a dated view that corresponds to the classic age of geopolitics, and one that crucially underrates the role of agency. The history and the reality are far more complex and, to an extent, more hopeful. The call to understand the challenge is sometimes dismissed as a sign of weakness or even 'going native'. But the alternative, attempting to enforce supposedly universal principles on situations wrenched out of context, and setting military taskings accordingly, is a naïve response to the complexity of international relations.

Dating Western success

Reassessing relations between Europe and the Islamic world, and even more, the Orient, helps underline the marginal character of the West within Eurasia prior to the nineteenth century. Then, the British both came to dominate India and used it as a base for further expansion, while Russian power pressed on every power from Turkey to China. This earlier marginal character helped protect Europe as a whole after the ebbing of the Ottoman threat following the death of Suleyman the Magnificent in 1566. There were short-term crises within Europe over the real or apparent hegemonic intentions of European powers – the Habsburgs of Spain and Austria in the 1620s, Louis XIV of France in the 1680s, Emperor Charles VI of Austria in the 1720s, Napoleon in the 1800s – but no need to fear the conquest of all or much of Europe by external forces. There was no crisis for Europe as a whole, certainly prior to the outbreak of the French Revolutionary Wars in 1792, which was a crisis within Europe – comparable to that of Ming China in the 1640s–50s and Safavid Persia in the 1720s, when they were overthrown by the Manchu and Afghans respectively. This contrast does not prove a greater strength for European militaries, but rather suggests the need also to consider a different political context, both domestically and internationally.

Indeed, no such European superiority on land was demonstrated over other 'gunpowder states' until the defeat of the Turks in the 1680s and even more, 1690s. Even then the 'real turning point' has recently been located as 'only by the late eighteenth century'.[23] It is far from obvious that a comparable superiority existed in India until the 1750s and, more clearly, the 1790s and 1800s, and in China until the 1830s and, more clearly, 1860. Prior to that, rather than assuming any European superiority, whether or not based on (or amounting to) a military revolution, it is more appropriate to note the more complex, contingent and varied nature of relative military capability, and also to give due weight to the non-military factors for differential regional success.

Firearms and native allies

This argument at once queries the technological interpretation of Western success, in the shape of the role of firearms, and its cultural counterpart, which argues that it was only in Europe that there was a sustained transformation of the culture of war, whereas elsewhere firearms were adopted as useful force multipliers without altering the underlying culture of war. This is a difference traced to, and resting on, contrasting organizational factors in the shape of drill and discipline,[24] in other words firing on command and operating as units, with consequences for battlefield cohesion, control and tactical flexibility. The argument relies, however, on a primitivization of the other, in this case the 'non-West', as it assumes contrasts in these factors and effects that have not been adequately demonstrated.

Furthermore, this approach underrates the capacity of non-Western powers and peoples to respond to Western forces. In some cases, adopting firearms, or improved firearms, without altering the underlying culture of war was not, as it is usually presented, a source of weakness, but rather a valuable enhancement to traditional fighting methods that took advantage of terrain and other local factors, and were also adapted to local social practices and mores, as on British India's North-West Frontier. Indeed, to be effective, Western forces themselves frequently had to adapt to local fighting methods, a process that has received insufficient attention. This led in particular to a move away from the mass of Western battlefields and instead to a use of small fighting units and an emphasis on mobility, as with the French in mid-nineteenth century Algeria. It has been necessary for modern Western militaries to re-learn this lesson from nineteenth-century colonial conflict.[25]

The process of matching the adaptability shown by Western militaries in the nineteenth century has been made more difficult for their modern counterparts because there is no equivalent to the hybrid militaries deployed by Western imperial powers that included large numbers of troops raised in the colonies. The equipment and training of the latter need to be considered with the politics that made it possible to raise these numbers, thus relating an organizational perspective to the wider character of imperialism. In 1850, Charles Napier, the British commander in India, wrote to the Governor General, Lord Dalhousie, threatening to resign as a result of a dispute over the compensation of the *sepoys*: 'seeing the great peril to which the Indian Government was exposed, by the mutinous spirit which has appeared among the troops, it seemed to me that the greatest caution and the promptest decision on my part was necessary'.[26]

In understanding the political context of modern Western force-projection, it is also important to note the experience of the nineteenth-century imperialists, namely that it is rarely viable to imagine that total peace could be obtained. Instead, it is appropriate to note the variety of military cultures with which Western forces came (and come) into contact. As Dalhousie pointed out, with reference to the North-West Frontier of (British) India:

> . . . with a population so long inclined to turbulence as the border tribes, and so little accustomed to show submission to any of the governments under which they have successively passed, I conceive that we must be prepared to expect from time to time risings among the tribes over whom our rule has been proclaimed, and plundering inroads by those which lie close to our frontiers.[27]

Sources and topics for study

The nature of the sources for conflict between Western and non-Western powers poses a major problem, as they are largely Western. For example, there is no Zulu account of the battle of Isandlwana in 1879 to match that left by Henry Curling, one of the few British survivors.[28]

Nevertheless, African roles in the Boer War were probed with considerable success in centennial works,[29] while Herero views of the struggle with the Germans in South West Africa (now Namibia) in 1904–7 have been assessed thanks to work on memory and ritual.[30] For more recent conflicts, it is possible to employ interviews, such as those with veterans and their wives used in Ashley Jackson's *Botswana 1939–1945: An African Country at War* (Oxford, 1999), but the use of such material is time-limited. Jackson's work on Botswana, however, is part of a major development in the historiography of the 'non-West': a focus on the contribution of these societies to Western militaries. This has become particularly prominent and although there are still important gaps, much is now known about the operational contribution of these forces. Some of the work extends to include scholarly study of the life of these troops and an investigation of their changing attitudes.[31]

As far as North America is concerned, there are few Native American accounts of their way of war. Part of the problem was that Native Americans did not want to talk about their battles with Whites because they feared retribution. Thus, there were no Sioux or Cheyenne accounts of what transpired at the Little Big Horn battle until the 1920s because participants were afraid they would be held responsible for the death of Custer and his cavalrymen in 1876. The Apaches, in contrast, were readier to talk freely, as with Jason Betzinez's *I Fought with Geronimo* (Harrisburg, Pennsylvania, 1959) and Keith Basso's edition of *Western Apache Raiding and Warfare, from the Notes of Grenville Goodwin* (Tucson, 1971): recollections of Apache warriors told to an anthropologist. There is much more information on the Native way of war in works by non-Native writers.[32]

Decrying Eurocentricity on the grounds that the military history of much of the world is underrated, if not obscure, does not mean that Western military history is necessarily well-covered. The authoritative treatment recently devoted to the battle of Salamanca (see p. 30) is not the case with many battles or campaigns, certainly in so far as a questioning examination of the sources are concerned. More generally, while many aspects of the military history of the West remain obscure and repay attention,[33] particularly for Eastern Europe,[34] even familiar episodes, such as pre-1914 German war planning,[35] and the Japanese attack on Pearl Harbor in 1941, appear to be more problematic, or at least more controversial, than was once assumed. In addition, scholarship over the last two decades has led to fundamental re-evaluations. This is true, for example, of World War One conflict on the Western Front, with, more particularly, a positive assessment of the British development of artillery–infantry coordination.[36] There has also been an extensive re-evaluation of the Eastern Front in World War Two, in particular of the fighting quality of the Red Army and the limitations of the German *Blitzkrieg*. Yet, compared to the scholarship devoted to the military history of the West, most of the rest of the world has been neglected, especially when it has not clashed with Western powers.

This can be readily seen in the case of World War Two. There has always been a disparity in the case of the treatment of the war against Germany, with a disproportionate attention devoted to British and American conflict with Germany, seen not only in scholarship but also in the availability of visual material. This is but part of the problem posed by an interpretation of Europe that focuses on Western Europe. Nevertheless, there has also been extensive work on the Eastern Front, and if this has become more marked since the fall of the Communist regime made it easier to examine Soviet archives, it was already the case that important work had appeared earlier. The situation is less happy as far as the war with Japan is concerned. There the overwhelming focus on conflict with the USA and, to a lesser extent, Britain and Australia, has been matched by a neglect of the war in China, despite the length of the latter, the large number of Japanese troops involved and the heavy casualties suffered. The war in China did not lead to Japanese defeat, but had Japan been victorious there it would have been more difficult for the West to achieve the peace terms it desired.

The Western dominance of military history can also be seen in the emphasis of scholarly attention in studies of World War One. Thus, the campaigns in Africa have generally received insufficient attention, although less so recently,[37] while some aspects of the war have been largely ignored. This is true, as far as Western readers are concerned, of the revolts of 1916 in Russian Central Asia against the recruitment drive for labour battalions in the army. In Kazakhstan, organized rebel forces reached a peak strength of about 50,000 men. The conflict as a whole throws light on the possibilities of counter-insurgency operations: the mobile and experienced government forces benefited from their opponents' lack of organization, training and arms.[38]

The post-1945 world also shows aspects of the same bias. For example, in wars that involved Western forces, it is their contribution that is emphasized. This is true of both the Korean and the Vietnam Wars. In each case, the extent to which the war was a civil conflict has been underplayed. This is a problem not only as it limits the possibility of creating an accurate record, but also because the analysis of the struggle as a whole is affected as a result. Thus, the stress on the important American role in the Vietnam War leads to an underplaying of the extent to which it was an Asian war, with the Viet Cong and North Vietnamese focusing on operations in the field, including against the South Vietnamese, and having only limited interest in trying to influence opinion in the USA. The scholarly focus on Western warfare is accentuated by the commercial pressures discussed in the previous chapter, and this is enhanced by the cult of the anniversary: accounts of fifty- and then sixty-year-old World War Two battles,[39] will be followed by bicentenary anniversaries of Napoleonic battles, and then by centenaries for World War One counterparts.

The Orient

The sole variant on the global scale has been the popularity of the *Art of War* attributed to Sun Tzu (*c.*500 BCE), allegedly a Chinese commander, although he may have been simply a writer. This work has appeared in several English translations over the last half-century,[40] in part because it provides short and apparently profound sayings that meet Western demands for such aphorisms, which have, indeed, also been applied to business, sporting and other forms of competition. The American publisher Westview Press's publicity leaflet for *The Seven Military Classics of Ancient China* (Boulder, 1993); *The Complete Art of War. Sun Tzu: Art of War* (Boulder, 1994); *The Tao of Spycraft. Intelligence Theory and Practice in Traditional China*, and *One Hundred Unorthodox Strategies. Battle and Tactics of Chinese Warfare* (Boulder, 1996), declared them 'The most thought-provoking works of strategy ever written' and 'the most profound studies on warfare'. The appeal of the *Art of War* also taps longstanding beliefs in the wisdom of the Orient, while its brevity, clarity and aphoristic style make it a welcome alternative to Clausewitz. The emphasis in Sun Tzu on operational flexibility and on out-thinking opponents appeared particularly attractive to Western commentators and readers keen to welcome theory and doctrine likely to lead to limited casualties. In *Sun Tzu and the Art of Modern Warfare* (Oxford, 2001), Mark McNeilly, who had already written *Sun Tzu and the Art of Business: Six Strategic Principles for Managers*, set out to show the relevance of Sun Tzu to modern warfare, drawing parallels with Dien Bien Phu and Desert Storm.

American fascination with Sun Tzu was in part fuelled by the fact that the Chinese Communist leader Mao Tse-tung was known to have read Sun Tzu, while Che Guevara, the exponent of 1960s revolution in Latin

America, read Mao. Thus, Sun Tzu appeared as a key to understanding not only the modern Chinese but also guerrilla warfare. Sun Tzu still appears relevant, although there is nothing in the work not found in the Graeco-Roman tradition of stratagems. To the American military, however, the same doctrine in Frontinus, Polyaenus or Xenophon is irrelevant, an instance of cultural bias in reverse.

The appropriation of Sun Tzu by Western publishers has not led readers to study Lao Tzu's *Tao te Ching*, which is the philosophical basis of the *Art of War* and is difficult for Westerners to understand because of the use of paradox, which Westerners interpret differently to how the paradoxes were originally intended to be read. Nevertheless, other aspects of Oriental warfare attract interest. Like the *Art of War*, the *Book of Five Rings* by Musashi Miyamoto, a seventeenth-century samurai, is popular and it is promoted as containing Japanese wisdom applicable to more than swordsmanship or war. The appeal of this model was such that, in 2003, Hollywood was willing to make an epic, *The Last Samurai*, about conflict in Japan in the 1870s, with an American deserter joining the samurai to fight the Japanese army.

Sun Tzu and Mao Tse-tung both played a leading role alongside Clausewitz in the major American work on strategic thought, Michael Handel's *Masters of War. Classical Strategic Thought* (3rd edn, 2001), although, in part due to his background in political science, the comparisons he offered across time were ahistorical. The previous year, Mao's *On Guerrilla Warfare* (1937) had appeared in a new American edition, with the editor, Samuel Griffith, a retired general, providing an introduction that considered the importance of guerrilla warfare for American policy. Work on Sun Tzu is also part of a wider probing of the strategic culture of that period in Chinese history, which within the limits posed by the nature of the sources, indicates how much can be recovered.[41]

Chinese work on the country's military history draws on a very different legacy to its Western counterpart, not least because of a contrasting academic tradition and a very different public market. Up until the early years of the twentieth century, Chinese military history was treated within the larger framework of statecraft, politics and ethics that was considered the proper subject of historical study. A traditional history, such as Sima Guang's *Zizhi tongjian* (*Comprehensive Mirror for Aid in Government*; late eleventh century), discussed many battles and campaigns but the focus was elsewhere. The élite officials responsible for writing most of the histories had little experience, knowledge or interest with regard to military matters – hence their battle narratives tended to emphasize colourful, elaborate stratagems while neglecting routine tactics and weapon handling. The histories from the Han period (206 BCE–220 CE), however, contain biographies of generals and treatises on military institutions, while in the Liu Song period (420–79 CE) there are separate sections in the compiled primary sources on documents relating to military campaigns, broken down by emperors.

Ancient Chinese military treatises contain relatively few illustrative examples drawn from history. With the Tang dynasty (618–907 CE), however, military treatises and encyclopedias increasingly included examples of the application of strategic and tactical principles culled from the pages of the histories. From the Tang, there were also extensive military sections in the institutional histories.

In the twentieth century, China learned the art of writing staff histories as part of its experience of importing European methods. The military establishments in both Beijing and Taipei (the capital of Taiwan) have produced many massive, multi-volume studies of the civil wars and the war of resistance against Japan. They have also done similar studies of the military history of pre-modern China, running to ten or twenty volumes in a set.[42] Ancient texts are currently used in Chinese officer training and at the highest levels of planning in developing and teaching deception theory. The ethnocentric character of Chinese thought encourages their belief that their tradition of stratagems in military theory is unique, and leads to an underplaying of Frontinus, Polyaenus and the Graeco-Roman tradition of stratagems. Western work is affected by language barriers, as well as by the Chinese reluctance to open documents, although the Chinese embrace of modernization has made its military history less inaccessible.[43] Furthermore, American concern about the challenge from China has encouraged research and publication.

South Asia

Most of the world outside the West is far more poorly catered for than China. The practice of military history outside the West varies greatly, but, in general, is very much affected by political considerations, in the sense of political control over the academic world and publishing, the impact of recent history, especially de-colonization struggles and subsequent politics, and with reference to the disruption caused by contemporary internal conflict. On the whole, military history has emerged only slowly in post-colonial settings. For example, in India and Pakistan, at the academic level, military history is only just now starting to establish its credibility. This owes much to the longstanding domination of Indian historiography by the great questions of nationalism and resistance. Regular armies generally raise uncomfortable questions within such a context, particularly so in India where large numbers served in the army, especially in World War Two, rather than heeding nationalist calls for opposition to British rule. In India, a focus on nationalism in turn led to an emphasis on social and economic history, much of which concerned the period after 1885. The emergence of the so-called Subaltern Studies group in the 1980s did little for military history; what military history was being done was largely by ex-officers and the like.

But with the renewed attention to the role of the state that can be seen from some Indian scholars who had worked in Britain came opportunities for military history to be treated as an acceptable field within Indian universities. Both Jawaharlal Nehru University and Delhi University have produced some good theses in the area, and scholars such as Kaushik Roy have demonstrated the academic credibility of military history. Recent collections include *Warrior Saints: Three Centuries of the Sikh Military Tradition* (2000), edited by Amandeep Madra and Parmjit Singh, and *The British Raj and its Indian Armed Forces, 1857–1939* (New Delhi, 2002), edited by Partha Sarathi Gupta and Anirudh Deshpande. But most of this work tends towards the social and institutional.

The government of India is still very sensitive about military topics (operational or otherwise) and scholars may find themselves fighting an uphill struggle to obtain funding and to gain access to the sources. Research visas have been denied to Western scholars because their topics were deemed to be too controversial. Historians in Pakistan are more constrained than their counterparts in India, but, in keeping with the traditions of the old Indian army, a number of retired officers have produced narrative histories and regimental accounts.[44]

Ottoman warfare

Different problems are posed by the military history of the Ottoman (Turkish) empire. The situation is not helped by the extent to which military history is the domain of the army in modern Turkey, as the army has little interest in Ottoman conflict. The nature of the sources, however, is also a serious problem, particularly in trying to uncover past attitudes. Surviving literary evidence for the Ottoman view of warfare is largely a question of tales of past glories, although a few chroniclers took a deeper interest in war. The anonymous author who left an account of the campaigns of the Zlatitsa Pass and Varna (1443–4) provided many details of Hungarian tactics, while Tursun Bey (d. after 1488) provided details of military encounters amidst his flowery style, and Pechevi (d. after 1640) was closely interested in warfare. There does not seem to be a tradition of military chronicles in which there is a focus on the technical details of warfare, but there is still much research to do on Ottoman records.[45] Nevertheless, the potential offered by Ottoman archives to throw light on hitherto obscure campaigns has been clarified by work such as Caesar Farah's *The Sultan's Yemen. Nineteenth-Century Challenges to Ottoman Rule* (2002), which indicates the difficulties faced in attempts to enforce direct rule.

Africa

Indigenous military history is weaker in many other countries, particularly in South-East Asia, the Middle East[46] and Africa.[47] As far as the last is concerned, military history is far less extensive than for Europe, and most of it is written by Western scholars. Given that Africa is the world's second largest continent, it is not surprising that what there is tends to be regionally focused.[48] Much of the literature on African conflict is not by historians at all, and is often decidedly ahistorical in methodology and style. Western anthropologists have made a valuable contribution,[49] not least because of the need to work from oral data.[50] African oral traditions offer memories of war that provide much material about conflict. Thus, the *Kano Chronicle*, an Arabic text written in the nineteenth century but based on oral traditions that may go back to the beginning of the fourteenth century, gives accounts of past battles and connected them with explanations of current situations. Oral traditions from the Interlacustrine Area, especially Buganda, contain a wealth of military history and have been carefully edited. One of Buganda's leading native officeholders under colonial rule, Sir Apolo Kaggwa, helped facilitate wider awareness of these oral traditions. Political scientists have also sought to study modern African military history:[51] there are many treatments of recent military regimes and coups.

The relative neglect in Western scholarship of those conflicts in which Western powers did not take a role has been particularly marked in sub-Saharan Africa. Some recent conflicts there, such as the genocide in Rwanda in 1994, have belatedly engaged Western attention for humanitarian reasons, but others, such as the conflict between Ethiopia and Eritrea from 1998, have attracted little study. Furthermore, the possible lessons that these conflicts between non-Western powers might offer to military historians have been slighted because of the emphasis on the paradigm–diffusion analysis. By thus downplaying the multiple political contexts and varied military character of war, this neglect has led to an account of conflict that is seriously misleading.

Diversity is a matter not only of large-scale warfare, but also of the wider question of the relationship between such warfare and the role of conflict in societies. Much of the work on the latter focuses on Western societies,[52] but there have also been important studies for other cultures, many of which draw on anthropological insights. This can be seen with Western work on pre-colonial African warfare. In the scholarship on this subject, there is a tension between the argument that much – probably most – African conflict was qualitatively different from Western warfare, what John Lamphear has termed 'raiding war', and the claim that Africans practised 'real' warfare, similar to that practised in the West, and not simply what is dismissed as raids. This discussion is linked to the applicability or otherwise of Western notions of significance. Without appreciating their effectiveness, past Western commentators were apt to be dismissive of non-Western forces, in large part because they did not conform with Western practices. Reflecting opinion in Gibraltar, the visiting British cleric Dr John Swinton wrote in his diary: 'The siege of Fez in 1727 by Muley Hamet Deby's army, which made so much noise in Europe was carried on by an undisciplined rabble, who had only one mortar, and three cannon amongst them, and who did not know how to use them.'[53]

Brazil

Eurocentricity is also an issue within the Western world, with a tension between the teaching and treatment of the subject in terms of European and North American examples and paradigms, and the use of indigenous counterparts. Thus the trend toward a genuine Brazilian history of Brazilian military affairs was disrupted by a French Military Mission, which influenced military education between 1920 and 1939 and had gained control of the curricula of the military schools by the mid 1930s. As a result, Napoleon and European warfare gained more space.[54]

Recovering non-Western warfare

Redressing Eurocentricity in part entails challenging the notion that a Western style or way of war, developed in Europe by European peoples, spread across the globe 'to be the war of our own time'.[55] Such a challenge may seem counter-intuitive, and, indeed, there has been first-rate work on this spread, presenting it as a significant step in modernization.[56] Nevertheless, as recent decades have abundantly shown, non-Western styles of war continue to enjoy considerable autonomy and vitality. In addition, the argument relates not only to the last half-millennium but also to earlier episodes in which styles of war spread and how they should be assessed. For example, in his study of the evolution of Japan's military from 500 to 1300, William Farris argued that there was an active drawing on Chinese models,[57] but that the difficulty of assessing the options that existed makes the analysis of why this occurred problematic.

The spread of archaeological research and the use of anthropological methodology has helped throw much light on pre-modern societies (including in the West, for example, the early Byzantine military). In particular, they have brought much insight into cultures for which written sources are lacking or limited. Thus, there have recently been major advances in the understanding of pre-Columbian warfare in the Americas.[58] In chronological terms, this is different from the use of archaeological material to throw light on ancient warfare, especially, although not only, in the Near East and China, but whatever the period, the uncovering of such material and the re-interpretation of existing finds continue to be important.[59]

Primitivizing the Middle Ages

The emphasis on cultural factors in warfare discussed in the last chapter makes the choices that were made by non-Western societies about how best to wage war harder to elicit and explain, certainly in terms of the models Western scholars have devised, which are essentially based on their own culture. Indeed, the issue of Eurocentricity is one way to consider the question of 'the explicit relationship between the ways societies wage war, and the ways in which they write about these wars, whether historically or theoretically'.[60] Furthermore, there are instructive comparisons with the treatment of conflict within the West itself. In this, in chronological terms, the Middle Ages plays the part taken by the non-West geographically, being treated as a largely inconsequential, if not primitive, period. This approach has a long legacy in Western military history, owing much to Renaissance confidence in its own novelty and to the legacy of the Renaissance construction of what came earlier as an Other against which progress had reacted. This

Eurocentric chronology also reflected the Cronus tendency in European intellectual culture from the Renaissance, to abandon the practice of viewing past ages as golden, and instead to disparage the past, or at least to regard the present as better than the past and a graspable future as likely to be better than both. The Renaissance was understood as a recovery of the Classical period, but this energy and vision was directed at surpassing what was presented as an inadequate intervening period. Furthermore, the Classical period was sufficiently distant and obscure that it could apparently serve as a model for a tendency that was not, in fact, conservative. Thus, Georg Heinrich von Berenhorst (1733–1814), in his widely read *Betrachtungen über die Kriegskunst* [*Reflections on the Art of War*] of 1796–9 presented the Middle Ages as a backward slough after the achievements of the Classical age.

This approach to the Middle Ages drew both on views of medievalism and on a sense of the transforming character of gunpowder. As a consequence, the Middle Ages themselves, which were studied within Europe in terms only of Europe, were presented in terms of this transforming character, with a teleological emphasis on the development of infantry and on archery as progenitors of the subsequent introduction of hand-held gunpowder weaponry. This led to a slighting of the variety of medieval warfare, and to a misleading analysis of its development.

Medieval warfare was also seen as different to what was then modern conflict, and thus alien because of its supposed ethos. Particular attention was focused on the Crusades, which were regarded as distinctive. For Edward Gibbon, in his *Decline and Fall of the Roman Empire* (1776–88) and for other historians of the Enlightenment, the Crusades were a regrettable expression of irrational superstition and violence that was different from both the Classical world and modern times.

Although there has been an important re-evaluation of medieval European warfare, with an emphasis on its art of war,[61] still to this day assertions of a particular cultural characteristic for European/Western warfare, most prominently that by Victor Davis Hanson, fail to engage adequately with the Middle Ages.[62] He is also all too typical in neglecting Byzantium, an important military power with a strong tradition of military commentary and theory,[63] on which research tends to stand apart, as a form of area studies rather than being incorporated into the mainstream. John Lynn also ignores Byzantium in his study *Battle. A History of Combat and Culture* (2003). The recent re-evaluation of medieval European warfare includes a useful discussion of its capacity to interact with Islamic methods[64] and a helpful engagement with Islamic responses to the Crusades.[65]

Revising Western military history

A more complex presentation of the European Middle Ages can be seen as an aspect of a shifting assessment within which non-European history can be accommodated and, to complete the revisionist process, can be matched by an account of subsequent Western military history in which the focus is not on a process of baton exchange (paradigm shift) from one leading power to the next, but on militaries not seen as at the forefront. Recent examples of first-rate work related to this theme include Gregory Hanlon's *The Twilight of a Military Tradition: Italian Aristocrats and European Conflicts, 1560–1800* (1998), Peter Wilson's *German Armies. War and German Politics 1648–1806* (1998), Gervase Phillips's *The Anglo–Scots Wars, 1513–1550* (1999), and Christopher Storrs's *War, Diplomacy and the Rise of Savoy, 1690–1720* (2000). Thus, Phillips's dismissal of the notion that the English armies were intrinsically backward or less tactically capable than their Continental counterparts is a qualification of the 'meta-narrative' tradition of military history, with its focus on a unitary account of good practice and its tendency to erect a hierarchy based on the adoption of this practice; while Wilson's stress on the value of the collective security arrangements offered by Imperial institutions and German political culture questions the emphasis on Prussia and Prussianization as the course and cause of German modernization, and thus the notion of the paradigm power.

There is also now an understanding of the value of private entre- preneurs in the organizing and support of past and even present Western militaries. The confidence that was expressed in the 1980s and earlier that public provision and state organization were necessarily better, and therefore the goal of past military and governmental development, is now seen as the projection of a particular set of contemporary values. It is, instead, now possible to draw attention to the weaknesses of Western public provision, not least of state structures focused on clientage, and to the limitations of governments. This revisionism provides an important perspective for reconsidering the global situation, not least underlining the need to assess the character of public–private provision and its specific capabilities, and also challenging the view that Western systems were automatically better because of the nature of public provision.

Modern revisionist approaches towards Western military history thus offer much of value for considering the non-Western world, which has also shared in the primitivization of areas within Europe, especially, from the eighteenth century, Eastern Europe.[66] Thus, explaining the failure of military observers to appreciate many of the tactical lessons of the Balkan Wars of 1912–13 that would become very important during World War One, especially the role of field fortifications, Richard Hall noted 'the assumption that events in regions of lesser development such as the Balkans could do little to instruct the Great Powers'.[67] This was even more the case for campaigns not involving Western powers.

Non-Western perspectives

These issues throw light on the treatment of the 'non-West', but it is also necessary to avoid a monolithic reification of the latter and, instead, to consider how best to address its variety. It has been suggested that military cultures have been constructed by misleading external categorization:

> For some reason, militarism has captured the minds of a majority of the people studying Mesoamerican history. In seeing the Maya, the Zapotecs, the Mixtecs and all the others through a filter of militarism and militarisation, the scholars give shape to their cultures and provide them with a set of characteristics. In the East Asian and the Southeast Asian cases, other filters were used, and completely different societies emerged.[68]

This leads to a more general questioning of the typology employed in judging difficult societies, both in the West and in the 'non-West'. In so far as there is to be an emphasis on the inherent military cultures of particular societies, the issue of construction is of great importance. It offers the benefit of further directing attention to the extent to which war-making was culturally specific in particular societies.[69] As a related topic, this focus can also shed light on particular factors that increased or diminished (or were believed to do so) the chances that, if defeated, particular societies could be conquered, and if conquered, be absorbed into the empires of others.

The issue of typology also suggests a bridging of West and non-West, as common elements at particular moments are considered together. For example, the following passage: 'Defence against diffused threats required a degree of military and administrative decentralization and the establishment of local defensive systems' refers 'to the origins of medieval Europe's fragmented political landscape',[70] but could equally be applied elsewhere. This is one way forward in lessening Eurocentricity: not simply studying the 'non-West', but also considering common themes, and without any assumption of Western superiority.

Most war, both in the past and today, occurs in the multiplicity of environments grouped together as the non-West, and this has become increasingly the case since 1945, although the Bosnia and Kosovo conflicts of the 1990s briefly suggested otherwise. The areas of highest population growth will continue to be the most volatile, not least because resource pressures will be most acute there, while there will also be a high percentage of the population under 25, the male cohort that it is easiest to persuade to risk death. Despite the Revolution in Military Affairs (RMA) fantasy of a one-sided banishment of the risk of casualties, the last is an essential precondition for conflict: it is relatively easy to get people to kill others, but far less so to lead them to risk death over a long period.

Conclusions

The issue of Eurocentricity is addressed in large part by focusing on the diversity of military histories and cultures, but it is also pertinent to note common themes that bridge divides. One such is the use of war in order to win prestige and to affirm rank and privilege. This characteristic of bellicose societies focused on heroic conceptions of royal, princely and aristocratic conduct in wartime. The resulting glory and honour were important to individuals and families, and past warrior-leaders were held up as models for their successors.[71] Thus, the reputation of the Ottoman Sultan Murad IV (r. 1623–40) rested on his having led the successful campaigns against Safavid control of Erivan and Baghdad.

Searching for comparisons depends, however, on more work on the 'non-West': Western military history cannot be used as a palimpsest for the remainder of the world. Thus, Western periodization does not necessarily apply elsewhere, and the notion of a staged modernization, as if the West set the pattern for development, is certainly unconvincing other than for aspects of the military history of the last two centuries. Again, research is required on the 'non-West': even for China, there is a lack of adequate periodization, as the dynasties do not always conform to helpful divides.[72]

The impact of a focus on the West is further revealed by the 'face of battle' and 'war and society' approaches. Particularly for outside the West (although, to a considerable extent, also for there), we have only a thin mosaic for such topics as the experience of battle and for combat motivation. There is a potpourri of such studies across time, of varying quality, with an emphasis on the West and a strong focus on the American Civil War and on World Wars One and Two, but the possibility of a systematic analysis using other disciplines is limited by the restricted nature of the work on the 'non-West'. If the basic methodology of critical history is a Western construction, however, then there will be more profound methodological limits to a truly global military history. Thus, a rethought military history may ultimately be a Western project.

Whatever the approach, it is necessary to consider the different perspectives that a plural focus offers. In 1738, Edward Trelawny, Governor of the British colony of Jamaica, reported on operations against the Maroons, runaway, or in some cases freed, slaves, who controlled much of the interior of the island: 'The service here is not like that in Flanders or any part of Europe. Here the great difficulty is not to beat, but to see the enemy . . . in short, nothing can be done in strict conformity to usual military preparations, and according to a regular manner; bushfighting as they call it being a thing peculiar by itself'.[73] This difference is also noted in fiction. In his novel *The Kleber Flight* (1981), Hans Koning has an American officer write: 'Perhaps we have to be the underdogs, the natives, for a generation or two before we can start writing history objectively, and before we dare compare the assassin's dagger in the night with the cavalry charge at high noon'.[74]

Notes

1 See also *The Russo–Japanese War: Reports from British Officers* (3 vols., 1904–5); *The Russo–Japanese War . . . Prepared in the Historical Section of the German General Staff. Authorised translation* (7 vols, 1908–14); G.C. Cox, 'Of Aphorisms, Lessons, and Paradigms: Comparing the British and German Official Histories of the Russo–Japanese War', *Journal of Military History*, 66 (1992), pp. 389–401; and for the cultural dimensions of Japan's previous war, S.C.M. Paine, *The Sino–Japanese War of 1894–1895: Perceptions, Power, and Primacy* (Cambridge, 2003).

2 For the neglect of China, H. van de Ven, 'Introduction' in his (ed.), *Warfare in Chinese History* (Leiden, 2000), pp. 1–11.

3 See, for example, articles in *The Times*, 14 Sept. 2001, pp. 6, 8.

4 J. Belich, *The Victorian Interpretation of Racial Conflict: The Maori, the British, and the New Zealand Wars* (1999).

5 B.C. Hacker, 'Military Technology and World History: A Reconnaissance', *The History Teacher*, 30 (1997), p. 462.

6 S. Morillo, '*Milites*, Knights and Samurai: Military Terminology, Comparative History, and the Problem of Translation', in R.P. Abels and B.S. Bachrach (eds), *The Normans and their Adversaries at War* (Woodbridge, 2001), pp. 167–84, quotes pp. 179, 183–4.

7   J. France, 'Recent Writing on Medieval Warfare: From the Fall of Rome to *c*.1300', *Journal of Military History*, 65 (2001), pp. 450, 454.

8   M. Khodarkovsky, *Where Two Worlds Met. The Russian State and the Kalmyk Nomads, 1600–1771* (Ithaca, 992), p. 51.

9   M.C. Paul, 'The Military Revolution in Russia, 1550–1682', *Journal of Military History*, 68 (2004), pp. 36–7.

10   G. Phillips, 'Douglas Haig and the Development of Twentieth-Century Cavalry', *Archives*, 28 (2003), pp. 142–62.

11   Pearson to his parents, 19 July 1857, BL. Indian Office papers, Mss Eur. C 231, p. 51.

12   J. Gommans, *Mughal Warfare. Indian Frontiers and High Roads to Empire, 1500–1700* (2002), e.g. pp. 202–5.

13   R.J. Barendse, 'Trade and State in the Arabian Seas: A Survey from the Fifteenth to the Eighteenth Century', *Journal of World History* (2000), pp. 210–11.

14   D.K. Abbass, 'Horses and Heroes: The Myth of the Importance of the Horse to the Conquest of the Indies', *Terrae Incognitae*, 18 (1986), pp. 21–41, esp. 40–1.

15   Liddell Hart to Brian Melland, 29 May 1961, LH, Liddell Hart papers, 4/31.

16   See, for example, M. Knox and W. Murray (eds), *The Dynamics of Military Revolution* (Cambridge, 2001).

17   For example A. Wheatcroft, *Infidels: The Conflict between Christendom and Islam, 638–2002* (2002).

18   R. Fletcher, *The Cross and the Crescent. Christianity and Islam from Muhammad to the Reformation* (2003).

19   D.M. Witty, 'A Regular Army in Counterinsurgency Operations: Egypt in North Yemen, 1962–1967', *Journal of Military History*, 65 (2001), pp. 401–39.

20   See, for example, T.J. Barfield, *The Perilous Frontier: Nomadic Empires and China, 221 BC to AD 1757* (Oxford, 1989).

21   R.D. Sokolsky and J. McMillan, 'Policy Implications and Recommendations', in Sokolsky (ed.), *The United States and the Persian Gulf. Reshaping Security Strategy for the Post-Containment Era* (Washington, 2003), p. 146.

22   J.M. Black, *The World in the Twentieth Century* (2000).

23   G. Ágoston, 'Early Modern Ottoman and European Gunpowder Technology', in E. Ihsanoglu, K. Chatzis and E. Nicolaidis (eds), *Multicultural Science in the Ottoman Empire* (Turnhout, 2003), p. 27.

24   J.A. Lynn, 'The Evolution of Army Style in the Modern West, 800–2000', *International History Review*, 18 (1996), p. 505; D. Showalter, 'Caste, Skill, and Training: The Evolution of Cohesion in European Armies from the Middle Ages to the Sixteenth Century', *Journal of Military History*, 57 (1993), pp. 407–30; H. Kleinschmidt, 'Using the Gun: Manual Drill and the Proliferation of Portable Firearms', *Journal of Military History*, 63 (1999), pp. 601–29.

25   J. Lamphear, 'The Evolution of Ateker "New Model" Armies: Jie and Turkana', in K. Fukui and J. Markakis (eds), *Ethnicity and Conflict in the Horn of Africa* (1994), p. 89; T.R. Moorman, *The Army in India and the Development of Frontier Warfare, 1849–1947* (1998).

26 Napier to Dalhousie, 22 May 1850, BL. Add. 49016, fols. 107–9.
27 Dalhousie to Napier, 24 Dec. 1849, BL. Add. 49016, fol. 57.
28 A. Greaves and B. Best (eds), *The Curling Letters of the Zulu War* (Barnsley, 2001).
29 For example J. Gooch (ed.), *The Boer War. Direction, Experience and Image* (2000); D. Lowry (ed.), *The South African War Reappraised* (Manchester, 2000).
30 G. Krüger, *Kriegsbewältigung und Geschichtsbewustein: Realität, Deutung und Verarbeitung des deutschen Kolonialkriegs in Namibia 1904 bis 1907* (Göttingen, 1999).
31 M. Bodin, *Les Africains dans la guerre d'Indochine, 1947–1954* (Paris, 2000).
32 For a selection, B. Mishkin, *Rank and Warfare among the Plains Indians* (New York, 1940); H.H. Turney-High, *Primitive Warfare: Its Practice and Concepts* (Columbus, Ohio, 1971); J. Ewers, 'Inter-Tribal Warfare as a Precursor of Indian–White Warfare on the Northern Great Plains', *Western Historical Quarterly*, 6 (October 1975), pp. 397–410; R.B. Ferguson, *Warfare, Culture and Environment* (New York, 1984); E. Wallace and E. Adamson Hoebel, *The Comanches: Lords of the South Plains* (Norman, Oklahoma, 1988); L.V. Eid, '"A kind of running fight": Indian Battlefield Tactics in the Late Eighteenth Century', *Western Pennsylvania Historical Magazine*, 81 (1988), pp. 147–71; A.J. Hirsch, 'The Collision of Military Cultures in Seventeenth Century New England', *Journal of American History*, 74 (1988), pp. 1187–1212; A. McGinnis, *Counting Coup and Cutting [Out] Horses: Intertribal Warfare on the Northern Plains, 1783–1889* (Evergreen, Co., 1990); P.M. Malone, *The Skulking Way of War: Technology and Tactics among the New England Indians* (Baltimore, 1991); N. Ferguson and N. Whitehead (eds), *War in the Tribal Zone: Expanding States and Indigenous Warfare* (Santa Fé, 1992); F.P. Secoy, *Changing Military Patterns of the Great Plains Indians* (Lincoln, Nebraska, 1992). I am most grateful for the advice of Bruce Vandervort.
33 E. Greenhalgh, 'The Archival Sources for a study of Franco–British Relations during the First World War', *Archives*, 27 (2002), p. 171.
34 P. Bushkovitch, 'The Romanov Transformation, 1613–1725', in F.W. Kagan and R. Higham (eds), *The Military History of Tsarist Russia* (Basingstoke, 2002), pp. 42–3.
35 T.M. Holmes, 'Asking Schlieffen: A Further Reply to Terence Zuber', *War in History*, 10 (2003), pp. 464–79.
36 See, for example, P. Griffith, *Battle Tactics of the Western Front: The British Army's Art of Attack, 1916–1918* (New Haven, 1994) and J. Bailey, *The First World War and the Birth of the Modern Style of Warfare* (Camberley, 1996).
37 H. Strachan, *The First World War. I. To Arms* (Oxford, 2001), pp. 495–643.
38 S. Kudryashev, 'The Revolts of 1916 in Russian Central Asia', in E.J. Zürcher (ed.), *Arming the State. Military Conscription in the Middle East and Central Asia, 1775–1925* (1999), p. 142.
39 For example S.E. Ambrose, *D-Day, June 6, 1944: The Climactic Battle of World War II* (New York, 1994); S. Bungay, *Alamein* (2002).
40 L. Giles (ed.), *Sun Tzu on the Art of War* (1910); S.B. Griffith (ed.), *The Art of War* (Oxford, 1963), R.T. Ames (ed.), *Sun Tzu: The Art of Warfare: The First English Translation Incorporating the Recently Discovered Xinque Shan*

Texts (New York, 1993); J.H. Huang, *Sun Tzu: The New Translation* (New York, 1993); R.D. Sawyer (ed.), *The Art of War* (Boulder, Co, 1994). This is not an exhaustive list of relevant works, and new translations of Sun Tzu are in preparation.

41 R.D.S. Yates, 'New Light on Ancient Chinese Military Texts: Notes on Their Nature and Evolution, and the Development of Military Specialization in Warring States China', *T'oung Pao*, 74 (1988), pp. 211–48; R.D. Sawyer (ed.), *The Seven Military Classics of Ancient China* (Boulder, 1993).

42 I am most grateful for the advice of David Graff and Peter Lorge.

43 E.A. Feigenbaum, *China's Techno-Warriors: National Security and Strategic Competition from the Nuclear to the Information Age* (Stanford, 2003).

44 I am most grateful to Douglas Peers for his advice.

45 I am most grateful to Colin Imber for his advice.

46 J.W. Jandora, *Militarism in Arab Society: An Historiographical and Bibliographical Sourcebook* (Westport, 1997).

47 I am most grateful for the advice of David Killingray and John Lamphear.

48 For example J. Ajayi and R. Smith, *Yoruba Warfare in the Nineteenth Century* (Cambridge, 1964); R. Smith, *Warfare and Diplomacy in Pre-Colonial West Africa* (1976); J.P. Smaldone, *Warfare in the Sokoto Caliphate* (Cambridge, 1977); R. Reid, *Political Power in Pre-Colonial Buganda: Economy, Society and Warfare in the Nineteenth Century* (Oxford, 2002).

49 K. Fukui and D. Turton (eds), *Warfare Among East African Herders* (Osaka, 1979).

50 J. Lamphear, 'Brothers in Arms: Military Aspects of East African Age-Class Systems in Historical Perspective', in E. Kurimoto and S. Simonse (eds), *Conflict, Age and Power in North East Africa. Age Systems in Transition* (Oxford, 1998), p. 96.

51 A. Mazrui, *The Warrior Tradition in Modern Africa* (1977).

52 For example J. Ruff, M.D. Meyerson, D. Thiery, and O. Falk (eds), *'A Great Effusion of Blood?' Interpreting Medieval Violence* (Toronto, 2003).

53 Wadham College, Oxford, Swinton's Diary, 25 Nov. 1730.

54 I am grateful for the advice of Frank McCann.

55 J. Carman and A. Harding, 'The Future Study of Ancient Warfare', in Carman and Harding (eds), *Ancient Warfare* (Stroud, 1999), p. 245.

56 D. Ralston, *Importing the European Army. The Introduction of European Military Techniques and Institutions into the Extra-European World, 1600–1914* (Chicago, 1990), p. 173.

57 W.W. Farris, *Heavenly Warriors. The Evolution of Japan's Military, 500–1300* (Cambridge, Mass., 1995), p. 357.

58 B.R. Ferguson and N.L. Whitehead (eds), *War in the Tribal Zone: Expanding States and Indigenous Warfare* (Santa Fé, 1992); R. Hassig, *War and Society in Ancient Mesoamerica* (Berkeley, 1992); S.A. LeBlanc, *Prehistoric Warfare in the American Southwest* (Salt Lake City, 1999).

59 For example E.L. Shaughnessy, 'Historical Perspectives in the Introduction of the Chariot into China', *Harvard Journal of Asiatic Studies*, 48 (1988), pp. 189–237.

60 T.R.W. Kubik, 'Is Machiavelli's Canon Spiked? Practical Reading in Military History', *Journal of Military History*, 61 (1997), p. 29.

61 M. Strickland (ed.), *Anglo-Norman Warfare: Studies in Late Anglo-Saxon and Anglo-Norman Military Organisation and Warfare* (Woodbridge, 1992); J.F. Verbruggen, *The Art of Warfare in Western Europe During the Middle Ages* (2nd edn of translation, Woodbridge, 1999).

62 For example V.D. Hanson, *Carnage and Culture: Landmark Battles in the Rise of Western Power* (New York, 2002).

63 Best approached through A. Dain, 'Les strategists byzantins', *Travaux et Mémoires*, 2 (1967), pp. 317–92; G.T. Dennis (ed.), *Maurice's Strategikon: Handbook of Byzantine Military Strategy* (Philadelphia, 1984); and a steady stream of subsequent English translations of Byzantine military theory, e.g. E. McGeer, *Sowing the Dragon's Teeth: Byzantine Warfare in the Tenth Century* (Washington, 1995).

64 J. France, 'Crusading Warfare and Its Adaptation to Eastern Conditions in the Twelfth Century', *Mediterranean Historical Review*, 15 (2000), pp. 49–66, esp. pp. 61–2.

65 C. Hillenbrand, *The Crusades: Islamic Perspectives* (Edinburgh, 1999), and, at the popular level, D. Nicolle, *The Crusades* (2001).

66 L. Wolff, *Inventing Eastern Europe: The Map of Civilization on the Mind of the Enlightenment* (Stanford, 1994).

67 R. Hall, *The Balkan Wars, 1912–1913: Prelude to the First World War* (2000), p. 134.

68 D. Harrison, *Social Militarisation and the Power of History: A Study of Scholarly Perspectives* (Oslo, 1999), p. 194.

69 L.E. Grinter, 'Cultural and Historical Influences on Conflict in Sinic Asia: China, Japan and Vietnam', in S.J. Blank *et al.* (eds), *Conflict and Culture in History* (Washington, 1993), pp. 117–92.

70 J. Landers, *The Field and the Forges. Population, Production, and Power in the Pre-industrial West* (Oxford, 2003), pp. 274–5.

71 C. Vivant, 'Henri IV the Gallic Hercules', *Journal of the Warburg and Courtauld Institutes*, 30 (1967), pp. 176–97; S. Gunn, 'The French Wars of Henry VIII', in J.M. Black (ed.), *The Origins of War in Early Modern Europe* (Edinburgh, 1987); D.A.L. Morgan, 'The Political After-Life of Edward III: The Apotheosis of a Warmonger', *English Historical Review*, 112 (1997), pp. 869, 876.

72 J.K. Fairbank and F.A. Kierman Jr. (eds), *Chinese Ways in Warfare* (Cambridge, Mass., 1974), p. 5. I am most grateful to David Graff for letting me read his unpublished paper 'History as *Gingfa*: A Tang Contribution to Chinese Military Thought'.

73 Trelawny to Thomas, Duke of Newcastle, Secretary of State for the Southern Department, 4 Dec. 1738, PRO. Colonial Office, papers 137/56.

74 H. Koning, *The Kleber Flight* (New York, 1981; London edn, 1989), p. 202.

Chapter 4

Qualifying technology

> The principle of the modern world – thought and the universal – has given courage a higher form, because its display now seems to be more mechanical, the act not of this particular person, but of a member of a whole. Moreover, it seems to be turned not against single persons, but against a hostile group, and hence personal bravery appears impersonal. It is for this reason that thought has invented the gun, and the invention of this weapon, which has changed the purely personal form of bravery into a more abstract one, is no accident.
>
> Hegel, 1821[1]

> One salient fact stands out throughout history . . . whichever side can throw the greatest number of projectiles against the other is the side which has the greatest chance of winning.
>
> J.F.C. Fuller, 1915[2]

The move away from Eurocentricity discussed in the last chapter necessarily leads to a downplaying of the role of Western military technology in military history, which very much qualifies the dominant tendency of scholarship in recent decades.[3] Downplaying, however, is not the same as denial, and it would be naïve to neglect the value of military *matériel*, both in quality and in quantity, and thus of changes in both. The technological perspective entails work on how weapons actually worked, a subject that is more obscure than is generally appreciated,[4] and were produced and improved, as well as assessing their impact within the context of a situation in which human beings develop and use technology for some purpose. This is related to the organization of resources for war and how innovations in organization are achieved. Technology was often very important in human efforts to organize resources more efficiently, but the driving force behind it was not technology appearing from nowhere, but human needs and desires that focused minds on some kind of change where technology was a part. The role of technology in helping to create capability gaps in force projection and battlefield effectiveness is greater in naval[5] and air than in land warfare, and underlines the importance of the force structures and goals stemming from policies and strategic cultures.

Many problems are faced when discussing technology and its role in warfare, not least that we have been 'educated' since the 1960s to expect technological solutions to be definitive. Prior to the 1960s, technology seems to have been viewed more pragmatically. Assessment is also complicated by the problems of analysing the initial introduction of new technology. Many inventions are, in fact, re-inventions, which is why patent law defines what an invention is. There are numerous examples of such re-inventions: working submarines (1776, 1797, 1879),[6] the percussion hand grenade (1861 and 1905), flamethrowers (424 BCE, 1910 and 1940s), and breech-loading rifles (for instance 1740s, 1750s, 1780, 1839), although it can be argued that all the re-inventions were 'new'.

How something works can be more important than what it does. Much of new technology did (and does) not work effectively when first introduced (this is equally true of patented inventions). For example, the great constructional problem with the breech-loading rifle was the escape of gas at the breech, and this was the cause of the major delay in its adoption in the nineteenth century. Similarly, the tendency of the gatling gun to jam delayed its large-scale introduction. As a result, it is important to discuss whether the important date was the date of invention, the date it worked effectively for the first time (and how was/is 'effectively' defined), or the date military thinking changed in order to take advantage of what the new device allowed the operator of it to do what he could not previously do.

There is also the issue of production. To create an effective weapon and to lead to a relevant change in tactics and, even, doctrine, is only part of the story. It is also necessary to be able to manufacture large numbers of a new weapon, and at a consistent standard, in order to replace losses both in victory and in defeat, and to provide the resources for new operational opportunities. The development of true firearms in thirteenth-century China did not lead to the rapid displacement of pre-firearm gunpowder weapons, because of problems with effectiveness, reliability, cost, and availability. With firearms, it was necessary to deploy a number of production technologies: weapon, ammunition, ignition, and propellant all had to be considered.[7] Although Alexander

Forsyth patented the use of fulminates of mercury in place of gunpowder as a primer for firearms in 1807, the initial impact of the percussion cap, coated with fulminates of mercury, was limited, and the mass-produced metal percussion cap dates from 1822. The rush on the part of the Germans to force the V-2 rocket into service in 1944 helped lead to a high margin of error.

Furthermore, it is important to be able to supply and repair weapons, as an example of their functionality and fitness for purpose. The records of the Teutonic Order from the late fourteenth and early fifteenth century provide ample and systematic evidence on logistics, including statements about the costs of supply and repair. New weaponry posed particular problems of supply and repair. It was difficult, for example, to maintain the Girandoni breech-loader, magazine-fed rifle, which was an innovative weapon; in general, the loading mechanism of eighteenth-century breech-loaders were susceptible to clogging by powder. Much of the importance of the introduction of single-shot breech-loaders in the mid-nineteenth century, followed by that of repeating firearms, stemmed from the ability to mass-produce rifling, sliding bolts, magazine springs, and chain-feeds to a high standard, and also to provide the large quantities of ammunition required. Effective mass-production provided a major advantage over craft-manufactured firearms, however good the latter were on an individual basis. This required a major change in the production process. When American gun-makers modernized Russian small arms after the Crimean War, they provided not only machinery but also skilled workers and advanced production techniques.[8]

In turn, improvements in technology seek to respond to the problems confronting production. Ease of manufacture in quantity can entail the avoidance of tight engineering tolerances, which require skilled workers. Skill and quality are not fixed factors, but vary according to circumstances. Their evaluation depends in part on the capacity of manufacturing systems, and on how these interact with quality control: a vital function of twentieth-century manufacture was inspection, which required skilled inspectors using precision-made testing tools. But under the pressure of war, innovations in manufacturing processes were introduced.

There is also the question of how technological innovations were perceived at the time. Within Western states, the institutionalization of military systems, particularly for artillery from the eighteenth century, ensured that the utility of new weapons and systems was carefully probed. Thus, in 1848–9, British officers commanding regiments with rifle companies reported to the Secretary of the Military Board on the best form of rifle ammunition. Investigation did not necessarily ensure appropriate usage. Conservatism on the part of French military engineers thwarted proposals for new fortification architecture in the late eighteenth century.[9] Automatic rifles, around since the end of the nineteenth century, were, when tested by the British during World War One, viewed as nothing more than weapons in which the burden of opening and closing the bolt had been automated. That is not how automatic rifles are viewed today.

In judging technological change, there is also the issue of differentiation between similar devices. If, for example, all bolt-action manually operated rifles are viewed as being essentially the same, it means that the Dreyse rifle of 1840 was the same as the SMLE No. 4 of a century later, when clearly they were very different. There is the question of degree of change within a given technology. For example, weapons such as bills, halberds and swords evolved over time according to changes in armour and alterations in use. Some developments were abandoned, while emulation created differences as well as similarities. More generally, differences in the technicalities of the technology concerned, so that the original or the copy might be technically better, could alter the way a weapon was used: there is always the danger that what looks the same is regarded as being the same.

Furthermore, hindsight is one of the difficulties in assessing similar inventions; theorizing about the impact of any new development needs to take this into account. For example, there were different models and varieties of the composite bow over the centuries, which was first attested in the West in Mesopotamia in about 2200 BCE. Storing compressive and tensile energy by virtue of its construction and shape, allowing it to be smaller than the long bow, the composite bow was a sophisticated piece of engineering that seems to have been invented in different places by different peoples, although there was probably some interchange of ideas. Thus, the Turkish bow was different from the Chinese bow. The bow was more effective than the simple bow because its stave of wood was laminated, but it was labour-intensive to manufacture; it is not safe to be too technologically deterministic and to claim that the composite bow drove out other types of bow; it did not.

There is also the question of how change occurs. It would be mistaken to suggest that we must choose between whether technological change is incremental, based on current knowledge, as with cannon in Europe in the eighteenth century,[10] or revolutionary. Instead, it is both at different times and in different settings. Nevertheless, the issue of emphasis has to be addressed. The concept of revolutionary change is particularly problematic. For example, there was a considerable overlap of flint with copper, copper with bronze, and bronze with iron, rather than a sudden and complete supplanting of one technology by another. In addition, the metallurgical aspects of making and processing the metals and alloys were not static, while different metallurgical processes developed in particular parts of the world. Thus, steels are not the same, geographically or historically. More generally, revolutionary change may be illusory: the timescale may be far greater than it appears to be, and the process of change may have been far from straightforward. The machine gun provides an instance of incremental change, with inefficient earlier models being improved and used more effectively.

Possibly the term 'a lateral leap' is more helpful than 'revolutionary', as the question of whether something is revolutionary is subjective and is very difficult to address because of the difficulty with keeping hindsight from biasing the answer. And technical change is not always 'forwards' in the conventional sense. Furthermore, sometimes technological advance entails simplification, although there is a tendency for it to lead to greater complication. Simplification can seem an advance, but can also appear not to be innovative. Whatever the level of complexity, supposed technical superiority may be incidental or, indeed unnecessary, if the new weapon increases the amount of damage that can be inflicted to such a level that the enemy cannot tolerate it. The latter, however, is far from clear: perception plays a major role in the consideration of the effects of weapons on targets, and this affects use of the weapons, tactically and operationally.

Another aspect of incremental development that can entail simplification is relating new weaponry to training. For example, Royal Navy recruiters in Britain in the early 2000s produced postcards depicting modern weapons with captions such as 'Controlled by a Team of Operator Mechanics it can stop a MiG-27. Without them it couldn't stop a 27 Bus' and 'Awesomely Powerful. Deadly Accurate. But Without Highly Trained Weapons Specialists about as Lethal as a Pork Sausage'. Recruitment material indeed charts different attitudes to military history: since the 1960s there has been scant emphasis on past glories. Training soldiers to clean and maintain weapons is also important to effectiveness.

The understanding of the term 'technology' varies. Engineers and historians are apt to give different answers: part of the problem is perspective, part is perception, but part is also understanding. There is a misleading tendency to treat technology as simple, or to regard a technical understanding as unnecessary. Alongside the underrating of the incremental character of technological advances and applications, there is also a tendency to focus on one technology or weapon at the expense of the cumulative nature of advances and application, and the extent to which weapons systems bring these together and need to be considered from tactical, operational and strategic perspectives. Thus, R.J. Barendse has pointed out, with reference to the seventeenth century:

> The armament of English ships was superior to that of Indian ships, and their naval stores in general. . . . It seems that the use of the telescope and the compass, which were rarely used on Indian vessels, better maps, and cartographic techniques – like measurement by degrees – enabled English ships to sail new routes that were generally shunned by Indian vessels.[11]

The assessment of technological change and its impact on military capability is even more complicated on the global scale: much of the talk about technology completely ignores anything outside the West. Yet it is acknowledged that gunpowder and, later, military rockets, the 'explosives technology' that has been seen as so important in Western military history, are Oriental in origin. There are examples of earlier Oriental technologies, such as the composite bow and the stirrup, that were arguably superior (although the definition of 'superior' is problematic) to contemporary Western technologies, but which are not presented in most general histories of war as winners in the way that later Western technologies are generally so treated, and there is room for a methodological debate on how best to assess 'paradigm-shifting' weaponry. Medievalists, however, have been all too ready to assume that everything superior in a technological sense came from the East and rather reluctant to accept Western ingenuity. In fact, although there were Islamic advantages,[12] naval technology was better applied, as far as the Mediterranean was concerned, by Western powers in the eleventh to the thirteenth and, even more, the fourteenth centuries, and it was not until the Ottomans that the balance was redressed. Technology itself was, and is, not an issue that can be readily separated from the need for organizational support if naval strength was to be sustained.[13]

As far as old technologies, such as arms and armour, are concerned, where there is little or no documentary evidence of how it was made or used, the technologies tend to be neglected, although there have been advances made from the study of surviving examples in collections.

Thus, early sixteenth-century muskets have been used for tests.[14] It is intriguing to note that the technology of sword production in western Europe in the tenth and eleventh centuries is lost, and that no one can now make sword blades of the same flexibility and strength that will hold an edge. There are records showing the presence of Viking swords for sale in Baghdad in the tenth century. This evidence seems to confirm the attraction of Viking swords in the Arabic world, which was itself remarkable for its sword-making techniques.

When military technology works there is a tendency to think that it is a war-winner. The American use of 'smart munitions' in the 2003 Iraq War is a good example of this, but just because the munitions do what they were designed to do (and it had taken more than forty years to achieve the level of reliability and precision seen in Iraq – and that was not 100 per cent), does not mean that these things will solve the basic military problem of defeating the enemy. Similarly, the major expansion in aerial and automatic surveillance in the late twentieth century, and the resulting enhancement in the quantity of intelligence information, did not necessarily lead to improved analysis. More generally, there is a widespread belief that superior technology is always the answer without understanding what the question is. Bigger, faster and higher are seen as the ultimate criteria, but such data exists in its own world of unreality.

This was seen with American intervention in Vietnam, where technology was heralded by the Americans as the ultimate means to defeat the enemy. They expected to be able to remove American soldiers from the battlefield and still win – a flawed analysis, ironically so as ever-increasing numbers of American ground troops became involved. Huge technical advances were made, with smart munitions to destroy bridges that iron bombs had failed to hit after many air raids, electronic countermeasures to defeat radar and SAM anti-aircraft missiles, and airborne cavalry carried into contested landing zones by the ubiquitous Huey, which led to the development of helicopter gunships. In all these instances, technology was harnessed to provide solutions to known problems, but the tactical and operational use of that technology did not lead to success on the ground. The North Vietnamese and Viet Cong adapted to the threat by using supposed American strengths against the Americans, frequently the resort of the weaker combatant and therefore, in the context of decolonization struggles, an un-Western approach to battle. The Americans, in turn, responded by using ever more sophisticated technology, but faith in technology contributed to their failure. The extent of the impact of technology in asymmetrical contexts has become more important, because the development of atomic weaponry, especially in large quantities, has introduced a factor discouraging (though by no means preventing) conflict between states armed with such weapons.

Mostly, technology is overrated by the military, the press and general public. And the military does not necessarily use a new weapon or even a better version of an existing one, in a revolutionary way.[15] Aside from the implications for war-making, this indicates the need for caution in seeing new military technology as a cause of social transformation.

Nevertheless, providing troops with better arms than their opponents not only enhances their effectiveness but also their morale, a point that is frequently ignored. Thus, during World War Two, the availability of radar helped create a sense that the Germans could be beaten in the battles of Britain and the Atlantic. Furthermore, technology, force structure, doctrine, and tasking are in a dynamic relationship. The greater capability provided by advances in weaponry makes it possible to envisage and carry out missions that hitherto had been impractical. In 2001, the Americans were able to use helicopters to lift troops into combat from ships in the Arabian Sea to Kandahar in Afghanistan, a distance of 450 miles.

Non-military technology

Technological advances have had a major impact not only in terms of weaponry but also in the varied fields on which war and military technology draw, for example advances in food preservation, medical treatment and communications. Indeed, to reverse the usual emphasis in the discussion of war and technology, it can be argued that, far from weaponry being the key sphere for the successful application of technology in order to enhance military capability, it was these other fields in which application was most important, not least in terms of force projection, command and control, and in sustaining the level of military commitment. Much of this entailed not the specialized usage of military developments but, rather, the employment of advances in other fields, such as barbed wire,[16] advances that therefore did not require heavy investment from military–industrial complexes or, often, government as a whole.

This counter-intuitive point serves as a reminder that the inherent strength and adaptability of economies, societies and states may be more important than the particular characteristics of their military systems. The value of this strength has been underlined as the result of a more positive focus on the role of private entrepreneurs in mobilizing resources for war on land and at sea.[17] This has an application in the shape of the strength of the West on the global scale after the demise of European colonial empires, for this is largely a matter of economic, fiscal and cultural power, rather than of military strength. Looked at differently, such power helps ensure that war can be a forcing house for the application of developments, so that, for example, medical advances have been pushed hard in wartime, as blood typing was in World War One.

In 1927, Sir Frederick Barton Maurice, a former major general, gave his inaugural lecture as the Professor of Military Studies, a newly created chair at King's College, London. Maurice declared:

> History shows that great changes in the character of war are normally brought about by other forces than the power of weapons (I am here speaking of war as a whole, not of the tactics of the battlefield), for the tendency is that sooner or later an antidote is found for each new form of attack.
>
> . . . the deadlock of trench warfare of 1915–1918 was a revolution, which changed the character of war. But the prime cause of that change was only partly weapons, it was still more numbers; and the reason why armies of millions could be maintained in the field was, I think, first the development of railways, roads, and mechanised transport of all kinds, which enabled supplies to be brought to the front in almost unlimited quantities, and secondly the progress of medical science, which has almost eliminated the danger of epidemic disease. . . . With certain reservations as regards the sea, I would say that the changes which affect the daily lives of peoples, such as developments of transport and of communication, tend to affect war much more than do changes of weapons.[18]

The reporting of war

Bearing in mind that it is the effect of technology that matters in warfare, not the technology itself,[19] the impact of technology on war is far from a constant, but instead is affected by the multiple contexts of the latter. In particular, the impact of technology is culture-specific. There has to be a desire for change, and technological change is therefore affected by cultural responses to innovation. Indeed, the Western expectation of technological change was important to developments in military capability and war-making over the last century. This is true not simply of the global consequences of Western advances, but also of changes within the West today. For example, democratization in the reporting and commemoration of war has been taken a stage further with technology, but this is fundamentally an enabler, in the shape, in particular, of the more speedy and insistent reporting of news, while the democratization itself is the product of social shifts. Thus, the twentieth century brought newsreel, radio, television, and then e-mail to war reporting, and advances in filming and transmission made real-time reporting easy. In the attempted coup in Moscow in 1991, Boris Yeltsin's speech from the back of a tank was reported live on CNN, preventing the junta trying to seize power from suppressing the news.

Newsreel and radio first took further the nineteenth-century innovation of the war correspondent, with all the attendant problems of news management that this posed for government. Indeed, as a positive public perception was important to a sense of victory, in fact increasingly a definition of it, so the immediacy that first radio and then television brought created important problems. The public, however, was still at a distance, as institutions were involved in the management of news. Thus, John Turner, a British newsreel cameraman in World War II, took striking film of the torpedoing by a German submarine of the battleship HMS *Barham* in 1941, in which 869 lives were lost, only to find that the film was censored. His belief that it was necessary to take the picture even if it was of death or failure did not extend to the aftermath of the landing of a V2 rocket near Selfridge's department store in London: he declined the offer for a picture of a thumb a bystander had picked up.[20]

The internet has changed this. Now soldiers in the field are able to communicate with family, friends and others at home, and this creates serious problems in news management. These were made abundantly clear in 2003, when the problems that American occupation forces faced in Iraq were rapidly communicated, gravely undercutting the sense of victory that the government had sought to inculcate. This also suggested that in the future, the views of the military will play a greater role in the perception of victory and, indeed, as a result, that the process of conflict will be much more closely involved in this perception. Thus, rather than victory as a response to the result of war will come victory as a response to the process of war; with all the problems that this entails for cultures, or at least constituencies, that have little idea what to expect. In short, audiences as well as soldiers will have to be 'blooded' to ensure success, an issue that underlines the shifting interaction of war and culture. In earlier periods, direct observation or participation in conflict, or indirect participation via the military service of male older relatives, prepared much of the public for the experience of war, but in a very different fashion.

The personalization of events is a problem with war reporting, so that the personal view of the soldier on the ground or, more usually, that of the journalist, is considered more important and more pertinent than a more considered view from someone at headquarters who has access to more facts: experience is valued more than intellect. The latter tends to be mistrusted by the public, which is liable to view information and remarks from senior staff officers as intentionally propaganda, while the front-line view is thought to be pure and untainted, a belief that itself is susceptible to the insidious manipulation of information. Greater ease of personal communications on the part of individual soldiers may also lead to a degree of interaction in the field that poses problems for morale and discipline, and in a few cases, to direct communication with the enemy.

Technology, adaptation and tasking

The relationship between West and 'non-West' involved, and involves, far more than force, and force involves more than technology, but the role of the latter should not be neglected. It is instructive to note how far, especially after 1850, non-Western powers sought access to Western military technology, although the role of this diffusion has led to an underplaying of the extent to which weaponry, new and old, and both in and outside the West, became operative in particular contexts, and needs to be considered in this perspective. These contexts owed much to pre-existing tactical conventions, institutional practices and military cultures. Thus, in 1940 French strategic and operational inadequacies, rather than deficiencies in weaponry, ensured that interwar German efforts at innovation, which had aimed at incremental improvement, produced instead a 'striking and temporarily asymmetrical operational revolution'.[21]

The extent to which the failure to make the adaptations necessary to make the best use of weapons has compromised the ability to exploit change, and therefore limited capability, has become a standard theme in much of the literature. The issue, however, could be re-examined in order to ask whether the need for such adaptation did not vitiate, in whole or part, the adoption of such weaponry. Indeed, there has frequently been a clash between newly fashionable ideas about the acquisition and use of apparently appropriate state-of-the-art weaponry, and less modish, but more pertinent, questions of adaptability. These range from specifics, such as cost and the necessary level of logistical support, for example the availability of ammunition, to the general issues of existing practices, and the continuities and interests they represent.

When this tension is considered alongside the role that tasking, or the setting of goals, plays in military history (see Chapter five), then it becomes clear that the impact of technology in the military history of societies is so varied, as well as profound, that it undermines much of the commonplace analysis of enhanced capability in terms of new weaponry. For example, the double-tracking of railways in Europe prior to World War One was important in speeding mobilization and deployment, but is apt to be forgotten in the focus on the machine gun. Yet this enhanced capability in communications affected doctrine and tasking. The German ability to mobilize more rapidly than the Russians encouraged the German military leadership to regard the launching of war as a reasonable option. Earlier, Moltke the Elder, Chief of the Prussian General Staff from 1857 to 1888, had grasped the interaction of technological advance and planning, as he became proficient at appreciating how the use of railways enhanced the possible precision of planning, and thus changed the nature of the decision loop. As a reminder of the complexity of explanation, however, so also did the organizational development by the Prussians of an effective General Staff and the use, at lower headquarters, of chiefs of staff answerable to the General Staff in order to create an integrated army.

The fascination with military change, particularly in weaponry, and the conviction of its value, seen in much of the literature, is somewhat subverted by research on how institutions really adapted to the actual problems of conflict. Jenny West's conclusion about the British Ordnance Office in the mid-eighteenth century, a period when Britain became the military power most effective at global power projection, that the Office's traditional and unchanging methods, rather than new departures, helped it to respond effectively to the very great demands it faced in the Seven Years' War, is more generally applicable. The issue of objectives is immediately apparent, in that lengthy and widespread conflicts were not anticipated when Britain began hostilities in 1739, 1754 and 1775. More generally, greatly fluctuating demands for gunpowder created problems for both the Ordnance Office and gunpowder makers, while whether in power or in opposition, politicians were unwilling to extend the power of government in the crucial sphere of gunpowder production and distribution, even though they were aware of their inadequacy.[22] In short, the optimal effectiveness of the system was affected both by the goals that were pursued and by the parameters of the politically possible.

This point is of value for analysis of the earlier introduction and spread of gunpowder firearms. While this process has frequently been discussed in terms of a military revolution and the onset of modernity,[23] it is necessary to emphasize its long-term nature, not least the difficulty of establishing both an effective system of gunpowder production and a practical means of battlefield application by infantry. Once due attention is devoted to the complexity of gunpowder, then it ceases to be a simple agent of historical change and becomes instead the product of a complex process, which, as with the discovery of the means to measure longitude, was an interaction of intellectual achievement and practical knowledge, in the context of political and social circumstances, and with respect to particular strategic cultures. The German philosopher Hegel's argument, cited at the beginning of this chapter, that weapons arise from ideas and that the factors that frame the latter require consideration, is instructive. With firearms, the net effect of the application of knowledge[24] was incremental, rather than revolutionary, change; and the same was probably true of the earlier introduction of the stirrup, an issue that, like gunpowder, benefits from an understanding of the variety of device and practice thus summarized.[25] Incrementalism involved not only technical improvement but also matching the pace of introduction, adaptation and deployment with tactical and operational adjustments. There has been a major advance in the understanding of Chinese military technology,[26] and it is clear that gunpowder did not cause a radical restructuring of government or society there; but the situation is less happy for many other parts of the world.

The process of change

What was supposedly wrought by revolutionary change requires careful consideration alongside the very process of alleged revolution. The combination of these rethinkings is to replace a 'big bang' or triumphalist account with an understanding of the degree to which incremental change poses its own problems, for both contemporaries and scholars, of assessing best practice; as well as the difficulties of determining whether it was appropriate to introduce new methods. Models of the quasi-organic search for best practice and its subsequent diffusion, as well as the language of adaptation, whether or not expressed in Darwinian terms, both make change appear far less problematic than was the case, and distract attention from the significance for military history of the understanding of novelty. This is true for both new weaponry and for related organizational changes; while, in addition, the political rationale of both has to be borne in mind,[27] as do their cost. These points are also related to the question of continuity, which greatly interests historians; for example continuity in Europe from the Classical period to the Middle Ages, and then into the 'early modern' period.

An emphasis on organizational factors as crucial to the understanding of the opportunities offered by weaponry, as well as to the application of technological innovation, does not relate only to recent European history. Indeed, it is central to much of the discussion of Classical and medieval warfare, although limitations with the sources create difficulties in probing the issue, while it is also necessary to avoid making capability and the course of conflict overly clear-cut. Philip II of Macedonia is generally presented as beating the squabbling Greek city states because he controlled a better all-arms army and ensured unity of purpose for his powerful monarchy, but Philip's victory over Thebes and Athens at Chaeronea (338 BCE) was not easy nor a given. Similarly, the Romans defeated the Macedonians not because of the superiority of the legion over the phalanx, as Polybius claimed, but because of better manpower, resources, willpower and organization. Even so the three most serious battles, Cynoscephalae (197 BCE), Magnesia (190 BCE) and Pydna (168 BCE), were all close-run.

A cross-cultural, historical perspective suggests that the diffusion of military practice has been as important, if not more so, than that of weaponry; although precision is limited not only due to a paucity of comparative research but also because the development of military institutions in response to foreign examples is variously due to both weaponry and practice. Whatever the country and period, the understanding of technological proficiency entailed cultural issues, as the acceptance of weapons and their usage interacted with the varied appreciation of what was necessary. Thus, in the USA, as subsequently in Europe with World War One, 'soldiers' expectations in the Civil War evolved from a series of heroic contests to an incessant, machine-like battle' in 1864–5.[28] An important cultural variable was presented by the degree to which a society was keen to engage with modernity in the form of new elements of a material culture, and the attitudes to go with them.

The perception of change

Until the late-eighteenth century, the notion of beneficial change in time did not always embrace modernity, but instead could lead to the idea of improvement through turning back. This itself, however, took a variety of forms, and frequently had a more complex relationship with modernity than simply rejecting it. The past could offer a frame of reference in which new ideas and practices were expressed, or, even, had to be expressed.

During the sixteenth century, the printing revolution in Europe was followed by the widespread 're-discovery' and availability of Classical texts, for example Xenophon's *Peri Hippikes*, a guide to horsemanship useful for cavalry, and Onosander's first-century CE treatise on generalship. The prestige of ancient Rome was such that ideas and vocabulary associated with it were applied in the European world in order to validate developments. For example, Battista della Valle's *Vallo Libro Continente Appertinentie à Capitanij, Retenere e Fortificare una Città con bastioni*, a very popular work on fortifications that went through eleven editions from 1524 to 1558, drew heavily on Classical sources.

Contemporary European warfare could be understood in Classical terms: the Greeks, Macedonians and Romans did not have gunpowder weapons, but their forces did have a mixture of infantry and cavalry, cold steel and projectiles. In his *Art of War* (1521), which was frequently reprinted, Nicolo Machiavelli tried to update Flavius Vegetius's fourth- or fifth-century *Epitoma Rei Militaris* [*On Military Matters*] by focusing on the pike and treating the arquebus as similar to missile weaponry; indeed, the major problem in comparing Renaissance with Classical warfare was set by the major role of French heavy cavalry in the fifteenth and sixteenth centuries, not by that of firearms. As the large-scale use of the pike in the early-sixteenth century in Western Europe in many respects represented a revival of the Macedonian phalanx, the key development in European infantry warfare of the period was apparently organizational, rather than technological. At the close of the century and in the early seventeenth centuries the military reformers linked to the House of Nassau in the United Provinces, Nassau, the Palatinate, Baden, Hesse–Cassel and Brandenburg, consciously used ancient Greek and Roman models for their efforts to improve military organizations. Their limited sense of changing conditions was matched by the contemporary theoretical work of Justus Lipsius, de la Noue and Patrizi on the ancient Roman military.[29]

This habit of referring back in Europe was not limited to the sixteenth and early seventeenth centuries. In 1736, the British envoy in Berlin reported: 'They make frequent parallels here between the Macedonian troops and theirs.'[30] Maurice, Comte de Saxe (1696–1750), the leading French general of the 1740s, called his ideal formation a legion as a Classical affectation and was interested in the re-introduction of armour.

Jean-Charles Chevalier de Folard (1669–1752) saw his advocacy of shock tactics in part as a commentary on Polybius, specifically on the latter's account of the clash between Macedonian phalanx and Roman legion. Folard wanted to bring back the wedge (*cuneus*), while the column he advocated was a form of the phalanx. Folard and Saxe were also interested in reviving the pike, as was the *Encyclopédie* (1751–65), the repository of fashionable French opinion; while there was also support for the idea at the time of the French Revolution: the use of shock action relying on cold steel was seen as a more vigorous means of fighting than a reliance on firepower.

Although in the eighteenth century the practice of using the past as a source of ideas is readily apparent, its extent is unclear,[31] while referring back was not the same as learning from the past. Nevertheless, the process of validation was one in which the balance between modernity and history was very different to the situation today. The tradition of Vegetius appears to have made historical study difficult in the sense of detecting, describing and analysing change. In the eighteenth century, Folard found it normal to debate with Vegetius as if he were a contemporary, as Christine de Pizan, Jean de Meung, Alain Chartier, or William Caxton as Christine's translator had done earlier. In eighteenth-century Germany, Franz Miller, an influential military theorist and the author of *Reine Taktik der Infanterie, Cavallerie und Artillerie* (Stuttgart, 1787–8), regarded the Roman military as if it were an army of his own time that he sought to improve.

There appears to have been only a limited awareness of historical change. In *The Wealth of Nations* (1776), Adam Smith related differences in military organization to those in social structures,[32] but such a historicism was not generally matched elsewhere. In Germany, histories of war, such as those of the Seven Years' War by Johann Wilhelm von Archenholtz (1793) and Georg Friedrich von Tempelhoff (1783–1801), included the word *Geschichte* in the title, but they did so in the established usage of narrative (as with the contemporary English use of history) rather than as historical description and analysis.[33]

Technology, organization and the pursuit of victory

It is useful for scholars to adopt a chronological perspective that permits a reconsideration of novelty, as with the consideration of the early modern period in Europe against a medieval background.[34] Both in this case and more generally, there is the question of how weaponry impacted on organization, an issue that brings together technological capability and the factors that affect institutional culture, not least social context and political goals. As a good example, the capability of the Napoleonic military was not so much due to new weapons, though the standardization of the French artillery in the late-eighteenth century was important. Instead, organizational and command issues were crucial, not least the development of all-purpose infantry, the massing of firepower at the tactical level and the use of mixed-armed units: their superiority over unitary structures was clearly demonstrated in the Napoleonic wars, and the mass warfare of that period had important repercussions for contemporary and subsequent debate over the organization of armed forces.[35]

The processes by which change and debate took place are themselves open to discussion and, indeed, provide one way to look at the question of military history. Intellectual and cultural factors are important for technological and organizational enhancement, not least in terms of how problems are perceived and solutions constructed. There is traditionally a teleology at play, notably with reference to the use of science, including the very employment of the concept of military science. While being wary of such teleology, it is worthy of note that a self-conscious method of rational analysis was applied in European discussion of warfare and weaponry, particularly, but not only, from the sixteenth century. Paolo Giovio, in his *Eine warhafftige Beschreyhung aller namhafftigen Geschichten* (Basle, 1560) combined narrative with comments about military matters. In his discussion of the Schmalkaldic War he emphasized the importance of military drill and praised the lansquenets (German pikemen) for their discipline. Mathematics was used with great effect in ballistics and navigation, while, from the sixteenth century, a 'knowledge nexus' had developed that was of particular value in the projection of European power, as cartography and navigation were employed to gain conceptual understanding of the space of the world. This self-conscious rationalization also affected some military history, with a move from narratives of glory and prowess, in which the emphasis was on manliness, to attempts to discern and dissect underlying characteristics of success. These could, however, be ahistorical in preferring the search for supposed inherent causes of victory to the acceptance of complexity and variety, an approach that remains influential today.

The emphasis on knowledge provides more than one way to discuss the place of technology, for it includes the issue of how conflicts were analysed differently in order to provide contrasting views on best practice,[36] and also focuses on how goals were assessed. This is linked to the reversal of the standard approach for explaining change, by arguing that, instead of weapons dictating tactics, strategy, doctrine, and tasking, it is the assigned tasks that determine doctrine and force structure. The latter process is even more the case now than earlier, as the range (and cost) of procurement options in weaponry are greater than hitherto. Furthermore, the institutional nature of military systems, and the particular interests and political weight of military–industrial complexes, ensure that there are bureaucratic interests and lobby groups able to press for each option, which returns attention to the role of choice in policy-formation, and thus of strategic and organizational cultures.[37]

Technology also links to the role of culture, not only in considering a willingness to appreciate, understand and adapt new advances, but also as an aspect of a more general sense of flux and new capability. Thus, in an article on the 'Future of War', in the American popular news journal *Newsweek* on 25 December 1944, J.F.C. Fuller, who contributed a series of articles to the journal in 1944, wrote: 'Before the present century has run its course, there is nothing fantastic in suggesting that complete armies will be whisked through pure speed a thousand miles above the earth's surface, to speed at 10,000 miles an hour toward their enemy'. Earlier, visiting India in 1926 on behalf of the British War Office, Fuller had emphasized the need for the Indian Army to mechanize, and had presented this as at once an aspect of modernity and a necessary response to a public opinion that, in the aftermath of World War One, did not want to face heavy casualties. Fuller argued that the navy and air force 'were mechanized forces, materially highly progressive', but he thought the Indian Army reflected 'its surroundings' in being Oriental,[38] a process and term that amounted to condemnation.

More recently, in response to the attacks of 11 September 2001 on New York and Washington, John Keegan offered, alongside references to past campaigns in Afghanistan and the American capture of Okinawa and Iwo Jima in 1945, a sense of the capacity of technology to pose new challenges, if not of what had seemed the future already present: 'The World Trade Centre outrage was coordinated on the internet . . . If Washington is serious in its determination to eliminate terrorism, it will have to forbid internet providers to allow the transmission of encrypted messages. . . . Uncompliant providers on foreign territory should expect their buildings to be destroyed by cruise missiles'.[39] This was not the only example of military historian as unsuccessful predictor, but it vividly presented an awareness of change. The sense of flux and new capability offered by the prospect of new technology can challenge established norms about conflict, although these challenges have generally been con-tested by the nature of military practice and institutional culture. Indeed, Christopher Marlowe's theatrical protagonists, especially *Tamburlaine* (1587), have been seen as depictions of such a challenge, while Marlowe's *Dr Faustus* (*c*.1589) reflects the threat from knowledge.[40]

As a result of the increase in points of contact with opponents that reflects the capability for force projection of modern advanced militaries, the pursuit of objectives frequently brings technologically very different militaries into conflict in what is known as asymmetrical warfare. This poses a variety of challenges, not least depending on the degree to which the less-powerful combatant resorts to guerrilla warfare or terrorism. Both negate the concentration of effort in order to produce an overwhelming application of force, which is generally valuable in conventional warfare with its focus on capability for battle. Instead, with guerrilla operations and terrorism, war becomes a much more protracted process, one where it is necessary to bring political and military strategies into line in order to lessen support for opponents. To this end, technology is very useful, not least aerial surveillance and the mobility provided by airborne forces, as with the Americans in Afghanistan in 2001–2, but state-of-the-art weaponry alone can achieve only so much, both against guerrillas[41] and against terrorists. Furthermore, a small increase in the numbers of either of the latter can make a major difference to their effectiveness.

The idea that state-of-the-art weaponry can act as a substitute for troop numbers makes more sense for symmetrical warfare than against guerrillas or terrorists, but even for that it has limitations. In 1939, Sir John Dill, commander of the British I Corps in France, complained about the 'incalculable' harm done by Liddell Hart, writing:

> Thanks largely to Liddell-Hart's advice battalions were cut down. The argument was that it is fire power, not man power that is wanted on the battlefield. That may be true up to a point but at night, in fog and when the enemy uses smoke one must have men on the ground.[42]

Asymmetrical warfare

To turn to asymmetrical warfare, the limitations of an advanced military in conflict with motivated irregular forces are scarcely novel. In the case of Western forces, they can be found before the cultural shift in Western attitudes towards war seen from the 1960s, which includes a reluctance to cause civilian casualties, which makes it difficult to counter opponents who are not readily differentiated from the general population. The failure of Italian forces against Bedouin opposition in Libya in 1911–12 and of the American expedition of 1916–17 to find the Mexican guerrilla Pancho Villa, are instructive indications both of the more general problems confronting conventional forces and of their earlier impact prior to the 1960s.

Furthermore, today, in the case of opposition from a domestic terrorist force, it is not very helpful to resort to the politics of high explosives. Domestic terrorism indeed poses in a particularly acute form the problem that faces all militaries: war involves obliging others to heed one's will, but victory in engagements is only so useful in this process. Like superior weaponry, it is far better than the alternative; but victory does not ensure that the defeated accepts the verdict, while in operational terms, it is difficult for victorious forces to impose their timetables on opponents who resist occupation. Instead, the victor can find itself in an unresolved situation, unable to obtain closure but denied a clear target whose defeat will ensure it. This has been the fate of the Israeli military since the Intifada, the rebellion in occupied territories that began in 1987: a force successfully developed to win quick victories over Arab states, and with a strong operational and tactical focus on mobility, has found an adjustment of doctrine and force structure difficult, in part, but certainly not only, because it has to implement policies in the face of constraints posed by domestic and international opinion.

The role of such constraints in limiting success should not be exaggerated, because there are instances where they have been weak but where success has still been elusive: this was true of Napoleonic forces occupying Spain in 1808–13, of Germans occupying Yugoslavia in 1941–4, and of the problems affecting the Japanese in China in 1937–45. Although Chinese conventional forces were defeated, the Japanese were surprised, and frustrated, by their failure to impose victory, and within occupied areas, Japanese control outside the cities was limited. These are the instances of success, but the stress should be on the inherent difficulty of the task of counter-insurgency. It is far from clear why such campaigns should be slighted in the classic canon of military history and treated as not 'real soldiering'.

Conclusions

The impact and role of technology, therefore, can be qualified from several perspectives. In particular, there is often a tendency to assume that in some way 'technology' is an absolute, independent of other factors. The human element is often overlooked, but in practice there is a complex relationship between observation, experience, perspective, and perception, an aspect of technology that is under-explored. For example, to employ the same weapon does not mean that its use is understood, and this can lead to a failure to reproduce results. Whether something is adopted successfully may be decided by all sorts of reasons unconnected with technical merit: it is not the technology itself, but the response to it that drives change.

Furthermore, technological change is often used selectively, in that only the successes are considered, while unsuccessful or less successful ideas, inventions and developments, such as the plug bayonet, early iron cannon, caseless ammunition, and the anti-missile laser, are overlooked or neglected. Instead, failure plays an important role in the pursuit and process of change. More generally, the assumption that there is a continuity in technological improvement is simplistic. There may be no pattern other than the one subsequently imposed after the event in order to explain what has happened.

Technological change comes about mostly in response to problems that need to be solved. This is an aspect of the extent to which broader cultural, social and organizational issues are at stake. Indeed, alongside a perception of the essential socio-cultural foundations of technological success has come a view of technology as a direct 'social construct', with social-cultural forces shaping the technology.[43] Once adopted, societies and cultural norms are themselves shaped by that technology, not least through the consequences of economic growth and change, but the underlying initial influences remain strong. From this perspective, warfare – the form and structure that it takes, and the technology it uses – emerges as a social construct. Dethroning technology from the central position in the narrative and explanation of military capability and change, does not, however, entail denying its importance. Instead, it is necessary to adopt a more nuanced approach to the different factors that play a role, considering them not as reified concepts that compete, but, rather, in a manner that allows for the multiple character of their interaction.

Notes

1 G.W.F. Hegel, *Naturrecht und Staatswissenschaft um Grundrisse* and *Grundlinien der Philisophie des Rechts* (1821) [*Natural Law and Political Science in Outline; Elements of the Philosophy of Right*], translation from T.M. Knox (ed.), *Hegel's Philosophy of Right* (Oxford, 1967), p. 212.

2 Fuller to his mother, 18 [not 28 as in catalogue] Aug. 1915, LH. Fuller papers, IV/3/155.
3 For instances of this interpretation, S.T. Possony and J.E. Pournelle, *The Strategy of Technology: Winning the Decisive War* (Cambridge, Mass., 1970); M. van Creveld, *Technology and War: From 2000 BC to the Present* (New York, 1989); and, for an important review, A. Roland, 'Technology and War: The Historiographical Revolution of the 1980s', *Technology and Culture*, 34 (1993), pp. 117–34.
4 A. Williams, *The Knight and the Blast Furnace* (Leiden, 2002).
5 L. Sondhaus, *Navies in Modern World History* (2004).
6 There were already drawings of underwater vehicles in late fifteenth century editions of Vegetius.
7 B.J. Buchanan (ed.), *Gunpowder: The History of an International Technology* (Bath, 1996).
8 J. Bradley, *Guns for the Tsar. American Technology and the Small Arms Industry in Nineteenth-Century Russia* (DeKalb, Illinois, 1990).
9 BL. Add. 49016 fols. 7–26; J. Langins, *Conserving the Enlightenment. French Military Engineering from Vauban to the Revolution* (Cambridge, Mass., 2003), esp. pp. 325–57, 361–428.
10 M.H. Jackson and C. de Beer, *Eighteenth Century Gunfounding* (Washington, 1974).
11 R.J. Barendse, *The Arabian Seas. The Indian Ocean World of the Seventeenth Century* (Armonk, New York, 2002), p. 454.
12 J. France, 'Technology and the success of the First Crusade', in Y. Lev (ed.), *War and Society in the Eastern Mediterranean, 7th–15th Centuries* (Leiden, 1997).
13 L. Casson, *Ships and Seamanship in the Ancient World* (2nd edn, Princeton, 1986); G. Deng, *Maritime Sector, Institutions and Sea Power of Premodern China* (Westport, Connecticut, 1999); J.B. Hattendorf and R.W. Unger (eds), *War at Sea in the Middle Ages and Renaissance* (Woodbridge, 2003).
14 P. Krenn, P. Kalaus and B.S. Hall, 'Material Culture and Military History: Test-Firing Early Modern Small Arms', *Material History Review*, 42 (1995), pp. 101–9; T. Richardson, 'Ballistic Testing of Historical Weapons', *Royal Armouries Yearbook*, 3 (1998), pp. 50–2.
15 I am most grateful for advice from Anthony Saunders on this topic.
16 A. Krell, *The Devil's Rope. A Cultural History of Barbed Wire* (2002).
17 C.R. Phillips, *Six Galleons for the King of Spain: Imperial Defense in the Early Seventeenth Century* (Baltimore, 1986); J. Glete, *War and the State in Early Modern Europe. Spain, the Dutch Republic and Sweden as Fiscal–Military States, 1500–1660* (2002), esp. p. 215.
18 Maurice, *On the Uses of the Study of War* (1927), p. x.
19 E. Goldsworthy, 'Warfare in Context', *RUSI Journal*, 148, No. 3 (June 2003), p. 19.
20 *Filming History. The Memoirs of John Turner, Newsreel Cameraman* (2002).
21 W. Murray, 'May 1940: Contingency and fragility of the German RMA', in Murray and M. Knox (eds), *The Dynamics of Military Revolution 1300–2050* (Cambridge, 2001), p. 173; E.O. Goldman and L.C. Eliason (eds), *The Diffusion of Military Technology and Ideas* (Stanford, 2003), p. 349.

22 J. West, *Gunpowder, Government and War in the Mid-Eighteenth Century* (Woodbridge, 1991).

23 J.R. Hale, 'Gunpowder and the Renaissance: An essay in the history of ideas', in his *Renaissance War Studies* (1983), pp. 389–90.

24 For a useful case study, E. Lund, *War for the Every Day: Generals, Knowledge and Warfare in Early Modern Europe, 1680–1740* (Westport, 1999).

25 A.E. Dien, 'The Stirrup and Its Effect on Chinese Military History', *Ars Orientalis*, 16 (1986), pp. 33–56.

26 J. Needham and R.D.S. Yates (eds), *Military Technology: Missiles and Sieges, Science and Civilization in China* (Cambridge, 1995).

27 G. Rowlands, 'Louis XIV, Aristocratic Power and the Elite Units of the French Army', *French History*, 13 (1999), p. 330.

28 D.A. Mindell, *War, Technology, and Experience Aboard the USS 'Monitor'* (Baltimore, 2000), p. 144.

29 M.C. Fissel, *English Warfare 1511–1642* (2001), p. 285; F. Gilbert, 'Machiavelli: The Renaissance in the Art of War', in P. Paret (ed.), *Makers of Modern Strategy: From Machiavelli to the Nuclear Age* (Princeton, New Jersey, 1986), pp. 11–31.

30 Guy Dickens to Horatio Walpole, 18 Sept. 1736, PRO. State Papers, 90/41.

31 K.H. Doig, 'War in the reform programme of the *Encyclopédie*', *War and Society*, 6 (1988), p. 3; J.P. Bertaud, *The Army of the French Revolution. From Citizen-Soldiers to Instrument of Power* (Princeton, 1988), pp. 154–5; D.A. Neill, 'Ancestral Voices: The Influence of the Ancients on the Military Thought of the Seventeenth and Eighteenth Centuries', *Journal of Military History*, 62 (1998), pp. 487–520.

32 A. Smith, *An Inquiry into the Nature and Causes of the Wealth of Nations* (1776; Oxford 1976 edition), pp. 689–708.

33 I am most grateful to Harald Kleinschmidt for his advice. See also D. Hohrath, *Ferdinand Friedrich Nicolai und die militärische Aufklärung im 18. Jahrhundert* (Stuttgart, 1989).

34 A. Ayton and J.L. Price, 'The Military Revolution from a Medieval Perspective', in Ayton and Price (eds), *The Medieval Military Revolution. State, Society and Military Change in Medieval and Early Modern Europe* (1998), pp. 16–17.

35 D. Gates, *The Napoleonic Wars 1803–1815* (1997).

36 Re the Spanish Civil War, M.R. Habeck, *Storm of Steel: The Development of Armor Doctrine in Germany and the Soviet Union, 1919–1939* (Ithaca, New York, 2003).

37 B.R. Posen, *The Sources of Military Doctrine: France, Britain and Germany Between the World Wars* (Ithaca, 1984); M.E. Brown, *Flying Blind: The Politics of the US Strategic Bomber Program* (Ithaca, 1992); E. Rhodes, 'Do Bureaucratic Politics Matter? Some Disconfirming Findings from the Case of the U.S. Navy', *World Politics*, 47 (1994), pp. 1–41; K.M. Zisk, *Engaging the Enemy: Organisation Theory and Soviet Military Innovation, 1955–1991* (Princeton, 1993); P.J. Dombrowski, E. Cholz and A.L. Ross, 'Selling Military Transformation: The Defense Industry and Innovation', *Orbis*, 48 (2002), pp. 526–36.

38 Rutgers University Library, New Brunswick, New Jersey, Fuller papers, Box 4, report on India 1926, pp. 4, 48.

39 J. Keegan, 'How America Can Wreak Vengeance', *Daily Telegraph*, 14 Sept. 2001, p. 22. For a more considered response, M. Howard, ' "9/11" and After: A British View', *Naval War College Review*, 55 no. 4 (autumn 2002), pp. 12–13.

40 N. de Somogyi, *Shakespeare's Theatre of War* (Aldershot, 1998).

41 D.M. Drew, 'U.S. Airpower Theory and the Insurgent Challenge: A Short Journey to Confusion', *Journal of Military History*, 62 (1998), pp. 809–32, esp. pp. 824, 829–30; C. Malkasian, *A History of Modern Wars of Attrition* (Westport, 2002), p. 205.

42 Dill to Field Marshal Montgomery-Massingberd, former Chief of the Imperial General Staff, 25 Sept., 18 Nov., 1939, LH., Montgomery-Massingberd papers 10/14.

43 W.E. Bijker, T.P. Hughes and T.J. Pinch (eds), *The Social Construction of Technological Systems: New Directions in the Sociology and History of Technology* (Cambridge, Mass., 1987); D. Mackenzie, *Inventing Accuracy: A Historical Sociology of Nuclear Missile Guidance* (Cambridge, Mass., 1990); M.R. Smith and L. Marx (eds), *Does Technology Drive History? The Dilemma of Technological Determinism* (Cambridge, Mass., 1994); G. Spinardi, *From Polaris to Trident: The Development of US Fleet Ballistic Missile Technology* (Cambridge, 1994).

Chapter 5

Setting military objectives

So much of our work has to be done in uncivilized parts of the world that it is a mistake to pin faith to a type of unit largely dependent on civilized conditions, good roads and open country.

Earl of Cavan, Chief of the [British] Imperial General Staff, 1924[1]

To some extent, America and its NATO allies fought a virtual war because they were neither ready nor willing to fight a real one.

Michael Ignatieff, re the Kosovo conflict of 1999[2]

Displacing technology, the theme of the last chapter, means, in part, moving from a supply-side account of military history, one that is focused on capability and its impact on warfare. Focusing on tasking or the setting of goals, the subject of this chapter, in turn directs attention to a demand-led account. Such an account does not exclude the consequences of technology, although the emphasis is rather on the bounded efficiency and rationality of arms technologies that depend so much on the exigencies that emerge during the political and social process of armament. Instead, fitness for purpose, a key concept in weaponry, force structure and capability, is the major issue for evaluation, with the purpose for the military set not by the capability but by the task required. The latter, however, attracts only slight attention in popular discussion of warfare, as it appears self-evident that the task is victory, generally defined as total victory, and, therefore, that the best-prepared military wins. This though is an account that is of only limited value, for the very nature of victory is dependent on the purpose of the military and its particular objectives, and, thus, on the process of tasking; while, in more narrow terms, this process helps address the issue of prioritization between conflicting requirements. The selection of goals is also important to the issue of costs, as the constraints posed by the latter are made more or less serious by the needs that have to be addressed.

The goals set for the military vary greatly, inviting attention to the problems of how best to classify and to account for tasks. These are far from easy. A cultural interpretation of tasking, which employs the notion of strategic culture (see p. 56), and focuses on reasons for conquest, or, alternatively, for the avoidance of aggressive warfare, directs attention to the concepts and moods that help frame the formulation of tasks, as well as to the moments when decisions are taken: ideological factors, as well as political and military contingencies. Such an interpretation directs attention to variety between states, and thus diversity within the international system, and accentuates the methodological difficulties of devising a general theory of military capability and change, one that is valid across a number of cultures.

The American role in the Korean and Vietnam Wars provides a good instance of the problem in evaluating tasking even in the case of one state – without, in short, adding the problems of cross-cultural analysis. The debate as to whether the Americans could have been more successful had they followed less-limited approaches, most obviously in the Korean War (1950–3) by an advance into China, or amphibious or air attacks on China; or, in the Vietnam War (for the USA focusing on 1964–72), by a ground attack on North Vietnam or by unrestricted bombing, under-rates the impact of the political context within which the Americans operated and which set the military tasking. In neither case did the Americans seek anything other than a limited war; and, in particular, they did not want to see the outbreak of World War Three.

This reluctance reflected not only political factors but also military ones, especially the traditional reluctance of powers to weaken one area of commitment by overly-concentrating on another – an issue that tends to be slighted in popular-level campaign accounts: they are apt to minimize, if not ignore, the wider strategic situation and its consequences in terms both of goals and of operational practice. Thus, during the Korean War, the Americans feared that a more extensive commitment in East Asia would weaken the fledgling position of NATO (the North Atlantic Treaty Organisation) in Western Europe and, in the face of the large Soviet army in Eastern Europe, accentuate its vulnerability to attack. This problem of emphasis between commitments was repeated during the Vietnam War but, on the American side, there was also the apparent lesson of the Korean War: the hot-pursuit invasion of North Korea in 1950 had been, unexpectedly and seriously, followed by hostile and damaging intervention by China. It is unclear that American ground attacks on North Vietnam, another neighbour of China, would have had the same result, but the possibility had to be considered.

More generally, the limited character of warfare after 1945, and the preference for letting goals and tasks set commitments, was illustrated by the failure of any of the nuclear powers to use their nuclear forces: total military capability and force structure did not dictate strategy nor operational planning. Instead, the military approach was determined within the parameters set by the political nature of the task which, in the case of the nuclear powers, included the avoidance of full-scale war.

If this clear sign of the role of tasking emerges from a consideration of post-1945 warfare, it might be asked how far this is also valid for earlier periods. The intuitive conclusion might be 'not at all'. It can be argued that the restraints on military methods seen in recent conflicts reflect the particular factors of the post-1945 period, especially the growth in relevant conventions, the dominant strategic culture of the period – not least the role of deterrence – and the extent to which major powers were not faced by attacks, with the exception of an assault on a distant possession – the Argentinian invasion of the British-governed Falkland Islands in 1982, where the resulting conflict could be contained – and of rebellions in colonies and of terrorism.

The extent to which restraint indeed characterized post-1945 conflict is worthy of reconsideration from a non-Western perspective, both in so far as warfare between such powers is concerned, most obviously in the case of the Iran–Iraq War, and also with reference to their experience of Western war-making: in Vietnam total-war firepower was applied to a small-war problem. Irrespective of that, it is mistaken to see the pre-1945 period as one of total warfare where the sole task was victory, and in which strategy and military methods were set accordingly. This approach, in particular, also ignores earlier practices of limited warfare, underrates the distinction between international and civil conflict, and neglects the extent to which victory was, and is, variously defined and thus furthered by different means. In some contexts, the defeat of opposing field armies, or, indeed, a field army, is the crucial point, but in others it is seen as necessary to destroy the opponent's capacity to field such forces, while yet other contexts appear to require the occupation of particular points in opposing territory, if not much of it.

In the case of international conflicts, the end sought might be the absorption of another power, a goal that creates the task of conquest;

but most international conflicts were, and are, not pursued to this end. Instead, the ends sought are less than total and the task is that of achieving sufficient success to oblige the opponent to sue for peace and to accept particular terms. If conquest is not the goal, or at least the task at that moment, then the victor does not have to consider the problems posed by acting as an occupying power. These are obviously difficult for modern militaries, such as the Israelis in the West Bank and the Americans in Iraq, but it should not be imagined that they were not also serious difficulties on earlier occasions, although these tend not to attract attention and the necessary research. The problem posed for Prussian occupying forces by *francs-tireurs*, French irregulars, during the Franco–Prussian War of 1870–1 was prefigured by such episodes as Calabrian and Spanish resistance to Napoleonic occupation, but too little is known about the comparable situation facing non-Western forces.

German war-making, 1866–1945

The problems the Prussians faced after their initial victories in 1870 are a reminder that, for all Moltke's success in the Austro–Prussian War of 1866 in ensuring that the army was appropriate for the tasks it was expected to undertake, and that these were kept carefully in line with Prussian capability, it was difficult to plan for unexpected political eventualities, and that these could lead to difficult, if not unrealistic, tasks. Moltke's successors lost touch with his goal, tragically so in 1914. The younger Moltke and his colleagues in the General Staff then sought war and, by emphasizing future threats and claiming that Germany in 1914 was still able to defeat likely opponents, helped to push civilian policy-makers towards conflict. Thus the military set the task. The younger Moltke hoped that the resulting conflict would be the short and manageable war for which the Germans had been planning,[3] but also feared that it could well be a lengthy struggle, for which there were no adequate preparations.

The elder Moltke's predecessor, Count Alfred von Schlieffen, the Chief of the General Staff from 1891 to 1906, had not helped by allowing members of the General Staff to become military specialists at the expense of more general, non-military thinking. As non-military problems were consciously excluded from General Staff thinking, military decision-makers were allowed to plan with scant regard for the political situation around them.[4] There was a preference for operational over strategic considerations, a choice that repeatedly has caused problems for militaries, and that creates particular difficulties if initial plans go awry.

Interest in atrocities has directed attention to another, subliminal, aspect of tasking: the extent to which assumptions about the social context of operations affected military conduct, and thus, aside from leading to the harming of prisoners and civilians, could compromise operational effectiveness, not least by exacerbating popular opposition. The impact of morality on war thus influences its conduct. Atrocities also provide a way to probe military culture, such as that of Japan in 1931–45. German atrocities in Belgium and France in 1914 in part appear to have reflected fury that Belgium resisted and therefore affected the German advance. German losses at the hands of Belgian regular units led to reprisals against civilians, as well as the killing of military prisoners, while a high rate of drunkenness, confusion and 'friendly fire' among German units contributed directly to their belief that they were under civilian attack, which encouraged their attitude that it was acceptable, and indeed sensible, to inflict reprisals on the innocent.[5]

More generally, a hostile and violent response to conquered peoples was a central aspect of German war politics.[6] This was at once an aspect of a wider flaw in German tasking, namely an inability to consider adequately the nature of the likely response, and also a consequence of the overlap between operational and genocidal warfare.[7] Thus, in World War Two, especially from 1942, the inability of the Germans to deal with the practical difficulties stemming from insufficient resources, over-extended front lines, and the strength of their opponents' war-making and fighting quality owed much to the extent to which the Nazi regime had lost its way, with decision-making warped by ideological megalomania and strategic wishful thinking.[8] The Germans were not alone in failing to consider adequately the nature of the likely response and in not matching operational planning to feasible strategic goals, but their war-making proved particularly flawed under both heads. This directs attention to German strategic culture, especially the nature of Wilhelmine and Nazi policy-making assumptions and élites. The role of the German military in atrocities suggests the need for a new military history of Germany, and also raises a question mark about the notion of progress in military development.

Civil wars

Occupation is an issue not only in international conflict but also in civil warfare. The tasks posed by the latter tend to be underrated, not least because of a habit of seeing civil wars in terms of conventional warfare between regular forces, as in the English (1642–6, 1648) and American (1861–5) Civil Wars. Aside from raising the issue of the typicality of these conflicts in terms of civil wars, there is also the particular question of whether they were typical in terms of the relationship between conflict and the outcome of the struggle. Thus, in the English and American Civil Wars, it was important that there was the possibility of a clear exit strategy through the existence of an individual whose decision to surrender led to the end of the conflict: Charles I in 1646 and Robert E. Lee, the commander of the largest Confederate force, in 1865. As a result of this clear command structure, pursuing the factors necessary to secure these surrenders were sensible tasks for the opposing sides – the Parliamentarians and the Union respectively, and for their commanders – Sir Thomas Fairfax and Ulysses S. Grant respectively. In the absence of such clarity and discipline, however, it becomes far harder to secure the end of hostilities; and this poses serious problems for combatants in most civil wars. Again, it is unclear how far this situation has changed with time.

More generally, the field of civil warfare suffers from its neglect compared to its international counterpart.[9] This can be seen in particular in work on military thought, such as that of Azar Gat,[10] but is also true of military history as a whole. Furthermore, the international dimension of civil warfare is often exaggerated, certainly if it involves Western powers, so that, for example, the focus on insurrectionary conflict in the period 1946–75 is on opposition to Western forces, both in colonies and in the Vietnam War, rather than on resistance to native governments. In practice, concern about domestic challenges to authority, rather than external threats to power, are particularly important in many states, especially over the last half-century, as in Latin America. Western narratives of military history frequently present other states in terms of conflict with the West, but in many, for example nineteenth-century China faced with the Taiping Rebellion of 1851–66, it was domestic conflicts and developments that were crucial and deserve more attention.[11]

Changes in tasking

The entire question of alterations in military tasking is obscure. In considering the issue, there is the serious problem with the simplification, if not primitivization, of the other, in this case, as discussed in Chapter three, both the past (the period anterior to that under discussion) and the non-West. Thus, in asserting the importance of tasking, we have to be aware of the problem discussed in the Introduction, namely that, in replacing technology as an analytical, or, at least narrative, explanatory device by, for example, organization, culture or tasking, we create, in our turn, an overly-clear meta-narrative.

Furthermore, in the absence of sufficient research, there is a tendency, in this as in other aspects of military history, to provide a cause-effect account that underplays the complexities of process, not least the ways in which lessons were absorbed, goals reshaped and campaigns thus linked one to another. The selection and appropriateness of goals were affected by organizational factors that repay consideration. For example, Ross Anderson, in his effective operational account of *The Battle of Tanga, 1914* (Stroud, 2002), the first major clash in World War One in East Africa, castigates the amateurish nature of British planning and command, suggesting that there was an absence of adequate coordination between army and navy, and, more generally, that the peacetime system of planning and controlling operations was unable to cope with the strains of war. A path is traced between Tanga and the unsuccessful Gallipoli operation the following year, when the British failed to knock Turkey out of the war, but the margin between success and failure is always close and, although failure is generally readily explained, it is necessary to give due weight to the problems facing all operations. The far-better-prepared Germans after all did not win in 1914.

In considering tasking, there is the general question of how the purpose of war was understood in different cultures,[12] and the far more specific need to address the way in which tasks, such as the maintenance of internal order, were differently understood by particular commanders and units. These factors might appear less pertinent for international conflict, but that is not the case because, for example, the willingness to accept casualties in order to achieve goals has varied greatly. Thus, tasking cannot be separated from culture. This particular issue has to be handled with care, however, as, no matter how willing commanders may be to risk casualties, that does not mean that soldiers had a particular desire to become casualties or to embrace that fate.

Tasking and organization

The relationships between the selection and pursuit of objectives, and the range of factors summarized by the term 'culture' offers a rich field for research. As with other areas for study, it is necessary to focus on the double-nature of the military: internal culture, organization, goals, and the equivalent in terms of relations with the wider society. The links are multiple. Thus, conscription, as a form of organization set by the wider context, can create a culture of behaviour, such as attitudes to casualties, and to appropriate conduct in domestic operations, within which the formulation and execution of tasks can be affected. Similarly, attitudes to conscription reflect in part perceptions of how much, and how best, to secure preparedness and readiness, and definitions of both of these vary.

The relationship between tasks and organization is an issue not simply for recent military history but also for earlier periods, and there, again, it is necessary to be cautious about adopting simple cause and effect approaches to process, especially unproblematic assessments of adaptation. The relationship between tasks and organization was not uni-directional. Thus, the problematic, and certainly controversial, thesis of Bernard Bachrach stressed the sophistication of the early-Carolingian military system, and linked the nature of the military organization he discerned to the preference for a long-term strategy of territorial gains, rather than a short-term pursuit of supplies through the campaigning of looting. Bachrach argued that 'the militarised civilian population serving in the select levy' provided the overwhelming force necessary for operations that were aimed at permanent conquest. These operations 'required that the great Roman fortress cities of Gaul, Italy, and, later, Spain be placed under siege. Such warfare required very large armies' – although most early medieval armies were probably not very large. Charlemagne, indeed, was ranked as remarkable by contemporaries for having been able to bring together sizeable armies against the Saxons. Bachrach subsequently added a conclusion that is striking for its focus on organization rather than weaponry and tactics, although both the others were also discussed in his text:

> Even the most limited of campaign strategies, conceived by a successful commander, rests upon his knowledge that necessary human and material resources will be available when he needs them. Thus, the government that succeeds militarily, and particularly one that succeeds over the long term, must execute a matrix of military policies concerning the recruitment of soldiers and their organis-ation. In addition, troops must be highly motivated and have good morale. Finally, military success requires detailed planning, and government bodies must be organised to make these plans.[13]

Similarly, an emphasis on cultural factors has been seen in accounts that also stress institutional developments. Thus, for early-sixteenth-century

Europe, the Emperor Charles V's reputation played a major role in the choices he made, not least in resolving the conflicting priorities of the various Habsburg realms. In this, Charles was affected by his sense of honour (then a legal, not a moral, category) and reputation. Far from being a mere chivalric fantasy, this sense was 'the keystone in a conceptual arch forming the grand strategy that guided Charles and his advisers'.[14] By choosing to risk his own person in defence of his honour and reputation, Charles greatly increased the cost of his wars.

This is a valuable reminder of the personal role of the leader in the selection of goals; this role often drew on a sense of military history, as the past served to provide exemplary individuals whose achievements had to be matched or surpassed. This was an instance of the role of the past as model, rather than as it is generally employed currently in public discussion, as warning – but both reflected the place of history in providing a spur for action. The difference is that the aggressive purposes of past leaders sought registration alongside those of glorious predecessors: in Egypt in 1798, Napoleon wished to repeat the triumphs of Alexander the Great.[15] Modern counterparts who take that view are regarded as 'rogue' leaders. Their respectable colleagues tend, instead, to be driven by defensive goals, and thus see the past in terms of warnings, particularly about the need to respond to aggression.

The role of leaders is frequently exaggerated in popular works on war but underrated in academic studies, not least due to a stress on structural factors, particularly in works written from the perspective of political science. In the latter, the emphasis for sixteenth- and seventeenth-century Europe is on how professionalization and the development of permanent armies and navies led to problems, in terms of political and military organizational demands, that required the creation of structures and the devising of co-operative practices, but within the social, political and ideological parameters of the period. The support of the military became a central task of the state, leading to a very different military history to that of societies for whom the military was far less central, not least if it was raised essentially only to wage particular wars.

Once institutionalized, the particular social politics and strategic cultures of individual militaries could diverge from those of the state in question, a process accentuated by the roles of patronage and contact structures within militaries; this divergence could help frame goals. Thus, the social conservatism of nineteenth-century European and Latin-American militaries not only made it possible to use them politically against social revolution, but also ensured that they helped direct politics to that end. The divergence between militaries and states could be far more pronounced, which creates additional problems for the analysis of tasking. Militaries can be regarded as a drag, if not a parasite, on societies, while, in contrast, in some cases militaries have been seen as serving, deliberately or not, a crucial role in the modernization of states and societies. Analysis leads to debate. Thus, warlordism, far from necessarily being an anachronistic throwback, as generally presented, has also been seen as a response to new developments in early-twentieth century China.[16]

From the perspective of the development of the state, the role of tasking helps provide an alternative explanation to the war–statebuilding relationship that has concerned many political scientists and that is generally seen in terms of sociological modelling, not as a detailed study of interactions. Rather than new weapons having social, political, financial, and/or administrative consequences, an emphasis on goals ensures that the political demands of statebuilding can be put first. As a caveat, war, force and the military are not co-terminous, not least because, in many states, it has been forces other than the regular military that have been primarily responsible for maintaining governmental power and for enforcing policies.

Whichever approach is taken, it is necessary to note that changes in the social politics and political consequences of force were far from constant in their rate. Furthermore, tasking was a matter not only of changes among the dynamic and successful military powers, but also of the way their policies were shaped by the response they encountered, both internationally and domestically – a subject that has received insufficient attention. The emphasis in recent decades on counter-insurgency warfare[17] reflects a particular aspect of the long-standing relationship between conflict and statebuilding, and thus of the shaping of the consideration and use of force in terms of goals.

Tasking and strategic culture

Study of the definition and pursuit of objectives also offers a way to join strategic culture to operational planning, and thus to give chronological and analytical depth to military success and failure. For example, the deficiencies that helped lead to American failure to protect Hawaii and the Philippines from Japanese attack in 1941–2 can thus be related to the problems created by a defensive task unrelated to resource availability. What appeared rational to military planners – withdrawal from the Philippines – was not politically possible,[18] and discussion of the eventual military failure requires a consideration of this background, a process that the popular military approach does not allow for sufficiently.

The strategic cultures within which goals were defined were far from immutable. Instead, even in the case of autocracies, they were rather a focus of, and framework for, debate and contention;[19] debate, moreover, in which military history could play an important role as means, symbol and/or vocabulary for discussion. Indeed, this has been one of the most important roles for the subject, and it is one that continues, not only in public and political forums, but also in advanced educational military programmes. The political assumptions and discussions that were crucial to strategic cultures were, however, far from fixed, and often difficult to disentangle, and were also not in a simple causal relation with the military. Instead, these assumptions and discussions were, at least in part, affected by military developments, including new weaponry, although the latter played a role within geopolitical constructs.[20] These constructs were themselves transformed, not only by alliance politics and domestic political developments but also by geographical changes. Thus, the opening of the Panama Canal in 1914 transformed the strategic place of the Caribbean in naval plans, and greatly increased the flexibility of the American navy by making it easier to move warships between the Atlantic and the Pacific.[21] Air power had a more profound impact on geopolitics.

Earlier, naval history had provided a good instance of major differences in strategic culture and tasking affecting powers that had access to similar weaponry. Thus, Britain had to protect maritime routes that provided her with food and raw materials, while challengers, particularly France in the late nineteenth century, Germany in both world wars, and the Soviet Union during the Cold War, sought a doctrine, force structure, strategy, and operational practice that could contest these routes. The role of strategic culture also emerges clearly in the extent to which goals, and therefore doctrine, procurement and training, focused on amphibious operations. For example, the British did not develop an amphibious strategy in the early-twentieth century, and this ensured that the Gallipoli campaign of 1915 rested on a political drive and suffered from inadequate preparation, specifically the lack of a relevant planning and command structure. Paradoxically, failure at Gallipoli led to greater interest in such operations, but the plans for a landing on the Belgian coast in 1916–17 were not brought to fruition. In the interwar period, British amphibious tasking was, as so often, bound up with institutional politics, in this case providing a role for the Marines. The nature of capability, however, was driven by goals arising from British strategic culture: the lack of any apparent need for such amphibious operations encouraged a reliance on potential, rather than actual, capability, and this was to affect Britain's ability to respond effectively when the Germans invaded Norway in 1940.[22]

Strategic cultures were also important in the air, with different states placing an emphasis on strategic bombing or ground support, and tasking, as a result, determining doctrine, force structure, and strategic, operational and tactical goals. As on land and sea, there was also a varying emphasis on 'anti-' weaponry, tactics, strategy, and doctrine: in the case of air warfare, interceptor fighters, and anti-aircraft guns and control systems. This 'anti' or defensive tasking and capability tends to receive insufficient attention in military history due to a focus on the offensive. The difference in strategic cultures can also be shown by contrasts in force projection. The ability to fight wars far from their own territory (and thus the problem for the military historian of assessing long-range expeditionary warfare) has been limited to a small number of states, primarily Britain and the USA, but, to a lesser extent, also France, Germany and Japan.

More than technology, geography and security interests are involved. Attitudes to the appropriate nature and use of power also play a major role. Thus, the USA behaved for much of the twentieth century much as Britain had done in the nineteenth, although it had the option of isolating itself on the American continent – which, indeed, a section of American public opinion usually wishes it to do. As an example of the variety of strategic cultures, several decades after the end of its empire, Britain continues to put much emphasis on 'out-of-area' operations, whereas China has, for more than a half a millennium, developed little capability to wage wars far from its own territory.

Tasking and military history

The tasking of military history also deserves attention, in particular the search for supposedly universal principles through historical example and the development of military history in an institutional context. The conceptualization and practice of the subject in part reflects the tensions arising from these, and other, multiple taskings. For example, it is unclear how best to integrate the 'policy' approach to war with that of war and society: the state tends to feature in the latter as a product and moulder of social forces and compromises, rather than as an agency concerned with relations with other states; but the taskings of international conflict are set at the latter level. Another task for study is set by political scientists concerned with the role of war in state formation.

It is instructive to turn from the general question of how best to offer an historical approach to warfare to consider specific instances of present concerns. Using historical evidence to provide rapid support for policy advice is all too easy in a crisis, but, at the same time, it is valuable to offer an historical resonance to current problems. This has certainly been the case since 2001, years which have seen a flood of histories of terrorism, of Afghanistan, of Iraq, and of relations, particularly conflict, between Islam and the West. Some of the work has been of high quality, but much has been superficial, understandably so as commercial opportunity plays a major role, while there are also serious analytical problems. One of the most important issues is how best to relate, and yet also distinguish between, long-term perceptions of Islamic power and intentions, and more short-term (but still pressing) developments (see pp. 72–83).

The USA and Europe today: different strategic cultures, clashing tasks?

An historical perspective is also valuable in considering the role that differences in strategic cultures play in current controversies within the Atlantic Alliance. In this case, the problem appears clear as far as policy-makers are concerned. Contrasting post-Cold War strategic perspectives in the West are matched by serious capability gaps. In so far as the European Union is willing to address the latter, its remedies tend towards challenging rather than supporting the USA. Around this theme, many variations have been played, particularly since policy differences over Iraq rose into greater prominence in 2002–3, but the common note is one of failure, whether the perspective is that of American and European multilateralists anxious to maintain NATO and the Western alliance system, American unilateralists pleased to find backing for their policy prescriptions, European unilateralists anxious to distance themselves from American (and current British) policy, or opponents of the West keen to spot signs of its weakness.

The analysis is not without value. There are enormous, and well-rehearsed, capability gaps and strategic differences, and these are growing. The American defence build-up under President George W. Bush, driven forward as post-11 September 2001 security concerns, and related ambitious goals overcame fiscal prudence, was not matched in Europe. Even before the Bush burst took full effect, American military expenditure suggested a tasking very different to that of European powers: in 2000, according to the International Institute for Strategic Studies, the USA spent $295 billion on its military budget, and the seventeen NATO European powers $162.5 billion. Thereafter, the gap widened. In 2003, a $401 billion military appropriations package for 2004 was approved.

The quality of expenditure is also very different between the USA and Europe, which, again, reflects tasking, although the nature of technological and economic capability is also important. Drawing on a doctrine and culture that put an emphasis on technological solutions and paradigm leaps forward, and able to rely on an industrial base that is particularly suited to innovation, especially in information technology, the Americans invested heavily in research and development, creating an unmatched capability in this field. As a result, the gap between American and allied militaries looks set to widen further, with consequent problems for analyses of military capability (and history) that rely on the notion of the diffusion of the practices of the paradigm power. The results are very apparent in the use of satellites and related high-speed technology: the American satellite-based global positioning system employed for surveillance and targeting is not matched elsewhere, and is being strengthened as the USA invests in a new network of spy satellites. If future military historians refer to an age of space-warfare, they will, in fact, be referring to very few powers.

As a background to tasking, resource differences are matched by intellectual and doctrinal ones, as America's allies are not equally committed to the concept of the RMA (Revolution in Military Affairs). The net effect of difference between the USA and Europe is to challenge the inter-operability that is necessary in joint and coalition operations, and particularly important to the Americans, with their emphasis on technologically advanced weapons systems and sophisticated command and control methods.

If to this is added the differences stemming from policy disagreements, then the situation appears even more serious. The American redefinition of national security policy after the attacks of 11 September 2001 involved an attitude to international agreements and institutions, and a readiness to consider and advocate pre-emptive action, that were unwelcome to most other powers; while European attentions focused on the creation of an expanded and stronger European Union that is of little interest to the USA, and that appears to challenge the strategic culture, or at least practice, represented by NATO. Furthermore, there are important policy differences, or at least clashes, in assumptions between the USA and Europe, notably over the Middle East but also extending, for example, to Latin America, as over Cuba.

An historical perspective, however, suggests that the situation is more complex. In particular, it is all too easy to reify national attitudes and policies, and make them appear clearer, more coherent and more obviously based on readily agreed national interests than is in fact the case. In part, this is a response to the problem of space for analysis, and the fact that an endless qualification of terms leaves little room for anything else. But there is a more serious aspect to this issue. Concepts as varied as *zeitgeist*, national interests and strategic culture (and, indeed, strategy), encourage reification for reasons that are actively misleading; as, drawing on neo-Platonic assumptions about inherent reality, they assert a false coherence in order to provide clear building blocks for analytical purposes and also to present those who hold different views as failing to understand the necessary course of action. In short, polemic masquerades as analysis, a process that is particularly strong at present given the fascination of so much of the intellectual world with 'discourse'.

Instead, it is necessary to accept that in sophisticated societies – in other words, to use a modernist working definition, those that contain a large percentage of the population able to engage in discussion about politics – there will be a variety of views and a debate about policy. Furthermore, politics is likely to change, either for institutional reasons – so that, for example, George W. Bush will not be President of the USA, certainly from January 2009 – or because it is difficult for any one political party to maintain dominance in such societies for long: Portugal is not Paraguay, nor Germany Gabon. So, to talk of American or French interests or policy, as if these are clear-cut and long-lasting, is to ignore the nature of politics and the character of recent history, and to offer an overly fixed use of the concept of strategic culture, a concept that depends for its applicability on a degree of flexibility.

It is rather strange to see the capability gap and differences in tasking, or at least co-operating in tasking, held up as evidence for, or cause of, a breakdown in the West; for, in common with other alliance systems including a hegemonic power, there has been a serious gap and major differences throughout the history of NATO ever since it was established in 1949. The gap can be variously measured and, anyway, expenditure is not always the best indicator of value; but however measured, it was greater in the decade 1945–55 than it is today. World War Two had devastated the military resources and capability of Continental Europe west of the Soviet Union. The end of the war led to the abolition of the German military, while those of France, The Netherlands, Belgium, Norway, Denmark, and Italy had been ruined by the war. For example, the French and Italian fleets, impressive and modern forces in the 1930s, had been largely destroyed. Of the militaries that had not suffered war damage, that of Spain in 1945 was essentially configured for internal control, that of Portugal for colonial policing, and both were low-tech; while Sweden's and Switzerland's militaries were home-defence forces. Britain, with the second largest navy in the world, was still a major military force, but its capacity to maintain this position had been hard hit by the costs of the conflict and by the heavy indebtedness that carried these costs forward.

The Cold War, nevertheless, saw rearmament in Western Europe, particularly from 1955 in Germany, but already in the late 1940s and separate from the foundation of NATO, this had been driven forward for a different reason, as the European colonial powers sought to regain and/or defend their overseas position. Yet this was largely a failure; the French suppressed rebellion in Madagascar in 1947–8 and the British were to succeed in the Malayan Emergency (1948–60), but the French swiftly abandoned Syria, the Dutch failed in The Netherlands' East Indies, accepting their independence in 1949, and the French in Vietnam became heavily dependent on American financial support, and anyway were unsuccessful, abandoning the struggle in 1954.

The capability gaps within the West during the Cold War were enormous. The bulk of the Western European states were largely able to provide forces only for linear defence against the feared Soviet attack, while they also had essentially inshore navies. In terms of strategic air power, air-lift capacity and aircraft carriers, most of these states were weak or had no strength, and that was even more true in terms of nuclear weapons and missiles. From the American point of view, this was not an insuperable problem. Their prime requirement for the Europeans was the contribution of strategic depth and of land forces for a linear defence that was sufficient to delay the Red Army, so as to permit the Americans to use their air and missile assets to bolster the defence. However, concerns developed as the Americans advanced the concept of AirLand Battle in the early 1980s, because its requirements for mobility in attack and defence, and for air-ground co-ordination, required a weaponry, a command and control system, and an operational doctrine that most of the Europeans lacked and showed no signs of acquiring.

If these historic capability gaps have persisted, they have also become more important, with contrasting rates in signing up to the RMA, and because the American concern is now not with defence against the Soviet

Union but largely with a degree of force projection that most of the Western Europeans lack. Britain, France and Italy are committed to developing aircraft carrier capability, but progress in arranging air-lift capability has been limited, and the current German government is particularly hesitant about contributing to force projection capability on any scale and in 2004 announced major defence cuts.

These contrasts in military capability, force structure and doctrine reflect, in part, very different taskings. Although there are important variations between Western countries, and between political parties within individual countries, in essence the emphasis in Western Europe has not been on high-spectrum warfare to the extent seen in the USA. Instead, once the important stage of colonial anti-insurgency warfare ended in the mid-1970s, as Portugal and Spain abandoned their African colonies (Britain still had to defend a colony, the Falkland Islands, from external attack in 1982, but this was unexpected and played no earlier role in tasking, doctrine and force structure), the Western European militaries focused on the two other goals that had been important from the late 1940s: first, largely conventional defence against Soviet forces, and second, being the arm of the government. In short, these were mostly garrison states, very different to the USA, the expeditionary state.

Americans are apt to misunderstand the exceptional, not to say eccentric, character of their military (and military history), not only because they do not appreciate that the leading military and economic power is inherently exceptional, but also because, over the last century and, even more, the last thirty years, the regular military has played little role in internal policing. The availability of the National Guard is important here, as it provides a buffer between the regular military and internal policing, but so also are many aspects of American public culture. This is a democratized society, as opposed to simply a democracy, in which if a former general gains power, he does so as Eisenhower did in 1952, at the ballot box, puts himself up for re-election as Eisenhower did in 1956, and retires at the close of his second term. In 2003–4, another former general, Wesley Clark, put himself forward as a candidate for presidential nomination, but not, as similar campaigns would have been launched in many other states, by seeking military support.

As a consequence, the Americans frequently fail to appreciate the extent to which militaries elsewhere act as the arm of the state. This is true even of the British military, the European one that is closest to that of the USA in professionalism and force projection capability. From 1969, a major requirement on the British military was support for policing in a campaign in Northern Ireland against nationalist terrorism subsidized by Libya and by American private individuals, but, in addition, as recently as the winter of 2002–3, the army had to be deployed in order to maintain vital services in the face of 'industrial action', i.e. inaction: strikes by firemen, and this affected planning for operations against Iraq. In Britain, the domestic task of the military is discharged by the use of a professional military, but across much of Western Europe, the main domestic function of the military was fulfilled by the maintenance of conscription. This was seen to give identity to the nation, as well as binding populations to policies in many states. Conscription also fulfilled the important domestic function in states, such as Italy and Germany, that were suspicious of the right-wing tendencies of their officer corps, of ensuring a congruence between, on the one hand, civil society and civic politics and, on the other, military culture and practice.

From the perspective of commentators concerned about techno-logical and doctrinal progress, this priority was ridiculous, but, in fact, it was an appropriate response to the domestic fragility of post-1945 Europe: between 1945 and 1985, there was a successful coup in Greece (1967), an unsuccessful one in Spain (1981), a revolution in Portugal in which the military played a major role (1974), plans for a coup in Italy, and a crisis of control in France in 1968 in which the prospect of military intervention helped stiffen the government's determination to persist against large-scale agitation. Furthermore, conscription appeared the best military solution when the task was to produce large numbers of troops to counter the size of the Eastern bloc forces; it also carried with it the political benefit that citizen-troops could be expected to fight in defence of their homelands.

The end of the Cold War in Europe in 1989–91 removed the prime external military rationale of conscription, while at the same time its domestic basis was eroded as a combination of hedonism and individualism lessened the willingness to serve. Furthermore, the political rationale of countering conservative officer corps declined, as the latter were increasingly professional without the right-wing beliefs and activism of earlier decades. In the USA, conscription fell victim to the politics of the Vietnam War, while confidence in the force-multiplier consequences of American technology appeared to lessen the need for large numbers of troops.

Over the last decade, conscription has declined markedly in Western Europe, especially, but not only, in France. The goal of a fully volunteer professionalized military is now shared by major political parties, and as a result, the gap between the USA and Western Europe has markedly diminished. This is also true of the aspirations for operational effectiveness held by, and for, the military. Western European military leaderships and governments are committed to modernization of their forces to confront the post-Cold War world and, although expenditure is lower (as a percentage of GNP) than in the USA, the goals are similar, especially flexibility and mobility in doctrine and operational method. This is designed to give their forces an out-of-area projection capability, so that, individually or collectively, European powers are able to intervene elsewhere, again a goal shared with the USA.

Such a goal had not been pronounced during the Cold War. France demonstrated a continued ability to intervene in Africa, but due to its anti-Soviet focus, Britain faced considerable difficulties in responding to Argentinian aggression in 1982: the NATO-driven focus for the Royal Navy on anti-submarine capability in the North Atlantic combined with the use of submarine-based missiles for the British nuclear deterrent to ensure that the out-of-area capability earlier provided by fleet carriers had not been maintained; this seriously compromised the attempt to provide air cover for the recapture of the Falklands, although the availability of V/STOL (vertical/short take-off and landing) aircraft provided a valuable stopgap.

The end of the Cold War was rapidly followed by chaos in the confusion that had been Yugoslavia, and this encouraged the development of a European projection capability. So also did the return of European forces to fighting 'east of Suez' seen with the two Gulf Wars and with operations in Afghanistan, which NATO took military responsibility for in 2003, while concerns about Africa led to intervention: by Britain in Sierra Leone in 2000 and by France in the Ivory Coast two years later. In scale, this did not match the activities of the USA, but the goals were similar and the commitments considerable, most obviously by Britain in the two Gulf Wars.

The prime reason for the present emphasis on a gap between the USA and Western Europe stems not so much from military development as from political intention, which again reflects the nature of tasking. The nature of alliances is that powers differ, but, in the 2003 Iraq crisis, the USA, at least publicly, propounded a one-way approach to alliances that dismayed many of its friends and irritated others. The 'either you are with us or against us' approach is not one that works well in the intricate web that is politics.

As a consequence of the response of the French and German governments to the Iraq crisis there is an emphasis on difference, but there has always been a tension between America's policies outside Europe and the views of European governments, and these have greatly affected military goals. During the Cold War, the USA found these governments very reluctant to offer support to American policies in the Far East. Thus, Harold Wilson, the newly elected British Prime Minister, rejected pressure from President Johnson in 1964 for a deployment of British troops in Vietnam, and in January 1968 announced a withdrawal from east-of-Suez commitments that angered the Americans. In addition, differences over the Middle East predated the end of the Cold War, as shown, for example, in the differing willingness of NATO states to permit the use of bases and to grant overflying rights when the USA rearmed Israel during the Yom Kippur War in 1973. In Latin America, there were also clashes over policy, for example toward Cuba and Nicaragua.

The current emphasis on trans-Atlantic crisis reflects the lack of memory and historical judgement that is typical of most commentators – their inability to understand the present other than in terms of present-mindedness, and the fact that current differences are related to a challenge, particularly so far for the Americans, that has collapsed the boundaries between the simplicities of domestic debate and the complexities of foreign affairs. It is not so much that many Americans have been killed in the War on Terrorism – far more died in Vietnam – but rather that this war does not seem containable to 'out there'; which is paradoxical, as, despite the terrible drama of 11 September 2001, only a small portion of terrorism, indeed of Islamic terrorism, over the last decade has taken place on American soil.

If, in historical terms, it is important not to exaggerate the scale of present differences between the USA and Europe, it is also the case that past experience shows us that future prospects are unclear. From the perspective of 2004, it is possible to sketch a short term in which America pursues a degree of interventionism using small *ad hoc* 'coalitions of the willing'. This policy will enjoy considerable inter-national support, including from European governments, if, as in the Philippines, intervention is in support of a democratic government battling terrorism. There will be far less support for military action against sovereign states, whether sponsors of terrorism or not, but the difficulty of managing an exit strategy in Iraq is likely to discourage American attacks on Iran, North Korea, Sudan, and Syria, all of which are ruled by harmful, vicious and hostile regimes.

In much of the world, there is no serious clash between the USA and Europe. Goals are similar in Africa, the Balkans, Latin America bar Cuba, and, most significantly, in trying to end the danger of a war that could go nuclear between India and Pakistan. Similarly, despite protectionism on both sides of the Atlantic and very different policies on social welfare, there is a general commitment to capitalism and consumerism. This common basis offers important resources to the USA. European diplomacy can help develop links the USA does not wish to be seen to be pursuing, for example, in 2003–4, probing the possibility of engagement with the quixotic Libyan regime and its intolerant Iranian counterpart. In military terms, Europe also offers proficient force projection in areas where the USA prefers not to be committed, particularly West and Central Africa, as well as lower-tech/value forces that can be used for stabilization in the Balkans, and possibly in the future, in the Caucasus. NATO guarantees also help secure Poland and the Baltic Republics against Russia, and if it is unlikely that these guarantees would amount to much without American backing, it is equally the case that that backing depends, in part, on the willingness of Europe to contribute troops.

Indeed troops, not machines, is the answer to the question concerning differences in capability that is about complementarity rather than clash. American populist assumptions, well ventilated by commentators, focus on machines because they assume a hierarchy of military proficiency defined by technology. This is a misreading of military history, and another version of the mechanization of the military imagination that has been so potent since the advent of the aeroplane and the tank. It is obviously important to seize and develop every advantage that new weaponry can bring, but it is mistaken to imagine that a technological edge guarantees victory at low cost, or, indeed, victory at all. To be sure, advantages in weaponry are valuable in symmetrical warfare, but even then a host of other factors intrude, including strategy, tactics, leadership, unit cohesion, and morale – American superiority in all of which acted as a force-multiplier for technology in ensuring victory against Iraq in 2003, as well as contextual issues such as the respective determination of the powers engaged. In asymmetrical warfare, the advantages conferred by superior weaponry are curtailed.

The specific danger the USA faces in defining tasks is the conviction that the RMA will ensure that those who are beaten accept defeat. The occupation of Iraq in 2003–4 should have cured policy-makers of that, reminding them that war is a struggle of wills, not machines, and that triumph in battle is not sufficient unto victory. Furthermore, American strategy and operational practice, targeted at seeking swift decisions without much involvement of ground forces, deviates considerably from

Clausewitz's insight that any opponent not completely defeated will have at least a chance of regaining power.

Just as individual militaries benefit from a force structure that permits multiple tasking, so alliance systems also need this capacity. In the case of the contemporary Western alliance, the defects of the machine-bound doctrine of war ensure that there is much of value in looking to forces which, lacking America's technological lead, have pursued more appropriate doctrine for counter-insurgency and peace-keeping operations. Furthermore, the American focus on machines has starved their military of men and, in particular, led to a dangerous run-down in the size of the army. This makes the contribution of allies more useful, especially for deterrent garrison functions and for peacekeeping and counter-insurgency goals. For military reasons, therefore, the gap in capability encourages co-operation, indeed requires it if the USA is to pursue active policies around the world. Whether there is the political will and skill to accept the consequences for tasking is less clear.

Conclusion

The particular challenge from terrorism also encourages the search for co-operation. Terrorism appears to have collapsed space, and, using missiles or other means, several states and terrorist groups now have the ability to bring explosives and other dangerous warheads or bombs to large parts of the world, whereas only a few states are able, or seek, to deploy operational forces as instruments of a more sophisticated policy far from their own borders or coasts. In the struggle with terrorism, it is necessary to seek the support of local governments.[23] This serves as a reminder of the continued dominance of political perspectives in the purposes that both set military goals and help determine the perception of success, a point that emerges across the chronological span that forms the subject of the following chapters.

Notes

1 Cavan to Maurice, 6 Feb. 1924, LH, Maurice papers, 3/5/150.
2 M. Ignatieff, *Virtual War* (2001), p. 176.
3 D. Showalter, 'From Deterrence to Doomsday Machine: The German Way of War, 1890–1914', *Journal of Military History*, 64 (2000), pp. 679–710.
4 A. Mombauer, *Helmuth von Moltke and the Origins of the First World War* (Cambridge, 2001).
5 J. Horne and A. Kramer, *German Atrocities, 1914. A History of Denial* (New Haven, 2001).

6 V. Liulevicius, *War Land on the Eastern Front. Culture, National Identity and German Occupation in World War I* (Cambridge, 2000). For a less critical view, D. Showalter, ' "The East Gives Nothing Back": The Great War and the German Army in Russia', *Journal of the Historical Society* 2 (2002), pp. 1–19, esp. 15–16.

7 H. Herr and K. Naumann (eds), *War of Extermination. The German Military in World War II 1941–1944* (2000).

8 H. Boog, W. Rahn, R. Stumpf and B. Wegner, *Germany and the Second World War. VI. The Global War* (Oxford, 2001).

9 R. David, 'Internal War. Causes and Cures', *World Politics*, 49 (1997), pp. 552–76.

10 A. Gat, *Clausewitz and the Enlightenment: the Origins of Modern Military Thought* (Oxford, 1988), *The Development of Military Thought: the Nineteenth Century* (Oxford, 1992) and *Fascist and Liberal Visions of War* (Oxford, 1998).

11 P.A. Kuhn, *Rebellion and its Enemies in Late Imperial China: Militarization and Social Structure, 1796–1864* (Cambridge, 1980).

12 D. Dawson, *The Origins of Western Warfare: Militarism and Morality in the Ancient World* (Boulder, 1996).

13 B.S. Bachrach, *Early Carolingian Warfare. Prelude to Empire* (Philadelphia, 2001), pp. 83, 242.

14 J.D. Tracy, *Emperor Charles V, Impresario of War. Campaign Strategy, International Finance, and Domestic Politics* (Cambridge, 2002), p. 38.

15 R.L. Tignor (ed.), *Napoleon in Egypt* (Princeton, 1993), p. 161.

16 E.A. McCord, *The Power of the Gun: The Emergence of Modern Chinese Warlordism* (Berkeley, 1993).

17 See most valuably I.F.W. Beckett, *Modern Insurgencies and Counter-Insurgencies* (2001).

18 B.M. Linn, *Guardians of Empire. The U.S. Army and the Pacific, 1902–1940* (Chapel Hill, 1997), p. 246.

19 S. Pons, *Stalin and the Inevitable War. Origins of the Total Security State in the USSR and the Outbreak of World War II in Europe* (2002).

20 I.C.Y. Hsu, 'The Great Policy Debate in China, 1874: Maritime Defence v. Frontier Defence', *Harvard Journal of Asiatic Studies*, 25 (1965), pp. 212–28; A.J. Bacevich, *American Empire. The Realities and Consequences of U.S. Diplomacy* (Cambridge, Mass., 2002).

21 D.A. Yerxa, *Admirals and Empire. The United States Navy and the Caribbean, 1898–1945* (Columbia, South Carolina, 1991), p. 53.

22 D. Massam, *British Maritime Strategy and Amphibious Capability, 1900–40* (D.Phil. Oxford, 1995).

23 T.G. Mahnken, 'The American Way of War in the Twenty-first Century', *Review of International Affairs*, 2 (2003), p. 82.

Chapter 6

1500–1815

The old ammunition of bows and arrows, battering-rams and wooden engines, which were to be procured and made in all parts of the world, are now laid aside; though these were the artillery of the Grecian and Roman governments: But now the materials necessary for carrying on a war must be by the returns made by the foreign trade that one country drives with another . . . no nation can resist invasion, or get out of a just and necessary war with honour, but from the stores it either has, or must procure by trade and navigation.

Honest True Briton [London newspaper], 27 April 1724

The American dispute between the French and us is therefore only the quarrel of two robbers for the spoil of a passenger.

'Observations on the Present State of Affairs in 1756',
Literary Magazine [London], 15 August 1756

Beginning the chronological treatment at this period in time brings together the related issues of modernity, the nature and impact of Western expansion, the global role of firearms, and the consequences of printing. The latter is of particular relevance as it transformed the writing about war in Europe, though not in China where printing was invented. On the world scale, printing powerfully accentuated the contrast between the military memory in the European world, where printing developed most rapidly and comprehensively, and elsewhere – although the oldest extant fully-fledged drill manual for firearms was Japanese, *Inatomi teppô densho*, appearing in 1595.

Printing and literacy contributed to the development of a military public, in the sense of a public informed about military affairs and a military interested in public comment on their activities, although such a public was already present in Europe in the fourteenth and fifteenth centuries, before the advent there of printing technology and its application to military matters, while as late as the eighteenth century, many European military manuals existed only in manuscript. Printing, nevertheless, was important in strengthening the consciousness of a specific military tradition, not least as printed manuals on gunnery, tactics, drill, siegecraft, and fortification spread techniques far more rapidly than word of mouth or manuscript. Manuals also permitted a degree of standardization that both helped to increase military effectiveness and was important for cohesion and the utilization of military resources. More generally, printing and literacy fostered discussion of military organization and methods, and encouraged a sense of system.[1]

Printing and literacy encouraged the use of military history as a source of examples as well as exemplars, although military history in the West had always employed both. Vegetius, for example, drew on examples from military history. Furthermore, the quest for modernity, in the case of the culture of print in the form of learned knowledge, should not detract from the continued use of military history as a source of exemplary tales reflecting traditional concepts of military behaviour and renown. The focus in literature and art was on hand-to-hand combat, valour, cavalry and infantry charges, and leadership from the front;[2] unsurprisingly so when collective prowess and exemplary leadership were seen as the keys to success.

It is also important to turn to the cultural suppositions underlining the modern military history of the period covered in this chapter. It is frequently claimed that the armies, and even navies, of the period were unable to achieve major strategic or political goals, and that their operations were generally inconsequential. Such a discussion, however, risks present-mindedness: modern concepts of decisiveness owe much to the achievement of unconditional victory in World War Two, but that is misleading even as a description of twentieth-century warfare. Ultimately, the problem is cultural. It is difficult today for many to accept that warfare was 'for real' in a world in which artifice, convention and style played such a major role. This is particularly the case because it has been contrasted with the apparently more vital, clear-cut, and successful warfare of the Age of Revolution that began in 1775, more particularly the ideologies and forces of the American (1775–83) and French (1789–99) Revolutions. There is also a tendency to underrate the determination and ability of aristocratic societies, especially those that dominated the pre-Revolutionary eighteenth century. Though rarely expressed explicitly, such views are no less influential for that, but they fail to note the extent to which war in the period was neither inconsequential nor predictable.

Like other branches of history, military history has to consider not only how to explain its subject, but also what it is seeking to analyse. If the central narrative in most work has been the military history of the West (actually only of parts of the West), this has appeared particularly appropriate for modern history, modern being defined, in a somewhat circular fashion, as the period of Western dominance. Earlier ages are considered if they allegedly prefigured aspects of this, as with some modern discussion of Classical (i.e. only ancient Greek and Roman) history.

This approach was brought together with the technological emphasis that characterized much military history by focusing on gunpowder weaponry, but, aside from the extent to which the use of such weaponry was far from a Western monopoly, it is also important not to see firearms as an independent variable. Instead, in considering their development and use, it is necessary to look at the goals set by the perception of threats, as well as at cultural assumptions. Geography may also have played a role: the most recent global assessment has suggested that the development of firearms 'was affected by the degree to which an area was threatened by nomads instead of by infantry. Development was slower to the extent that the threat came from nomads';[3] while the latter's adaptation of firearms varied, in part because of opportunity but also due to military and social constraints.[4]

Comparative approaches have a worthy lineage but, given this period saw an hitherto unprecedented interaction of Western with non-Western societies, it is unsurprising that Eurocentric military history, when not focusing largely on Western developments, considers those elsewhere in terms of Western paradigms and of the interaction of non-Western powers with the West; these latter two factors being closely intertwined, although, of course, analytically distinct.[5] It might be thought that the discussion of developments in other cultures in terms of conflict with the West addresses the issue, but that is far from the case. Here, there is a linked empirical and methodological problem: as discussed for the Islamic world in Chapter three, there is a tendency to treat what frequently is marginal as if it was central. Thus, for both China and Persia, conflict with Western powers in the period covered by this chapter was episodic and relatively minor. This was not the case for the Ottoman Turks, but with them it is necessary to recognize the secondary nature of conflict with Christendom (as opposed to with other Islamic powers) in the sixteenth century, the first four decades of the seventeenth, and for the 1720s, early 1730s and 1740s, the last a period that tends to be neglected in Ottoman military history.[6]

More generally, in assessing impact there is the assumption that non-Western powers should have behaved like their (or rather some of their) Western counterparts. For example, China and Japan, both of which, alongside Korea, displayed considerable short-range naval capability during the Korean War of the 1590s (as well as the large-scale use of guns and cannon)[7], did not seek to match Western colonialization; but rather than treating that as evidence of failure, it is necessary to consider the goals of these, and other non-Western, states.

This illuminates the contrast between the trans-oceanic colonization and power-projection of the Atlantic European powers, and the far more land-based character of both non-European powers, some of which, such as China, Japan and the Ottoman Empire[8], had lengthy coastlines, and their Eastern European counterparts. Although Chinese colonies of traders settled at various places on the Malay peninsula, including Singapore, which was then known as Temarek, and though Japanese navigators and cartographers had a rather keen interest in the South Pacific, at the latest from the sixteenth century and probably earlier, neither China nor Japan created settlement colonies across the Pacific. This does not, however, indicate a failure of administrative capability. Indeed, in the 1750s, China achieved a success in the Eurasian heartland that exceeded those accomplished by Russia that century, when it overcame the Dzungars of Xinkiang, thereby demonstrating an impressive logistical capability that was the product of a sophisticated administrative system, and applying force at a distance with considerable success.[9]

The absence from the oceans appears a failure in Atlanticist terms, as it was across the oceans that Western power was most effectively projected, while the ability of Atlantic Europe to become central to new global networks of exchange gave a sharp stimulus to its collective borrowing and lending.[10] But the extent to which Atlanticist terms are appropriate as a means of judging societies that did not share these assumptions is unclear. Furthermore, the extent of European participation in, and control over, European–Asian trade links have been exaggerated; while true of maritime trade, overland links remained important and were dominated by Asians.[11] Indeed, the Western merchants struggling to gain entry to Oriental markets, or financing their purchases with bullion exports, would have been as surprised as were the Dutch expelled from Taiwan in 1661–2 or the Russians driven from the Amur valley in 1685–9, when told about Western dominance. Similarly, although the British occupation of Tangier from 1662 was important for the development of the army and for increased experience in distant naval deployment, they found it necessary, in the face of Moroccan pressure, to evacuate the garrison in 1684.[12]

A demographically reconceptualized world

This perception can be sharpened up by rethinking the world in 1500 and 1815 in terms of equal-population cartograms, which provide demographically weighted maps that are far more useful than the conventional equal-area maps. Furthermore, these maps would suggest that Western power was less central than the use of equal-area maps would imply. This is an important perspective, because the subliminal quality of cartographic images conveys impressions of importance that help dictate conclusions about success. In many respects, these are misleading. Rethinking the world spatially in terms of equal-population cartograms very much revises the impression of Western success. For example, the Russian conquest of much of Siberia from 1581 and, at the close of the period, the British conquest of part of Australia from 1788 become relatively inconsequential, as indeed does that of eastern North America from the Native Americans by the British, French and, to a lesser extent, Spaniards, Dutch, and Swedes – and, from 1776, by the (European) Americans.

Instead, the European achievements that repay attention are those toward the close of the period, particularly if the conquests of the Aztec and Inca empires are adjusted to take note of the impact of smallpox and other diseases on their populations[13] (and their size in terms of equal-area cartograms is therefore reduced). It is the British conquests in India in the second half of the eighteenth century that are crucial in demographic terms. As yet, there has been no extensive rethinking of world history in terms of equal-population cartograms, but it is important at all levels. It would also, indeed, repay attention at the European level, not least because such an approach would ensure that more attention is devoted to Italy than is usually the case in accounts of seventeenth- and eighteenth-century European warfare. Furthermore, an emphasis on gaining control of people helps underline the importance of sieges.

Outside Europe, as already indicated, the demographic approach encourages a reconceptualization of European expansion, but it is also important to the consideration of conflict between non-Western powers. This is true both at the macro- and at the micro-level. Inevitably, the demographic approach ensures that more attention is devoted to China, and indeed conflict within that country is, at this level, more significant than that between many European states. This is especially true of the ultimately unsuccessful Sanfen rebellion of 1673–81. This 'War of the Three Feudatories' was begun by powerful generals who were provincial governors, especially Wu Sangui, who controlled most of south-western China and rebelled in 1673, followed, in 1674, by Jingzhong Jimao and, in 1676, by Zhixin Kexi. The feudatories overran most of south China, but were driven back to the south-west by 1677 thanks to the use of Green Standard troops: loyal Chinese forces fighting for the Manchu emperor. Earlier, Manchu units had failed to defeat the rebels, and this failure, and the success of the Green Standard forces, helped in the consolidation of Chinese administrative techniques, personnel and priorities. Wu died in 1678, but the rebellion did not end until 1681.[14] It had come close to overthrowing the Manchu, but Wu and his allies were unable to translate their success in south China into the conquest of the north. In terms of the number of combatants and the scale of area covered, this war was more important than the contemporaneous Dutch War (1672–8) in Western Europe.

This rebellion was particularly serious because it arose from within the structure of the Chinese state as altered by Manchu conquest. Wu was a key Ming general who had joined the Manchu in 1644 and played a major role in the Manchu conquest of southern China in the 1640s and 1650s, being rewarded with considerable power and autonomy. In contrast, eighteenth-century risings in China, although still large-scale and important, especially the millenarian White Lotus rebellion of 1796–1805 in Shaanxi, and the Miao revolt in Hunan and Guizhou of 1795–1805, were not from within the political structure.

Defining the issues

Along with space, it is important to add the variable of time. It is all too easy to assume an early modern situation described and analysed in terms of European naval force projection and of the use of gunpowder weaponry. This runs together such episodes as the Spanish conquests of the Aztecs and the Incas in the early-sixteenth century with battles such as the British victory in Bengal at Plassey (1757), in order to produce a single situation that can be analysed in one fashion, an approach that encourages an emphasis on technology. This is misleading. First, it underrates the chronological as well as the geographical distinctiveness of episodes of Western success, such as the triumph of the *Conquistadores*,[15] and, therefore, the need to consider them separately. Such a disaggregation reduces the temptation to run together the largely patchy empirical evidence that tactical changes, in the shape of the invention of the volley and the re-deployment of firepower on the battlefield, made much difference in practice to the outcome of battles. Indeed, the role of firepower in the success of the *Conquistadores* has been heavily qualified.[16]

Second, the unitary approach fails to judge chronological developments alongside those in the 'non-West', and to understand their mutual dynamism. Thus the globalization of which Western power projection was an important aspect involved a strong degree of mutual dependence with aspects of the 'non-West', and, indeed, it is necessary to think not in terms of the West versus the Rest, but of specific Western initiatives and their interaction with the complex rivalries and relationships of local groups, peoples and states, a point also true of the expansion of non-Western Powers.[17] If it was Westerners and, especially in the eighteenth century, the British, who organized the new systems, they could not do so in a unilateral fashion. Instead, mutual dependence and power projection were in a dynamic tension, frequently shifting in balance.

Rivalry between the Western powers was important in this, not least in affecting the options for syncretic relationships. Rivalry with the Bourbons in the eighteenth century, and, even more, with Revolutionary and Napoleonic France,[18] led to an emphasis in Britain on power projection that helped reshape the terms of mutual dependence with non-European countries, although the nature and chronology of this reshaping varied greatly, as the contrasts between British relations with China and India, and later with China and Japan, indicated. In the nineteenth century, rivalry with Russia helped drive forward a similar process.[19]

Having made these theoretical points, it is time to turn to war outside the West in order to ask what were the master elements in the narrative. Here again, there is the issue of significance, in particular the question of whether lasting impact is the key topic to pursue, and, if so, how to define 'lasting' and 'impact'. For example, the fate of Safavid Persia, overthrown by the Afghan Ghazais in 1722, offered a dramatic episode, but its wider significance is unclear. The fate of Safavid Persia was important in the Persian Gulf, as well as to Oman,[20] Afghanistan, northern India, Central Asia, the Caucasus, and to the Ottoman empire, all of which experienced the campaigning of Nadir Shah of Persia in the 1730s and 1740s, but it is difficult to see this as playing a formative role in the nineteenth- or twentieth-century world, not least because neither the Afghan control of Persia that lasted until overthrown in 1729, nor the empire of Nadir Shah proved lasting: indeed, the last was very much an expression of individual military drive. More generally, the states of the region between the Ottoman Empire and Hindustan were unable to coalesce lastingly to provide a strength in the nineteenth century sufficient to thwart the growing interest, ambitions and power in the region of Britain and Russia.

A *longue durée* approach might appear to render redundant much of the history of the 'non-West'; but it is also necessary to consider its application to the more conventional cast of military history. If the Persia of Nadir Shah, whose campaigns have indeed received insufficient attention, is to be dismissed as of limited long-term significance (possibly alongside those of Alaung-hpaya of Burma in the 1750s and Tashin of Siam in the 1770s, both of whom had major successes), then it can be asked why Napoleon is worthy of consideration, as his empire rapidly ended in failure and certainly did not set the geopolitical parameters for the Western world. Again, if the context is institutional continuity, not individual genius, then it is worth asking why modern German military history deserves attention, as the General Staff presided over the disasters of the two World Wars, disasters that culminated in the unconditional surrender of Germany, the dissolution of the German military, including the General Staff, and the partition and occupation of Germany.

There is less excuse now for this conventional emphasis than there was during the early modern period, for European writers on war then knew little about developments outside Europe and, in so far as the latter were considered, they were understood in terms of the projection of Western power. The 'real military renaissance' detected in sixteenth-century Europe, with an interest in the classics of ancient military history, was seen not only as a way to enhance capability within Europe, but also as a means to multiply the effectiveness of troops against the Ottomans.[21]

Nevertheless, if the bulk of European discussion of warfare lacked any real understanding of non-European interests, it was still an instructive aspect of European military culture, which in part reflected a sense of continuity in practice. Furthermore, interest in contemporary works on military history encouraged translation. For example, Adam Heinrich Dietrich von Bülow (1757–1807), a former Prussian officer, wrote a series of studies in which he sought to offer a comprehensive analysis and explanation of war, most importantly, *Geist des neuern Kriegssystems* (1799), a presentation of the science of military operations, which was published in London as *The Spirit of the Modern System of War* (1806).

Although this period saw the West widely, if episodically, engaged with non-Western powers, conflict within the West dominated its intellectual and popular interest. Alongside the engagement with the Classical past, understood in terms of the worlds of Classical Greece, Alexander the Great, and Ancient Rome, that were seen (or, in modish modern terms, appropriated) as the roots of contemporary Western warfare, came an interest in the recent military past. Thus, in his influential *History of the Reign of the Emperor Charles V* (1769), the British historian William Robertson saw the Italian Wars (1494–1559) as the birth of the modern European international system.[22]

Naval developments

The problem of defining what was militarily significant in the early-modern period invites debate, and certainly underlines the questionable character of any Eurocentric emphasis for land warfare. The situation is different on the water, at least for deep-draught naval capability, although there is also need for study of this question, more particularly for shallow-water capability. Furthermore, the suggestion above of a cartographic reconceptualization can be extended to the watery sphere as a whole, with a need to place the emphasis on rivers, lakes, deltas, estuaries, lagoons and inshore waters, alongside the oceans that dominate Western attention and analysis. For the seventeenth century, it is important to consider not only the revival in the Ottoman fleet,[23] which covered the massive invasion of Crete in 1645, and the Chinese fleets that helped drive the Dutch from the Pescadores Islands in 1604 and 1624 and from Taiwan in 1661–2,[24] but also the formidable navy, with well-gunned warships, that the Omani Arabs created after they captured the Portuguese base of Muscat in 1650.[25] In terms of amphibious operations, some of the most impressive in the seventeenth century were by non-Europeans: the Ottomans against Crete; Coxinga, the Ming loyalist, against Taiwan, followed, in 1683, by its conquest by the Chinese under admiral Shi Lang; and, albeit against weaker opposition, the Omanis against Mombasa, which fell in 1698.[26] In South Asian waters, Mataram, Aceh, Mughal, and Magh fleets all played a local role, although Sultan Iskander Muda of Aceh was defeated when he attacked Malacca, then Portuguese-controlled, in 1629. Large squadrons of Mughal riverboats, carrying cannon, played a major role in defeating the fleet of Arakan in 1666, while the Marathas had a sizeable fleet in the late seventeenth century.[27]

In the eighteenth century, substantial navies were deployed by only a handful of non-European powers, principally the Ottoman empire, the Barbary states of North Africa, the Omani Arabs, and the Maratha Angria family on the Konkon coast of India. The ships of these powers had a greater range than war canoes and approximated more closely to European warships, but they lacked the destructive power of the latter. Tasking was important: the Barbary,[28] Omani and Angria ships were commerce raiders that emphasized speed and manoeuvrability, whereas the heavier, slower ships-of-the-line of European navies were designed for battle and stressed battering power, which in 1756 helped the British capture Gheria, the stronghold on the west coast of India of Tulajee Angria. When in 1735 the Pasha of Ottoman-ruled Basra defeated a Persian naval attempt to seize the port, he did so by commandeering British ships. On the other hand, the difficulties the English encountered in the 1660s in opposing corsairs off Tangier led to interest by them in the use of Mediterranean galleys.[29]

In many parts of the world, canoes were important. These boats were shallow in draught, and therefore enjoyed an inshore range denied to European warships. Their crews usually fought with missile weapons, increasingly muskets, and some canoes also carried cannon.[30] Areas where canoes were particularly important included inland waterway systems, especially in Amazonia; the eastern half of North America as well as its Pacific coastal region; the valleys of the Brahmaputra and Irrawaddy; coastal systems, particularly the lagoons of West Africa; and island systems, such as the Hawaiian archipelago.[31] By the end of the eighteenth century, the fleets of outrigger canoes of the Betsimisaraka and Sakalava of Madagascar raided as far as the mainland of northern Mozambique. As yet, these and other forces are not only largely unstudied but also scarcely mentioned in general accounts of naval power and warfare. Thus, a definition of capability is asserted rather than discussed: a common problem in military history.

Key geopolitical changes

To turn to another approach to assessing significance, geopolitical links were created and contested throughout the period. Alongside those that commonly dominate attention, especially the creations of a European Atlantic and of a maritime link between Europe and South Asia, it is important to focus on the creation of two relationships that were to help define the succeeding centuries, and were thus an important part of the legacy of the period. The rapid conquest of Egypt by the Ottomans in 1517 is generally treated with far less prominence than the achievements of Cortes against the Aztecs, but the battle of al-Rayda on 23 January, with the victory over the Mamluks achieved in less than twenty minutes, helped define the western Islamic world; it was the Omdurman (the battle in 1898 that ensured British conquest of Sudan) of its age, yet much more significant and lasting in its consequences. From Egypt the Ottomans rapidly extended their power along the coast of North Africa, down the Red Sea and into the Arabian peninsula, underlining their prestige by gaining the guardianship of the Holy Places.[32]

This linking of the Turkic and Arabic worlds helped give the Ottomans the resources, energy and confidence to press the Safavids hard to the east, and to drive forward against Christendom to the West, and it created a geopolitical system that in large part lasted until World War One; a reminder of the late-onset of 'modernity' if seen in terms of Western control. Egypt itself was not to be wrested from the Ottomans until the nineteenth century, and then initially by Mehmet Ali, the Viceroy, and only in 1882 by Britain; the earlier European impact – Napoleon's conquest in 1798 and the British counter-invasion in 1801 – was shortlived, and a British invasion in 1807 was unsuccessful.

The second relationship of lasting importance was that of the overcoming of the steppe challenge by the Chinese in the 1750s, an achievement that helped define the modern world: the threat from nomadic power was finally overcome when the Chinese crushed the Dzungars, and China gained strategic depth.[33]

Multiple capability and eliciting support

Mention of both the Ottomans and the Chinese underlines another important aspect of the achievement of major non-Western powers, and suggests a further way in which they can be judged: the range of physical and military environments in which they had to operate. Thus, the Ottomans fought not only the Safavids and Mamluks, but also the Europeans on land in Europe, North Africa and Abyssinia (where the Portuguese helped the Abyssinians in the 1540s), and at sea in the Mediterranean, Red Sea, Persian Gulf, and Indian Ocean, as well as fighting a series of less-powerful polities, ranging from Bedouin Arabs to opponents in the Caucasus. The Chinese fought in the arid steppes of Mongolia and Xinkiang, the high plateau of Tibet, and the forests of Burma and Vietnam. Such campaigns faced formidable logistical burdens. A failure to cope with them could offset any advantage in firepower. In 1602, Abbas I of Persia marched on Balkh (in modern north Afghanistan) with 40,000 troops, including 10,000 musketeers and about 300 cannon, but a lack of provisions and water caused problems that led to a humiliating retreat.[34]

The roots of success in multiple capability can be compared and contrasted with those of European Atlanticist powers. Like that of the latter, Ottoman capability drew on a military system that required a considerable measure of organization, especially in logistics,[35] although, alongside the logistical successes, especially supporting operations in Hungary, came failures that helped establish limits. For example, the unsuccessful attempt to capture Astrakhan from the Russians in 1569 was hit by a lack of sufficient provisions, and the Turks did not repeat it. The Ottoman military, however, was arguably more effective (here a comparative methodology is required) than the European Atlanticist powers in combining the strengths of different systems: organizational/ bureaucratic and fiscal strengths that benefited from the increasing monetarization of the Ottoman economy, alongside tribal forces, including allies and tributaries, especially the Crimean Tatars, whose cavalry became more important as Ottoman forces shifted their emphasis to infantry. The diversity of the Ottoman military system was an inherent source of strength, one linked to the breadth and depth of its recruitment system.

Similarly, in China, once conquered by the Manchu in the mid-seventeenth century, the combination of a number of separate forces and of successful logistical and organizational systems made the army particularly effective and also able to operate in a range of environments. The banner system enabled Mongols, Chinese and Manchu to work together as part of a single military machine. Organization meant not only military structures but also the ability to evolve and maintain a military organization that was adapted to the realities of the political situation, not least in its capacity to cope with the multiple crises that war brought.

In short, the powers best able to wage war were those who got close to a synthesis of military organization and political/administrative capacity – although that was far from being a fixed relationship, not least because political parameters varied depending on the degree of support for the goals of the war in question. The eighteenth-century British navy and the early eighteenth-century French army were good examples of well-adapted military organizations, as, more generally, was much of the European military of the period, whereas the situation had been less happy across much of Europe during the period 1560–1660.[36] That century is frequently presented in terms of a military revolution, variously in all or some of tactics, troop numbers and bureaucratic support,[37] but this is unconvincing. Prior to the floating of this theory, Georges Pagès had already pointed out that in 1660 the conditions under which the Elector of Brandenburg-Prussia led his forces were not far different from those of the fifteenth and early sixteenth century.[38]

The improvement in military effectiveness within Europe in the period 1660–1760 was important but limited, not least because of the financial constraints arising from the nature of the economic and fiscal systems and the size of the military forces that had to be supported. Lengthy wars exacerbated the problem, especially the Nine Years' War (1688–97), that of the Spanish Succession (1702–1714), and the Great Northern War (1700–21). Financial problems hit logistics and also led to troop mutinies, for example among the Austrian force in Spain in 1711. As a result of shortages of money, the Spanish army destined for Italy in 1741 faced multiple difficulties, including problems with the artillery. Furthermore, innovations that have been praised nevertheless had important limitations. The magazines developed to support French forces in the late seventeenth century generally only contained supplies able to support initial operations, which caused problems if the conflict was a lengthy one and it proved impossible to transfer the cost by operating in foreign states. The more financially secure British state also faced serious problems in maintaining its military: in 1729, the Regency Council had to discuss the shortage of magazines and powder in the garrison on Minorca.[39]

In evaluating these and other military organizations, it should be understood that it is not easy to rank organization in any objective way, but rather it is necessary to consider it in terms of adaptation to the particular political and social realities of the state. This point reminds us of the need to study specific details, and thus challenges simplistic attempts by political scientists to offer a typology of states based on the relationship between war and political developments.

Outside Europe, thanks to the profits of trade and to the ability to win local support, the European powers were to deliver something similar to the Manchu banner system, as a result of hiring, co-opting or allying with local forces, ranging from the sepoys and allied troops in India to Native American tribes, a practice that continued until the end of their empires, for example with the recruitment of native Africans in the late nineteenth and twentieth centuries. It is too easy, however, to underrate the difficulties inherent in this process, particularly in political and organizational terms.

Success and failure

The military emphasis, as seen with the use of the sepoys and, later, native Africans, but not with the allied Native American tribes, was the application of European standardized operating procedure focused on infantry volleys. This relative uniformity has customarily been seen as an aspect of Western superiority, but this needs re-consideration.

First, it is by no means clear that this uniformity provided an adequate adaptability that permitted an effective military response to different environments; indeed, as with imperial campaigning in the late-nineteenth century, this lack of adaptability can be linked to failure, for example Braddock's defeat in 1755 when a British force was ambushed and routed by the French and their Native American allies near modern Pittsburg. Geoffrey Parker has recently claimed that 'Time and again, infantry volley fire enabled Western troops to defeat far larger numbers of non-Western adversaries.' Indeed, he cites Arthur Wellesley, later first Duke of Wellington, who was victorious in India in 1803, as his evidence for this providing the basis of British strength in Asia.[40]

Yet, alongside success came failure, for example British defeats in India: by the Marathas at Wadgaon in 1779, and by Haidar Ali, Sultan of Mysore, at Perumbakam in 1780. Furthermore, successful campaigning in India required an ability to combine British firepower with the logistical capability provided by Indian entrepreneurs; allied Indian cavalry could also be important, as the British conflicts with Mysore in the 1790s indicated. The 'tipping point' toward European success in India came then and in the following decade. Until the 1790s, British success, although important, especially in Bengal in 1757–65, was far from amounting to a tide, and there had been significant setbacks, particularly at the hands of Haidar Ali. Indeed, it was unclear how far Britain would dominate post-Mughal India, as the East India Company was only one among a number of powers seeking to do so.

With the benefit of hindsight, it is possible to explain British success in terms of a number of factors that suggest an inevitable course. These include the fact that (with the exception, after 1761, of brief periods of French challenge) Britain was the sole power in India benefiting from a naval capability, trans-oceanic range and maritime commercial resources. Indeed, it was not until April 1942, when a Japanese fleet briefly entered the Indian Ocean, that this situation was to be seriously challenged. In the early modern period, there was no equivalent non-Western power, certainly not China or Japan. The closest was Oman, but the attacks mounted by the Omanis on the Portuguese bases in India in the late seventeenth century – Bombay was attacked in 1661–2, Bassein in 1674, and Diu was sacked in 1668 and 1676 – were not sustained, and the Omanis concentrated instead on the East African coast, where they sacked Mombasa in 1661 and captured it from Portugal in 1698. Naval capability and commercial interests played a role in another characteristic of British power in India, its wide-ranging character. With their three Presidencies, based at Bombay, Calcutta and Madras, the British were present on the coasts of both the Arabian Sea and the Bay of Bengal, and had a range denied such Mughal-successor powers as the Gurkhas, the successive Nizams of Hyderabad, and Haidar Ali and Tipu Sultan of Mysore.

In terms of battle in India, it has been argued that the British mastery of firepower tactics and their emphasis on infantry and artillery were crucial. The Western impact in India was seen in the spread of flintlock rifles, bayonets, prepared cartridges, and cast-iron cannon, and it was in the late eighteenth century that the advantage swung in India from cavalry to infantry armed with firearms, while artillery also became more effective. Superior firearms – flintlocks mounting bayonets – and effective tactics were important in this shift. It is noteworthy that Benjamin Robins, 'the central figure of the ballistics revolution',[41] died in 1751 while serving as Engineer General and Captain of the Madras artillery for the East India Company.

The trend thus seems clear, and, indeed, the eagerness with which several Indian rulers sought to adopt European weaponry has attracted attention.[42] That in turn creates another way to approach their failure, namely that they saw they had to innovate and failed to do so successfully. Instead, Westernization appears to have had detrimental military and political consequences. Warren Hastings, a prominent British Governor-General, was content for Indian states to try to emulate European infantry formations because he was confident they would never succeed and that it would take resources away from their cavalry and slow them up in the field. As Maratha armies became more professional, so the strategy based on living off the land became less feasible. Furthermore, the new infantry and artillery formations proved expensive, leading to developments in revenue administration, banking and credit that created serious political problems.

The situation appears readily apparent, but there is a danger that the analysis conforms to the standard approach to military history with its misleading tendency to attribute to winners all the strengths of superior political and military systems and greater resources, and all the skills of vision, strategic know-how, preparation and back-up; whereas losers tend to lose because they lose. There is a need, particularly, but not only, at the operational level, for continued reference to chance, and for the frequent use of terms such as 'perhaps' and 'maybe', and also for a measure of scepticism about the attribution of inevitability to long-term military history. This is especially important for India in this period, because it saw the most significant conflict between Europeans and non-Europeans.

At the same time, there is a danger in reading from the particular to the general: it is unclear how far the results seen in India were of wider applicability. As yet, there has been no serious study of conflict between Western and non-Western powers across the world in the period from 1790 to1820. Such a study could focus on Western successes, such as the American victories at Fallen Timbers (1795) in the Ohio country, and against the Creeks in 1813–14, Napoleon's victories in Egypt and Palestine in 1798–99, or Russian success against the Ottomans in 1806–12. But it is also worth noting failures, such as the British in Egypt in 1807, and, outside lightly-populated North America, it was only in India that major territorial gains involving large numbers of people took place. The Russians gained Bessarabia from the Ottomans at the Treaty of Bucharest in 1812, but this was marginal to Ottoman power, although it did take the Russians closer to the Balkans.

The case study of India

In India, from the 1790s to 1818, the British won a number of important battles, but these did not conform to the image of Western warfare in terms of defensive firepower bringing down attacking numbers, the position at Plassey. Instead, as in the American victories over the Creeks at Fallen Timbers and Horseshoe Bend (1814), and also with the Russian operational mode against the Ottomans developed by Count Peter Rumyantsev and used by him with great success in 1770, the emphasis was on the operational offensive and the tactical attack, and the use of bayonet charges as well as firepower was of importance. It is difficult to produce a comparative weighting of firepower and bayonet charges, both because of a lack of information (and research), and also due to the very confused nature of some battles, especially Arthur Wellesley's victory over the Marathas at Assaye in 1803. The attack was important there, as it also was in Wellesley's victory over the Marathas at Argaon (Argaum) in 1803, Lake's victory over them at Farruckhabad in 1804, and Malcolm's victory over the Marathas at Mahidpur in 1817.

British tactics, based on firing once or twice and then charging, had had an impact in India from mid-century. On the battlefield, speedy infantry attack helped compensate for numerical inferiority, while at the operational level, it was only through the use of the offensive that the British could hope to counter the Maratha cavalry.[43] The attack in the shape of storming was also important in the British capture of fortified positions, such as the Mysore capital Seringapatam in 1799, the Maratha fortresses of Alegarh and Gawilgarh in 1803, and, in the East Indies, the Sultan of Yogyakarta's *kraton* (royal residence) in 1812.

This might simply suggest that Western military superiority has to be considered in a wider fashion – to encompass offensive as well as defensive conflict. But this approach is complicated first by the quality of the Maratha cannon (and the skilful and brave nature of its use[44]), and second, by the non-military weaknesses of the Marathas, which compromised their effectiveness. Weakened by serious divisions, the Marathas suffered from a weak command structure and from a lack of money that hit discipline and control, just as divisions among Britain's opponents had helped in the conquest of Bengal.[45]

The latter point directs attention to the wide range of factors at issue. The British may well, as has been argued, have benefited from the degree to which they were less willing than earlier conquerors to absorb Indian political and military values.[46] The British administrative goals and methods certainly seem to have been different from those of Indian states,[47] and it has been argued that, in the case of Mysore, the Marathas and the Sikhs, there was an 'inherent weakness . . . that seriously impeded their efforts at adopting the Western military system . . . for all of these powers were essentially feudal in origin and had very little time to make the transition to a stable monarchy with a centralized bureaucracy', while the British were able 'to adapt and innovate on the basis of a vastly superior organizational and governmental infrastructure'.[48]

It is important, however, to be wary of judgements that assume a ready superiority in Western governmental systems as a result of fiscal demands generating institutional development, a point that emerges in comparative discussion of Europe and China.[49] Indeed, the East India Company was nearly bankrupted by the campaigns of 1803–4, recalled Richard Wellesley, the Governor-General, and sought peace with the Marathas. This is a reminder of the role of competing interests and ideas in the formulation of policy, in short of the dynamic nature of strategic culture. British territorial gains in India coincided with the declining influence of the East India Company vis-à-vis the British government and parliament. In the late seventeenth century, Sir Josiah Child, a key figure in the East India Company, argued against the building of fortresses on the grounds that they would frighten off local traders and thus be harmful to trade. In the early nineteenth century, in contrast, there was an emphasis on seizing territory. In the absence of a systematic comparative study of Britain and the other Indian powers, and indeed of Britain's Indian wars in the period, it is rash to make statements about military or governmental effectiveness or superiority, for example the claim that the greater continuity and institutional stability of the Company than those of native rulers was crucial to its military success.[50] The results were notable, but the causes are less clear.

Assessing effectiveness

For all major powers, success owed much to sensible tasking, the ability to adapt in response to challenges, as well as logistical capability and skill in managing combined arms operations. The role of chance, serendipity and opportunism, as well as of stupidity and the fear of making, or of appearing to make, mistakes, should, however, be considered more often in the outcome of battles and wars: human traits, rather than military skills or equipment, may be the key elements in the outcome. Europeans faced major disadvantages in meeting requirements for success when operating outside their homelands, although these could be lessened by winning local support, as, very importantly, with Cortes in Mexico and, on a longer timespan, the British in India: for example, in 1774, the British destroyed the Rohilla state in co-operation with Awadh.

To this example can be added the role of winning local support in the successes of the Mughals in India, the Manchu in China and a host of other non-Westerners, providing a reminder that there was no clear analytical division between Westerners and non-Westerners. Indeed the willingness to seek acquiescence in conquest, or at least co-operation with the creation of a new hegemony, was crucial to success, both Western and non-Western. In its absence, conquest could be reversed: Ming Chinese forces conquered Dai Viet in 1407, but were driven out two decades later. The ability of Dai Viet to acquire firearms capability to match that of the Ming was important, but so also was the political situation.

This approach is far removed from the usual stress on weaponry, specifically infantry firearms, but, aside from the problem that that approach mistakenly equates war with fighting, the focus on weaponry provides only limited guidance to military, and even battlefield, capability. More specifically, it underrates the continued importance of cavalry, and, in particular, first of horse-archers and then of cavalrymen armed with firearms.[51] Infantry gunpowder weaponry brought only so much change because, rather than a transformation of tactics or operational assumptions, there was often an attempt to use new weapons to give added force to existing practices, which were, in part, a response to social norms. Across the world, the notion of effectiveness was framed and applied in terms of dominant cultural and social patterns. The analysis latent in most military history that assumes some mechanistic search for efficiency and a maximization of force driven by a form of Social Darwinism, does violence to the complex process by which interests in new methods interacted with powerful elements of continuity, as well as the manner in which efficiency was culturally constructed, and the lack of clarity as to what defined effectiveness in force structure, operational method, or tactics. All of these are topics that require research, but for this period the key point is that techno-logical change was an enabler of attitudes and policies, rather than the driving force of modernity.

The weakness of the technologically driven account is shown by the most important conquest of the seventeenth century, that of Ming China by the Manchu. Nothing in the Western world compared to its scale or drama; there is something strange about the standard account of world military history with its heavy emphasis on the Thirty Years' War in Europe (1618–48) and its near total avoidance of the contemporaneous conquest of China – a point that can be repeated for the subsequent centuries, with the relative neglect of the Chinese defeat of the Dzungars in the 1750s, the Taiping rising in the 1850s–60s, and the Chinese Civil War in the late 1940s. The Manchu triumph was a victory for cavalry over the then military system of warfare of China, with its emphasis on positional warfare; and also a victory in which political factors, in the shape of a lack of Chinese unity, were important.[52]

A linear concept of military history[53] might see this as another triumph for barbarians and thus an anachronistic development that does not deserve subsequent scholarly attention. But this approach to cavalry-dominated systems is a mistaken one that is flawed by its assump-tion of a unitary model and a pattern of linear development, which is an aspect of the more general problem of the questionable application of modern criteria about effectiveness.[54] There is also an implicit racial stereotyping at work, which indeed bedevils much of military history and contributes to the Eurocentricity that is a serious problem.

Thus, the history of this period invites an explicit engagement with methodological issues, especially putting aside Western paradigms. Alongside the spreading role of firearms in, for example, eighteenth-century Madagascar, it is necessary to note campaigns and battles where firearms were far from decisive. Thus, at Amed Ber in 1787, an Abyssinian (Ethiopian) army equipped with cannon and thousands of muskets was defeated by the cavalry of the Yejju. By then, however, the world was changing. The Chinese victory over the Dzungars in the 1750s and the Russian conquest of the Crimea in 1783 showed that this was not simply a matter of the rise of the Atlantic powers. Instead, it is necessary to address cross-cultural comparisons and contrasts, while at the same time moving away from the mistake of assuming that the period can be read as a whole, and, furthermore, that knowledge of what was to come helps to establish relative capability and that that can then be used to explain success. Even more is this the case if war is understood as an attempt to enforce will, with battle treated as an important aspect of it (at least generally), but as in no way coterminous with conflict.

The last invites attention to the capacity of different systems for engendering and sustaining syncreticism, or at least winning or buying co-operation.[55] This issue is not separate from European military history: alongside the victories of Louis XIV of France (r. 1643–1715), it is necessary to consider the way in which conquered provinces, such as Artois and Franche-Comté, were assimilated, and the same was true for Peter the Great of Russia with Estonia and Livonia. Conversely, in the sixteenth century the disruptive political consequences of the Protestant Reformation was an important reason why state formation based on political incorporation did not work for the Habsburgs in early modern Europe. It was no accident that Spain was able to re-create its power and authority in Italy, where Protestantism scarcely existed, after its position there was challenged in the 1640s, but earlier had no comparable success in the Low Countries where Protestantism was far stronger. Such a point helps make military history an aspect of total history, and other branches of history an aspect of military studies. That, indeed, is the correct conclusion.

Notes

1 J.R. Hale, 'Printing and Military Culture of Renaissance Venice', *Medievalia et Humanistica*, 8 (1977), pp. 21–62; C. Wilkinson, 'Renaissance Treatises on Military Architecture and the Science of Mechanics', in J. Guillaume (ed.), *Les Traités d'architecture de la Renaissance* (Paris, 1988), pp. 467–76; H. Kleinschmidt, *Tyrocinium Militare. Militärische Körperhaltungen*

und- bewegungen im Wandel zwischen dem 14. und dem 18. Jahrhundert (Stuttgart, 1989).

2 J.R. Mulryne and M. Shewring, *War, Literature and the Arts in Sixteenth-Century Europe* (New York, 1989); S. Anglo (ed.), *Chivalry in the Renaissance* (Woodbridge, 1990); J.R. Hale, *Artists and Warfare in the Renaissance* (New Haven, Connecticut, 1990); M. Murrin, *History and Warfare in Renaissance Epic* (Chicago, 1994); S. Anglo, *The Martial Arts of Renaissance Europe* (New Haven, 2000).

3 K. Chase, *Firearms. A Global History to 1700* (Cambridge, 2003), p. 197. See, however, the review by Harald Kleinschmidt, *Journal of Military History*, 68 (2004), pp. 242–3.

4 M. Khodarkovsky, *Where Two Worlds Met. The Russian State and the Kalmyk Nomads, 1600–1771* (Ithaca, 1992), p. 49.

5 For an attempt to offer a different account, J.M. Black, *War. Past, Present and Future* (Stroud, 2000) and *War. An Illustrated World History* (Stroud, 2003).

6 Though see R.W. Olson, *The Siege of Mosul and Ottoman–Persian Relations 1718–1743. A Study of Rebellion in the Capital and War in the Provinces of the Ottoman Empire* (Bloomington, Indiana, 1975).

7 S. Turnbull, *Samurai Invasion* (2000).

8 Though see A.C. Hess, 'The Evolution of the Ottoman Seaborne Empire in the Age of Oceanic Discoveries, 1453–1525', *American Historical Review*, 75 (1970), pp. 1892–1919; and P. Brummett, *Ottoman Seapower and Levantine Diplomacy in the Age of Discovery* (Albany, New York, 1994).

9 P.C. Perdue, 'Military Mobilization in Seventeenth and Eighteenth Century China, Russia, and Mongolia', *Modern Asian Studies* (1996).

10 D. Christian, *Maps of Time. An Introduction to Big History* (Berkeley, 2004).

11 S. Chaudhury and M. Morineau (eds), *Merchants, Companies and Trade: Europe and Asia in the Early Modern Era* (Cambridge, 1999).

12 A.J. Smithers, *The Tangier Campaign. The Birth of the British Army* (Stroud, 2003).

13 A. Crosby, *The Columbian Exchange: Biological and Cultural Consequences of 1492* (Westport, Conn., 1969).

14 L.D. Kessler, *K'ang-hsi and the Consolidation of Ch'ing Rule, 1661–1684* (Chicago, 1976).

15 D.H. Peers (ed.), *Warfare and Empires: Contact and Conflict Between European and Non-European Military and Maritime Forces and Cultures* (Aldershot, 1997), p. xviii.

16 M. Restall, *Seven Myths of the Spanish Conquest* (Oxford, 2003), p. 143.

17 B.L. Walker, *The Conquest of Ainu Lands: Ecology and Culture in Japanese Expansion 1590–1800* (Berkeley, California, 2001), pp. 27–47.

18 E. Ingram, *Commitment to Empire: Prophecies of the Great Game in Asia, 1797–1800* (Oxford, 1981); P. Mackesy, *War Without Victory. The Downfall of Pitt, 1799–1802* (Oxford, 1984), esp. pp. 144–7; S. Förster, *Die mächtigen Diener der East India Company. Ursachen und Hintergründe der britischen Expansionspolitik in Südasien, 1793–1819* (Stuttgart, 1992).

19 M.E. Yapp, *Strategies of British India: Britain, Iran and Afghanistan 1798–1850* (Oxford, 1980).

20 L. Lockhart, 'Nadir Shah's Campaigns in Oman, 1734–1744', *Bulletin of the School of Oriental and African Studies*, 8 (1935–7), pp. 157–73.

21 T.F. Arnold, 'War in Sixteenth-Century Europe: Revolution and Renaissance', in J. Black (ed.), *European Warfare 1453–1815* (Basingstoke, 1999), pp. 41–4.

22 W. Robertson, *History of the Reign of the Emperor Charles V* (1769; 1782 edn) I, 134–5.

23 R. Murphey, 'The Ottoman Resurgence in the Seventeenth-Century Mediterranean: the Gamble and its Results', *Mediterranean Historical Review*, 8 (1993), pp. 198–200; K.M. Seton, *Venice, Austria and the Turks in the Seventeenth Century* (Philadelphia, 1991).

24 L. Blussé, 'The Dutch occupation of the Pescadores (1622–1624)', *Transactions of the International Conference of Orientalists in Japan*, 18 (1973), pp. 28–43; C.R. Boxer, 'The Siege of Fort Zeelandia and the Capture of Formosa from the Dutch, 1661–2', *Transactions and Proceedings of the Japan Society of London*, 24 (1926–7), pp. 16–47.

25 R.D. Bathurst, 'Maritime Trade and Imamate Government: Two Principal Themes in the History of Oman to 1728', in D. Hopwood (ed.), *The Arabian Peninsula. Society and Politics* (1972), pp. 99–103.

26 C.R. Boxer and C. de Azvedo, *Fort Jesus and the Portuguese in Mombasa 1593–1729* (1960), pp. 59–73, 81–3.

27 M. Malgonkar, *Kanhoji Angrey, Maratha Admiral* (Bombay, 1959), p. 17.

28 M. Vergé-Franceschi and A.-M. Graziani (eds), *La Guerre de Course en Méditerranée, 1515–1830* (Ajaccio, 2000).

29 D.F. Allen, 'Charles II, Louis XIV and the Order of Malta', *European History Quarterly*, 20 (1990), pp. 323–40.

30 L.R. Wright, 'Piracy in the Southeast Asian Archipelago', *Journal of Oriental Studies*, 14 (1976), pp. 23–33; B. Sandin, *The Sea Dayaks of Borneo: Before White Rajah Rule* (1967).

31 R. Tregaskis, *The Warrior King: Hawaii's Kamehameha the Great* (New York, 1973).

32 A.-C. Hess, 'The Ottoman Conquest of Egypt and the Beginning of the Sixteenth Century World War', *International Journal of Middle East Studies*, 4 (1973), pp. 55–76.

33 T.J. Barfield, *The Perilous Frontier: Nomadic Empires and China, 221 BC to AD 1757* (Oxford, 1989).

34 A. Burton, *The Bukharans. A Dynastic, Diplomatic and Commercial History, 1550–1702* (New York, 1997), p. 117.

35 C. Finkel, *The Administration of Warfare: Ottoman Campaigns in Hungary, 1593–1606* (Vienna, 1988), p. 309.

36 The key work is David Parrott's excellent *Richelieu's Army. War, Government and Society in France, 1624–1642* (Oxford, 2001). See also J.M. Black, *European Warfare, 1494–1660* (2002) and *Kings, Nobles and Commoners. States and Societies in Early Modern Europe. A Revisionist History* (2004).

37 See, in particular, M. Roberts, *The Military Revolution, 1560–1660* (Belfast, 1956).

38 G. Pagès, *Le Grand Électeur et Louis XIV 1660–1688* (Paris, 1905), p. 16.

39 Newcastle to Charles, Second Viscount Townshend, Secretary of State for the Northern Department, 27 June 1729, PRO. State Papers 43/78.

40 G. Parker, 'Random Thoughts of a Hedgehog', *Historical Speaking*, 4, 4 (2003), pp. 13–14.

41 B.D. Steele, 'Muskets and Pendulums: Benjamin Robins, Leonhard Euler, and the Ballistics Revolution', *Technology and Culture*, 35 (1994), p. 354.

42 E. Chew, 'Militarized Cultures in Collision. The Arms Trade and War in the Indian Ocean during the Nineteenth Century', *RUSI Journal*, 148, no. 5 (Oct. 2003), p. 91.

43 J. Weller, *Wellington in India* (1972), pp. 275–6.

44 R.G.S. Cooper and N.K. Wagle, 'Maratha artillery: from Dalhoi to Assaye', *Journal of the Ordnance Society*, 7 (1995).

45 S. Gordon, *Marathas, Marauders and State Formation in Eighteenth-Century India* (Delhi, 1994); R.G.S. Cooper, 'Wellington and the Marathas in 1803', *International History Review*, 11 (1989), pp. 36–8, and *The Anglo–Maratha Campaigns and the Contest for India. The Struggle for Control of the South Asian Military Economy* (Cambridge, 2003). See also, D.D. Khanna (ed.), *The Second Maratha Campaign, 1804–1805: Diary of James Young, Officer Bengal Horse Artillery* (New Delhi, 1990); K.G. Pitre, *The Second Anglo–Maratha War, 1802–1805* (Poona, 1990); A.S. Bennell, *The Making of Arthur Wellesley* (1997).

46 C.A. Bayly, 'The British military-fiscal state and indigenous resistance. India 1750–1820', in L. Stone (ed.), *An Imperial State at War. Britain from 1689 to 1815* (1994), pp. 324–49; S. Alavi, *The Sepoys and the Company. Tradition and Transition in Northern India 1770–1830* (Delhi, 1995), p. 4.

47 S. Sen, *Empire of Free Trade. The East India Company and the Making of the Colonial Marketplace* (Philadelphia, 1998).

48 P. Barua, 'Military Developments in India, 1750–1850', *Journal of Military History*, 58 (1994), p. 616.

49 R. Bin Wong, *China Transformed: Historical Change and the Limits of European Experience* (Ithaca, New York, 1997); K. Pomeranz, *The Great Divergence: China, Europe and the Making of the Modern World Economy* (Berkeley, California, 1999).

50 J. Lynn, *Battle* (2003), p. 176.

51 J. Gommans, 'Indian Warfare and Afghan Innovation during the Eighteenth Century', *Studies in History*, 11 (1995), pp. 271–3, and *The Rise of the Indo-Afghan Empire c.1710–1780* (Leiden, 1995); G.J. Bryant, 'The Military Imperative in Early British Expansion in India, 1750–1785', *Indo-British Review*, 21, 2 (1996), p. 32.

52 F. Wakeman, *The Great Enterprise. The Manchu Reconstruction of Imperial Order in Seventeenth-Century China* (2 vols, Berkeley, 1985).

53 Barton Hackler has referred to 'the common view of a straight-line historical development from the Greeks to us', *World Military History Bibliography. Premodern and Nonwestern Military Institutions and Warfare* (Leiden, 2003), p. ix.

54 K. DeVries, 'Catapults Are Not Atomic Bombs: Towards a Redefinition of "Effectiveness" in Premodern Military Technology', *War in History*, 4 (1997), pp. 475–91.

55 For example, B. Ganson, *The Guaraní under Spanish Rule in the Río de la Plata* (Palo Alto, California, 2003).

Chapter 7

1775–1918

> Your Lordship's words express, exactly, what is required at this moment: 'The thing I am most anxious about is the recovery of our military reputation in Afghanistan by some decisive success'. *That* is the one thing necessary.
>
> Major-General Charles Napier to Lord Ellenborough,
> Governor-General of India, 1842[1]

The chronological overlap between this chapter and the previous one is instructive for a number of reasons. First, it serves as an important reminder that chronological divides are artificial constructions, produced for analytical purpose, and that there is a danger that these divides will be used in pursuit of a misleading degree of abstraction. Second, the divides relate in part to the analytical practice and problem of modernity. The standard narrative of military history assumes the dual analytical strands of a move toward the modern, and modernization: goal and process being interrelated. Thus, chronological divisions are employed in order to record this process. The Middle Ages, which are seen in terms of limited progress, are divided from the modern by discussion of the major changes that are held to have ushered in the latter, establishing, as they did, what has subsequently been separated out as the early modern period.

If, in terms of the culture of Western military perception, modernity is identified with the gunpowder age described in the previous century, then that, however, does not offer a sufficient account of modernity to cover the last half-millennium. First, gunpowder weaponry was not a Western monopoly, and, in so far as a crucial aspect of modernity was Western control, the introduction of such weaponry could not provide a sufficient explanation for this on a global scale, although it could (however mistakenly) be employed with reference to the demise of the Aztec and Inca empires, neither of which deployed troops armed with gunpowder weapons.

Second, the very idea of gunpowder warfare itself as modern appeared increasingly less credible. Here, a crucial indicator was the standpoint of the observer. In the eighteenth and nineteenth centuries, particularly the first two-thirds of the latter, it was possible to see gunpowder warfare as modern, because the resulting weapons, tactics and operational methods did not seem very different from those of the contemporary world. This was particularly so at the tactical level and with the focus on the battlefield, which indeed received the bulk of attention. Even after the introduction of railway and telegraph, with the enhanced capability they offered operationally, logistically, and for command and control, battles continued to be dominated by blocks of troops, deployed in close-packed formations, whether line or column, and relying on firepower or striking power delivered in mass, with this mass achieved by density. In many respects, this was not too different from the combats of the Italian Wars (1494–1559) or the Thirty Years' War (1618–48). At sea, the extent to which steam power and iron ships might have changed the nature of naval warfare by c.1865 was unclear due to the paucity of naval battles over the previous decade.

The situation both on land and at sea changed, however, when the perspective was affected by the developments in warfare from the last third of the nineteenth century. At sea, the battles of the Sino–Japanese (1894–95) and, even more, Russo–Japanese (1904–5) wars revealed the extent of development in the destructiveness of naval gunnery. Far more significantly, the combined impact, over the following half century, of submarines and air power suggested a fundamental change in naval capability and in the tactical, operational and strategic aspects of naval power. As a consequence, the world of substantial fleets of large wooden warships, each with a heavy gunnery, that in the period 1793–1815 had seemed the acme of economic strength and organizational effectiveness, now appeared quaint, and certainly not modern. This was far more the case with the perception of the fleets and naval warfare of the sixteenth century.

On land, again, the changes from the mid 1860s to 1914, including the 'emptier' battlefield that apparently stemmed from a decline in the massing of forces, paled into apparent insignificance beside the major changes that were to come over the following half century. As a consequence, again, from the modern perspective, and whether it was that of the period 1860s–1914 or, even more, so 1914 on, the warfare of the early modern period appeared far from modern. As a result, it was historicized, a process that particularly happened to the conflicts of the Seven Years War (1756–63) and the French Revolutionary and Napoleonic Wars (1792–1815), which in the mid-nineteenth century had both, though especially the latter, still appeared full of contemporary relevance.

Creating the past

The process of historicizing did not only affect recent centuries. There was also a more defined chronology of military history, with the earliest book-length studies of medieval warfare as a distinct entity dating from the late nineteenth century: Germain Demay's *Le Costume de guerre et d'apparat d'après les sceaux du moyen-âge* (Paris, 1875), Charles Oman's *The Art of War in the Middle Ages, 378–1515* (Oxford, 1885), Paul Serre's *Les Marines de Guerre de l'antiquité et du moyen âge* (Paris, 1885–91) and Hans Delbrück's *Die Perserkriege und die Burgunderkriege* (Berlin, 1887); while Theodore Dodge's *Gustavus Adolphus. A History of the Art of War from its Revival after the Middle Ages* (Boston, 1895) suggested that there had been a major change since the Middle Ages.[2] These books about medieval warfare coincided with the beginnings of the scientific investigation of arms and armours: the study of examples in collections, rather than the uncritical acceptance of iconography. In *Ancient Armour and Weapons in Europe: from the Iron period of the Northern Nations to the end of the seventeenth century* (London, 1855–60) and *Dictionnaire raisonné du mobilier français* (Paris, 1874), John Hewitt and Eugène Viollet-le-Duc were the first to write about form and construction of arms and armour, while in *Handbuch der Waffenkunde* (Vienna, 1890), Wendelin Boeheim, drawing on sixteenth-century usage, identified different styles, or schools, of armour.

This process of historicizing left unclear, however, how best to assess and date modernity, and indeed, to treat what was seen as an early modern period. In terms of the battlefield, the modern was now located far more closely to the contemporary observer; sometimes indeed to the use of tanks and aircraft in the Allied offensives on the Western Front in 1918. Certainly, the conflicts of the period 1500–1815 no longer seemed modern, and this was underlined in 1985 when Arthur Ferrill discussed how Alexander the Great could have beaten the British at Waterloo, an ironic commentary on the apparent timelessness of conflict between the two periods, Ferrill conceded that the Classical world had lacked firearms, but he argued that the effectiveness of the latter in 1815 was not a quantum leap greater than those of the projectiles of the Classical period: arrows, spears and slings.[3] Visually, Napoleon was no longer perceived as modern, but rather, with the armoured breastplates of his cuirassiers gleaming in the sun, as a quasi-medieval figure – an impression enhanced by the paintings of Napoleonic combat, such as those of Antoine Jean Gros (1771–1835), who had travelled with Napoleon's armies, with their emphasis on bravery and glamour but certainly not the machine.[4] Cannon did not play a major role in these illustrations.

Chronological boundaries

Thus, from the perspective of the chronological delimitation in this book, it appears appropriate to group the French Revolutionary and Napoleonic period with the early days of mass–gunpowder warfare. Indeed, a case could be made for putting the Crimean War (1854–6) in the same chapter, and the Austro–French conflict of 1859 with the battles of Solferino and Magenta, as well as the bulk of the American Civil War (1861–5); before the last stage of that war in Virginia, especially the siege of Petersburg (1864–5), apparently ushered in the modern age of warfare. In technological terms, certainly, Waterloo (1815) was closer to the battle of Pavia (1525) than to that of Kursk (1943). Furthermore, if technology is understood not primarily from the perspective of the battlefield but as a more complex process of development, of which weaponry is but one aspect, then in so far as a 'big bang' is being sought, it occurred after 1815. The rapid introduction of railway locomotives, steamships and telegraphs (and, in terms of weapons, the Minié rifle and improved artillery) were all far more important than what had occurred in the forty years prior to 1815. The earlier period had witnessed innovations, but neither the submarine, the balloon, the use of the rocket in the West, nor the semaphore, had led to fundamental changes.

Yet, an overlap chronologically is appropriate because many late twentieth-century commentators found important signs of the onset of modernity – if not modern war – in the period 1792–1815, and indeed earlier, during the War of American Independence (1775–83). In particular, there was an emphasis on a social dimension of modernity. Modern war was seen as requiring the mobilization of society, and to be effective, this mobilization was seen as needing a degree of popular commitment that distinguished it from earlier warfare. From this perspective, the *levée en masse* ordered by the French Revolutionaries in 1794 appeared the outset of modern war. This commitment was seen as a strategic, operational and tactical enabler: strategic in that it permitted Revolutionary France to wage protracted warfare against a large number of opponents for years, a process continued by Napoleon; operational in that it was possible to campaign on the offensive in a number of directions simultaneously, particularly in Italy and north of the Alps; and tactically in that it was possible to mount attacks using columns. The last was seen as crucial, both in terms of attacking formation and offensive tactic, in overcoming the linear defensive formations of *ancien régime* warfare. Aside from winning victory on the battlefield, this was regarded as important to a high-tempo operational practice of seizing and using the initiative that was presented as central to Napoleonic victory.

In this argument, Napoleon lost when other governments were able to mobilize their societies to match the energy released by the French Revolution, especially with the German War of Liberation in 1813. Furthermore, Napoleonic France had earlier been successfully opposed by Britain and by the Spanish resistance because both had enjoyed popular support.

In addition, just as the last stage of the American Civil War was seen as an anticipation of World War One, so the American War of Independence was presented as an anticipation of the popular commitment of the French Revolutionary War. The War of Independence was similarly held to have provided the basis for a new warfare that thwarted its *ancien régime* predecessor in the shape of British regular forces. In this case, as so often, military capability was understood in terms of position along a clear linear process of progress.

Much of this analysis still holds sway, particularly, though not only, in popular accounts; but it is ripe for re-examination. This comes from a number of directions, both empirical and conceptual. In the case of the former, work on the warfare of the 1790s has suggested that the fighting quality and success of the *ancien régime* forces, in particular of the Austrian army, have been underrated,[5] while there has also been a re-consideration of the use of the column by the French and of its effectiveness as part of a more searching assessment of the French Revolutionary armies. Conceptually, there is also room for considerable disquiet about the assumptions underlying the conventional account, particularly the linear nature of progress and the clear-cut definition of modern warfare in terms of total war.

The latter brings us to the issue of present-mindedness, because to argue that modern war is no longer defined by the total conflict of World

War Two and the apocalyptic confrontation of the Cold War, but, rather, by more limited struggles, is to risk the response that the latter are simply, or at least possibly, a stage between more major conflicts. Nevertheless, at the very least, the situation since 1990 opens the way to a reconsideration of what is understood as modern war, and thus provides a new perspective on the chronological delimitation of earlier periods, in particular on the placing of 1775–1815. One crucial limitation of modern warfare, the widespread move away from conscription, is particularly significant for the last, as it makes attempts to raise large numbers of men through such systems, such as those seen during the Napoleonic period,[6] appear far from an anticipation of the present.

Last, at the global level, it is far from clear how best to consider the period 1775–1815. At one level it was a continuation of the early modern period discussed in the previous chapter; as yet, there were not the formidable developments in communications, in the shape of the ocean-going steamship and the telegraph, that later permitted the economic and organizational integration of the world on Western terms and thus fostered the imperialism of the second half of the nineteenth century. From this perspective, the earlier Western conquest of Australasia from 1788, or British success in India from 1798, is a matter of more-of-the-same, not a quantum leap forward. If, however, an accretional, rather than a big-bang, approach is taken, then it is possible to treat 1775–1815 as indeed a period of overlap: one sharing characteristics with what came earlier and later. If the emphasis is on the transformation of military organization, then it is also important to note important changes in France from the late 1760s, especially the development of a divisional system.[7]

Which narrative?

Western ideas of progress dominate the conventional assessment of the period covered by this chapter. The notion of the development of a more effective killing and controlling machine as constituting progress was one that most contemporaries were happy to accept – unlike the more divided situation today. Furthermore, there was no doubt that a monopolization of force by the state was seen as modernity. The standard narrative of military history for this period focuses on conflicts between Western conventional forces: the French Revolutionary and Napoleonic Wars, the Crimean War, the Wars of German and Italian Unification, and the American Civil War, closing with, first, developments that led to World War One and prefigured aspects of that conflict, and then with World War One itself. This focus displaces attention from two other narratives: first, conflict between Western and non-Western forces, and second, warfare between the latter. The reasons for this neglect lay in part in the analysis that accompanies the standard narrative, an analysis focused on proficiency understood in terms of relative effectiveness within the Western system – in short, a stress on the paradigm power or, at least, system. Having considered the Austrian and French armies in the half-century after Waterloo, the emphasis switches to the Prussian. Thus, the Austro–Prussian War of 1866 and the Franco–Prussian War of 1870–1 are seen as centrepieces of narrative importance and analytical weight.

As a result, there has been an attempt to work back to find causes from effects; and the varied character of the causes found tell us much about shifting interests in military history. Thus, in place of the earlier stress in the discussion of Prussian victory on weapons and railroads,[8] has come a more recent reassessment of the organizational culture of the Prussian military in terms of the understanding and application of power. Applied knowledge has recently been emphasized as a key element in Prussian success. In *Moltke and the German Wars* (Basingstoke, 2001) Arden Bucholz argued that Prussian war-making became more effective because Moltke the Elder, Chief of the General Staff from 1857 to 1888, made Prussian war planning a modern knowledge process that his opponents lacked. In particular, he claimed that Moltke interjected the concept of risk, and was able to define and manage risk based upon size, space, time, and technology. This skill rested on thorough planning: war games and strategic memos described a series of linked observations about the state of the war at some predetermined future time, and a series of counterfactuals were constructed and then criticized. This process also helped speed up response times.

The stress on Prussia, which from 1871 is usually referred to as Germany, is less convincing on the global scale. In part, this is because German warfare is misleadingly treated as a paradigm of Western warfare. In fact, to take the 1860s, a comparison of the Wars of German Unification, the American Civil War, and contemporaneous conflicts in Latin America – civil wars in Mexico (1857–60, 1862–7), the Paraguayan War (1864–70) and the War of the Pacific (1879–84) – indicate the variety of warfare and the weakness of attempts to use the paradigmatic approach. The employment of similar weaponry did not result in similar usage, not least because of the role of specific political, economic, social, and geographical contexts, and the way they moulded the particular strategic, organizational and social cultures of conflict.

For European states, the central narrative on the global scale was of the unprecedented projection of Western power, in which conflict had the unintended effect of entwining hitherto separated societies more deeply. This is not, however, a subject that has attracted sufficient attention in the standard narrative of military history, in part because neither Austria nor Prussia were at the forefront of extra-European imperial expansion, but, more seriously, because this has seemed less worthy of attention. Indeed, although there is much excellent work on imperial warfare, there has been an assumption of the inevitability of Western expansion, and thus that the major subject for analysis is of the changing distribution of power within the West.

The intra-Western and Western–non-Western approaches can be brought together by an emphasis on military-industrialization. This had a variety of aspects, including the mass-production of weaponry and the development of communication and logistical systems focused on telegraph, steamship and railway. In the Crimean War, Thomas Molyneux Graves wrote from the Anglo–French siege of the Russian fortress of Sevastopol in 1854: '. . . a few days will show an immense number of guns in battery and when our fire opens it will be tremendous . . . now I am so accustomed to the noise that I believe I could go to sleep in a battery when the enemy were firing at it'.[9]

The effect of the development of enhanced communication and logistical systems was to provide interacting force multipliers. These, however, also created major problems for effectiveness: the potential gap between well- and poorly-structured and commanded militaries grew, as it became necessary to consider how best to adopt, and to adapt to, new systems. Indeed, the modern military age began as 'fit for purpose' ceased to be a state that changed episodically and instead became both high-tempo and continuous. This had not been adequately anticipated by military commentators writing earlier in the century. Clausewitz and Jomini, the two most prominent, addressed the changes stemming from the mobilization of society seen with the French Revolution and the German War of Liberation in 1813, and also, a different point, from the high-tempo offensive war-making developed by Napoleon. Both were indeed important, but neither commentator devoted equivalent attention to the technological changes and, in part, industrialization of war that began in their lifetime but became more insistent and incessant thereafter.

Industrialization is indeed helpful in explaining European relative capability and power projection. This was the case on the battlefield, more famously described in Hillaire Belloc's couplet from *The Modern Traveller* (1898): 'Whatever happens, we have got/ The Maxim Gun; and they have not'; in logistics and communication, as with the steamships that sped troops as far as New Zealand; and with aspects of the rationale for expansion, especially the economic opportunities that seemed more tempting with a world economy that was increasingly integrated.[10] As with the situation within the West, discussed earlier in the chapter, the crucial period of change was the second half of the century. This was true of all the factors just cited, from the battlefield, where flintlocks were replaced by single-shot breech-loaders and then by repeating firearms, to the shipyards.[11]

While the stress on industrialization indeed focuses on important aspects of relative Western capability, it also distracts from other aspects of Western expansion. In particular, there is an emphasis on the Western 'push' rather than on the non-Western response, and linked to that, an 'expeditionary' approach to conquest: one that puts more of a stress on force projection and battle than on the processes by which control was ensured or, to employ a fashionable term, negotiated. An important military consequence of the latter was that many colonies became important sources of manpower,[12] with additional consequences for the military culture of imperial forces.[13]

Aside from rethinking the period on its own terms, it is appropriate to re-consider it in terms of more recent developments. Consideration of the current situation invites a shift of attention from the habit of treating the world as an isotropic plane, under the sway of the dominant military system, to a consideration of the complexities of military capability and warfare, and the problems this poses for all states and militaries, both Western and non-Western. This offers a perspective for approaching the clarity of much of the narrative of the 'rise' of the West, with its analytical focus on the triumphs of advanced industrial technology. Furthermore, this account appears more problematic as the age of Western colonial empire recedes, and its brevity appears more apparent. Instead, it is more important to consider Western victories within their political context, which frequently was an enabling one. For example, Anglo–French success against China in 1860 owed much to the weaknesses resulting from Chinese disunity in the shape of the large-scale civil war stemming from the Taiping rebellion.

Whatever the deficiencies in the treatment of Western expansion, they are as nothing to the standard neglect of conflict between non-Western forces. Indeed, as far as the 'non-West' is concerned, there is a unifying narrative in the shape of the adoption of Western weaponry and military methods, with an emphasis on Japan. Thus, the independent survival of non-Western powers is linked to their willingness and ability to adopt and adapt, and this factor is also used to create a hierarchy with, for example, Japan more effective and successful than China. The success of Ethiopia, the sole African country to resist Western control (it was not conquered until 1936), in repelling Italian attack in 1896 is in part related to the use of Western weaponry at the battle of Adua. The Japanese and Turks turned to Britain for naval advice, while as an indicator of relative capability, in 1910 Germany was able to sell Turkey superannuated warships.[14]

This approach is clearly important, but it is also insufficient. Among the problems is a running together of the entire century, which leads to an exaggeration of the importance of adoption and adaptation: prior to 1850 they were considerably less important, particularly in East Asia and sub-Saharan Africa, than they were to become. Conflicts such as those with Khoja and Kokand invaders in Chinese Turkestan in 1826–7 and 1830[15] cannot be related to this narrative. Thereafter, adoption and adaptation were not the sole reasons for victory: Ethiopian success at Adua also owed much to numbers and better generalship, including good use of the terrain. As a 1906 report on the Zulus noted, the adoption of Western weaponry posed problems for existing tactical systems,[16] while, as Charles Malet observed from India about the Marathas in 1792,[17] the combined strains of adoption and adaptation could seem to pose excessive pressures for armies and associated social practices.

While the adoption and adaptation approach is of value not only for conflict between non-Western and Western forces but also for warfare among the former, it is misleading to put too much stress on weaponry and related military organization. Instead, there is a need for a thorough study of conflict between non-Western forces, which varied greatly, not least in scale and goal. Although concepts of statehood have to be employed with care, there was a major difference in goal between warfare within polities, and those which pitched polities against each other. The former included civil wars in China and Japan, with the Taiping rebellion in China the largest-scale civil war of the century.

Although conflict between non-Western forces has attracted excellent work, it is nevertheless both smaller in quantity than studies of the other two categories already discussed, and also plays a totally inadequate role in the general narrative of the period. In large part, this is because there is an assumption that the non-West was the recipient, generally unwilling, of developments elsewhere, and that changes there had no causative impact elsewhere, not least because there was no feed-back mechanism by which warfare within the West was affected by Western conflict with non-Western powers, let alone struggles between the latter. In practice, service in colonial warfare did have an effect, not least in the French army, much of which served in Algeria, while Western military observers were very interested in the lessons to be learned from the Russo–Japanese War. Japanese victory also encouraged the 'Look East' policy of Indian nationalists, while earlier the Merina dynasty in Madagascar had sought to implement the Japanese model of modernization before the advent of French colonial rule. Irrespective of this, a reconsideration of the importance of the non-Western military narrative in recent decades necessarily directs attention to this narrative in earlier periods.

The study of war

Within the West, the development of both popular and academic/ institutional military history owed much initially to the interlinked need to come to grips with the supposed lessons of Napoleonic warfare (a task made more difficult by the lack of any systematic writing on the subject by the Emperor) and to provide material for the growing emphasis on formal practices in the education of officers and commanders. The two combined to ensure the birth of modern historical scholarship, with a pronounced emphasis on discussing recent warfare.

Although Clausewitz drew inspiration from Thucydides, and, more generally, the cult of antiquity continued to influence military writing, the sway of the Classical period or, more particularly, of Classical texts, which had characterized the sixteenth, seventeenth and eighteenth centuries, was not to be repeated to the same extent. In part this was because different issues came to the fore, not least the understanding of strategy, but also because of a different attitude to the past: one in which rhythmic and cyclical patterns of rise and fall were replaced by a linear notion of development. The corollary of the latter was not to deny the value of history but to emphasize, as Clausewitz did, the recent past, and thus to slight the supposed immutable characteristics of war. Instead, a sense of specificity developed, seeing war as bounded by the characteristics of a period.

This was linked to the particular state of Western technology, which contributed to a growing interest in future warfare that in turn suggested a new way to locate war past and present.[18] That, however, was not the position immediately after the Napoleonic Wars. Then the problem appeared how to explain the nature of war and its operational and strategic potential as seen in those conflicts. The two most influential writers, as far as war on land was concerned, were Antoine-Henri de Jomini and Carl von Clausewitz. The Swiss-born Jomini (1779–1869) rose into French service through the army of the Helvetic Republic (a French client state) and became Chief of Staff to Marshal Ney. He subsequently served in the Russian army. Jomini's influential works, which included the *Traité des Grands Opérations Militaires* (1804–9) and the *Précis de l'Art de la Guerre* (1838), sought to find logical principles at work in warfare, which was seen as having timeless essential characteristics, and, in particular, to explain Napoleon's success, the central theme of his *Vie Politique et Militaire de Napoléon* (1827). For Jomini, the crucial military point was the choice of a line of operations that would permit a successful attack. Napoleonic operational art was discussed in terms of envelopment – the use of exterior lines – and of the selection of a central position that would permit the defeat in detail (separately) of opposing forces – or interior lines. This, however, was an emphasis on battle-winning, rather than on the wider military and political mobilization that Napoleon had secured. Furthermore, Jomini failed to make sufficient allowance for changing aspects of war-making, not least the tactical and wider consequences of social, economic and technological change. He offered little guidance on what was to be seen as 'total war'.

Jomini's influence was widespread, and not simply in France, which became again an active military power in the 1850s and 1860s under Napoleon III. In Britain, William Napier wrote about Jomini's ideas in the *Edinburgh Review* of 1821, while Edward Hamley, who in 1857 became the first Professor of Military History at the recently-created Staff College, published in 1866 *The Operations of War*, which owed much to Jomini. Until 1894, it was required reading for Staff College entrance. In 1891, Major-General Sir Evelyn Wood wrote to John Frederick Maurice, then a colonel, about the latter's work on war: 'I thoroughly agree with your assertion as to the value of a study of Napoleon's campaigns, in spite of the change of weapon [*sic*] which time and science have brought about'.[19]

Jomini's influence was not restricted to Europe. His *Summary of the Art of War* was published in New York in 1854 and in Philadelphia in 1862, and he was much studied at West Point, influencing many of its graduates. These included Henry Halleck, who served as Union

Commander-in-Chief in 1862–4, translated Jomini's life of Napoleon (New York, 1864), and wrote his own *Elements of Military Art and Science* (1846). This, the first major American textbook on war, was updated by Halleck with reference to recent wars; *Critical Notes on the Mexican and Crimean Wars* were added for the second (1859) and third (1862) editions.

Clausewitz (1780–1831) was a Prussian officer who had also seen service in the Russian army and, from 1818, was Director of the War Academy in Berlin. His posthumously published *Vom Kriege* (*On War*) of 1832 was initially less influential than Jomini's works, in part because it was (and is) less accessible; in addition, it was not translated into English until 1873. A poor style was accompanied by philosophy, not an approach calculated to endear it to military readers; in 1857 Wilhelm Rüstow (1821–78), a former Prussian officer then writing on military matters, claimed that 'Clausewitz is much quoted but little read'. Furthermore, Clausewitz's specific discussion of campaigns could be found wanting. For example, his criticism of Wellington's dispositions and passivity in 1815 was rejected by the Duke, who had not sought a decisive battle but rather the preservation of Allied forces in Belgium so that they could take part in concerted action against Napoleon with other, advancing Allied armies.[20] Furthermore, the subsequent scholarly analysis of Clausewitz's work has to note the degree to which his ideas developed and were not therefore consistent. Except for Book I, his work was really a collation of manuscripts assembled by his wife.

Clausewitz, however, understood better than Jomini the need to relate war and the socio-political context, and thus to assess military capability and skill in terms of political objectives, and was ready to engage with these objectives. Furthermore, Clausewitz offered a more appropriate description of conflict. He emphasized uncertainty, and therefore risk, rather than Jomini's controllable environment, and pressed the need for a continuous process of planning that could take account of the dynamic and unpredictable character of events, and the importance of an individual of genius as commander. Clausewitz saw the French Revolution as having changed war. He regarded the direction of a national will, and the mobilization of a nation's resources that it made possible, as truly potent.[21]

As the prestige of German war-making rose with Prussian victories in 1864–71, so interest in Clausewitz increased, and this was important to the development of a canon of 'classic' texts in military affairs that were not simply Classical.[22] The place of formal education in the military was increasingly seen as important to professionalization,[23] and this encouraged the development of the canon. Thus, in Argentina, the foundation of the Colegio Militar in 1870 and the Escuela Naval in 1872 was followed in 1900 by that of the Escuela Superior de Guerra, a war college for senior officers, while German military missions and equipment became important.[24] German campaigns were studied in staff colleges, as in those in the USA, where they influenced the extended order advocated in the Infantry Drill Regulations of 1891 – although, across the Western world, the tactical lessons of the battles were inadequately grasped.[25] *Kriegspiel* (war games) was introduced at the British Royal Military College in 1871. At Oxford, the University *Kriegspiel* [War-Games] Club played war games on a set of Prussian official maps for the Sadowa campaign of 1866, and its President, Hereford Brooke George, was a pioneer of military history and geography at the university.[26]

Interest in Clausewitz survived the defeat of Germany in 1918 and the destruction of her military power in 1945. Indeed, there has been a marked revival in recent years, especially in the English-speaking world, a process helped by a good translation[27] and the publication of some excellent commentary. As his works are believed to offer lessons of universal validity, there has also been a willingness to look at their role for future conflict.[28]

Jomini and Clausewitz were not the sole writers on war. Others included the Prussian general Karl Wilhelm von Willisen, whose *Theorie des grossen Krieges* (Berlin, 1840) presented Napoleon and Jomini to German readers. Scientifically analysed, war, for Willisen and others, had to be prudent and rational. Alongside theoretical reflections, there was also much work on particular episodes of military history. Thus, the German General Staff produced a large number of works (Schlieffen, the Chief of General Staff, writing on Cannae, Frederick the Great and Napoleon[29]), and used military history as an integral part of training. In the early twentieth century, the German General Staff and its affiliated researchers were still comparing battles throughout history as if they were taking place contemporaneously. They despised the work of Hans Delbrück (1848–1929), Professor at Berlin from 1881, who insisted, especially in his *Geschichte der Kriegskunst im Rahmen der politischen Geschichte* [History of the Art of War within the Framework of Political History] (1900–20), that due consideration of changes of historical conditions was essential to the analysis of military history; he also argued that the subject should not be the prerogative of the military.[30] In addition, he was opposed to the doctrine of the war of annihilation cherished by the General Staff. Dozens of doctoral dissertations emerging from the school of Delbrück in Berlin in the early-twentieth century subjected sources on major battles to critical scrutiny in accordance with the idea of *Sachkritik*. The results of such dissertations found their way into Delbrück's history of war.

Military history benefited from the general institutionalization of the study of warfare, not only in military academies but also in universities. In 1909, Spenser Wilkinson was appointed the first Professor of the History of Warfare at Oxford. Three years earlier, a desire to analyse war in order to learn lessons had led to the creation in Britain of the Historical Section of the Committee of Imperial Defence, which was instructed to produce accounts of the Boer and Russo–Japanese wars. The institutionalization of the study of warfare provided a new twist to the issue of how far theory was applied in reality: the expectation that it should be rose greatly.

The market for military history

In addition, there was work designed for a commercial market, not least in Britain, where the purchasing public was particularly extensive. The Peninsular War (1808–13) gave rise to works such as the *Atlas Militaire: Mémoires sur les opérations militaires des Français en Galice, en Portugal, et dans la Vallée du Tage en 1809* (Paris, no date), William Napier's *History of the War in the Peninsula* (1828–40), and James Wyld's *Maps and Plans, Showing the Principal Movements, Battles and Sieges, in which the British Army was Engaged during the War from 1808 to 1814 in the Spanish Peninsula* (1840). Napier's history was translated into French, Spanish, Italian, and German, and several editions and abridgements appeared in English. Napier, who had fought in the war, consulted Marshal Soult, who arranged a French translation, and also received Joseph Bonaparte's correspondence from Wellington. Napier was also involved in controversy about Sir John Moore's campaign, publishing *Observations Illustrating Sir John Moore's Campaign* (1832) in response to criticism expressed by another veteran, Moyle Sherer, in his *Popular Recollections of the Peninsula* (1823). Sherer also published a commercially-successful *Life of Wellington* (1830–2), while Napier defended his brother's campaigning in India in *The Conquest of Scinde* (1844–6) and the *History of Sir Charles Napier's Administration of Scinde and Campaign in the Cutchee Hills* (1851). The controversies that these and his Peninsular volumes aroused testified to public interest in the conflicts.

Fascination with Waterloo led to William Siborn's successful *History of the War in France and Belgium in 1815, Containing Minute Details of the Battles of Quatre Bras, Ligny, Wavre, and Waterloo* (1844). In 1830, Siborn had been instructed by Wellington, then Commander-in-Chief, to undertake the construction of a model of the battlefield at Waterloo. He did so on the basis of thorough and lengthy research, living for eight months at the farmhouse of La Haye Sainte, a key point in the battle, and produced a detailed survey of the battlefield as the basis for his model. He also consulted those who had taken part. In 1833, however, the Whig government refused to allot funds for the work, and Siborn, who had only the time that he did not need to be at work as Assistant Military Secretary in Ireland, did not finish the model until 1838. It was publicly exhibited, but Siborn did not recoup the £3,000 the model had cost. Aside from the success of his two-volume 1844 book, with its accompanying atlas, this was not, however, the end of the family's engagement with the battle. In 1891, Siborn's second son, Major-General Herbert Siborn, edited a selection from the letters his father had accumulated under the title *Waterloo Letters: A Selection from Original and hitherto Unpublished Letters bearing on the Operations of the 16th, 17th, and 18th June 1815, by Officers who served in the Campaign.*

Alongside 'top–down' campaign histories, came memoirs by the less prominent. Some of these, such as *Recollections of Rifleman Harris* (1848), have been reprinted in recent decades, which is a testimony to modern interest in this perspective. Thus, *The Subaltern* (1825), an account of service in the Peninsular campaigns of 1813–14 by George Gleig was published anew in 2001. His writing career indicated the possibilities that military history offered. Gleig (1796–1888), who became Chaplain of Chelsea Hospital in 1834 and was Chaplain-General from 1844 to 1875, published a large number of works, including *Sketch of the Military History of Great Britain* (1845), *Waterloo* (1847), *Sale's Brigade in Afghanistan* (1847), and biographies of Clive (1848) and Wellington (1862). Captain James MacCarthy's *Recollections of the Storming of the Castle of Badajos* (1836) was reproduced in facsimile with an introduction in 2002.

Alongside memoirs came war literature and other aspects of the memorialization of war. One of the most prominent figures in British popular literature of the period, Frederick Marryat (1792–1848), a veteran of the Napoleonic and First Burmese wars, made his name with *The Naval Officer or Scenes and Adventures in the Life of Frank Mildmay* (1829), a narrative of naval exploits based on his experiences, which was a tremendous literary and financial success. Other naval adventures followed, including *The King's Own* (1830) and *Peter Simple* (1834), which drew on Marryat's service in the Napoleonic wars under the daring Captain Thomas Cochrane.[31]

Commemorating war and learning lessons

The impact of the recent Napoleonic war was also seen in Britain in the cult of Horatio Nelson, with Robert Southey's successful *Life of Nelson* (1813), monuments in Dublin, Edinburgh and London, and annual dinners, paintings and engravings, most famously Arthur William Davis' *Death of Nelson in the Cockpit of HMS Victory*. In 1823, the Painted Hall of the Greenwich Naval Hospital was established as a national gallery of marine paintings to mark the services of the navy: George IV provided over thirty canvases from the Royal Collection, and the gallery was soon receiving up to 50,000 visitors a year. Daniel Maclise painted *Wellington and Blücher at Waterloo* (1861) and *The Death of Nelson* (1864) for the Houses of Parliament; these works being thought an appropriate inspiration and backdrop for the empire's legislators. Art proved at once an important aspect of commemoration and a presentation of military history, and as a result was both a contested field, particularly with civil wars,[32] and one that charted different views of conflict.[33] Photography was to come to share this function.

Military history was also recorded in a different way across the West, as streets, bridges, buildings, and pubs took their names from war. In Britain, military leaders such as Napier, Wolseley and Roberts joined sites of martial glory, the Almas, Inkermans and Omdurmans, that survive as street names to this day. Parisian avenues and railway stations recorded victories such as Jena, Wagram, Solferino, and Austerlitz, while London had Waterloo station. Battlefields became the site of monuments and the destination of travellers. A gigantic statue of Arminius brandishing a large sword was finished in the Teutoburger Wald in 1875 to commemorate victory over the Romans in 9 CE: Arminius was presented as an exemplary assertor of national independence and thus a precursor of the new German state.

The memorialization and commercialization of war were aspects of its public interest and normative status. The wars covered stretched back across European history to the Classical period. Thus, Wilhelm Benicken, a retired Prussian captain, published an edition of Polybius on war as well as his own *Die Elemente der Militär-Geographie von Europa* (Weimar, 1821). The strong interest in the Classics reflected not only their weight in Western culture but also the belief in the timeless example of great commanders, such as Alexander the Great and Hannibal, and major battles, such as Issus and Cannae. Hannibal's triumph at the latter, indeed, had a particular fascination for German planners; significantly so as Hannibal won battles but could not defeat Rome.

The focus on a canonical tradition, however, had its drawbacks, not least because of the lessons to be learned from campaigns that were ignored. This was also seen with more recent military history. Thus, Continental European General Staffs and commentators underrated the lessons that could be learned from the American Civil War, treating it as a war waged by amateur militia,[34] and there has also been criticism that, earlier, American officers were overly willing to accept the value of a European paradigm of war, rather than developing an American doctrine useful in America.[35]

Reflecting the interaction of military culture and current goals that played, and plays, such an important role in the selection of conflicts for attention, there was a turn-of-the-century fascination in Britain with the American Civil War, in part because it appeared to show how a society without the background of conscription could rapidly create an effective military. Army staff candidates being taught at Camberley were expected to study *Stonewall Jackson and the American Civil War* (1898; 3rd edition, 1902) by the Professor of Military History, Colonel George Henderson, and to know the minutiae of Stonewall Jackson's Shenandoah Valley campaign of 1862, in which a mobile Confederate force had outmanoeuvred and defeated larger Union forces, a lesson that was believed to be relevant to the British military. Furthermore, Henderson was one of the first to try to revive interest in the benefits of speed and surprise in an age of fascination with Napoleonic masses and frontal assaults. What would now be termed lessons of operational theory underlie the book. The work of Henderson, who also produced a study of the Fredericksburg campaign, looked toward later British interest in the Civil War, including Frederick Barton Maurice's *Robert E. Lee, the Soldier* (1925) and, more particularly, J.F.C. Fuller's *Grant and Lee: A Study in Personality and Generalship* (1932), which was widely cited and also reprinted in America.

Within the USA, there was much interest in Civil War history and indeed in American military history as a whole. The lectures given by Matthew Steele at the Staff College at Fort Leavenworth were published as *American Campaigns* (1909), and this was then used as a textbook. Staff rides on Civil War battlefields, especially at Antietam and

Gettysburg where the War Department bought land and built observation towers, also played a role. In contrast, there was less interest in military history in the American universities, which were far smaller in scale than their modern counterparts. The session on military history held at the 1912 meeting of the American Historical Association led to an unrequited call for work in the field and, at that stage, the half-course offered intermittently at Harvard appears to have been the only one on military history in an American university.[36]

The public role of the Civil War was far greater. The memorialization of the war was politically loaded, with four Union generals (Grant, Garfield, Hayes, and Harrison) and one Union soldier (McKinley) becoming Presidents; all Republicans, as the party used their role in the war to justify their claim to guide the nation. Union victory was also marked in the erection of monuments, so that Washington became full of equestrian statues of generals, as well as in the celebration of anniversaries, especially Memorial Day, when graves were decorated and speeches listened to. There was also an ethnic dimension, as the contribution of African-Americans to Union victory was minimized, a process that, significantly, has been challenged in recent years.[37]

In the nineteenth century, wars outside the West received only limited attention from Western military commentators, as they felt that colonial campaigns were a lesser form of conflict. This was to have a long-term consequence in the lack of preparedness of metropolitan militaries for such campaigning. Nevertheless, Western readers were kept well informed, by newspapers and publishers, of campaigns involving their compatriots. Thus, British newspapers spent heavily on telegraphy to receive reports of conflicts, such as the Zulu War of 1879, while the publications of John Frederick Maurice included *A Popular History of the Ashanti Campaign* (1874). Maurice had been the private secretary to Garnet Wolseley in his victorious campaign in Asante in 1873–4. He went on to be Professor of Military History at the Staff College from 1885 until 1892, during which time he published a military history of the 1882 campaign in Egypt. His son, Frederick Barton Maurice, published in 1905 a history of the Russo–Turkish war of 1877–8.

Far less attention was devoted to warfare between non-Western powers. Non-Western states developing governmental forms and militaries on the Western model also established practices of military education accordingly. This was linked to a reconceptualization of military history in these countries, not least because, as in the West, past conflict was analysed for educational purposes. Furthermore, an account of history played a part in the affirmation of these new polities.

Japan

In Japan, the 1870s saw the creation of a national conscript army, the establishment of a compulsory primary school system, and the development of a national and local press. Thus, the nature of the military, the wars it could fight, and the character and extent of the reading public for military history were all changed radically. Modern, Western-style history began in Japan in the late-nineteenth and early-twentieth centuries. Much of it amounted to military history, in as much as it centred on samurai (warrior) development. A large proportion of the early scholarship reflected a complex perspective, simultaneously celebrating the military traditions of the Edo period (many of which, it now appears, were manufactured by historians and military officers), while lamenting it as a dark age of the degeneration of imperial rule. This offered an apparent parallel to European developments, and, indeed, treatments of medieval history were heavily shaped by European scholarship, which included the adoption of constructs like 'feudalism' and 'medieval period'.

The first international war fought by Japan in 300 years was against China in 1894–5. This was relatively bloodless and easy for the Japanese armed forces on the battlefield; most deaths came from infectious disease at the war's end. The early historiography of this war divided into two approaches. One was the simple narrative of troop movements and battles: traditional battlefield history. The second similarly focused on the army in movement and action, but gave considerable emphasis to the 'ordinary' soldiers and sailors as well as the great commanders. This heroic-style historiography, most common in popular instant histories during the war, linked the mass readership of Japan with the mass modern military.

A similar combination of approaches was used in and after the Russo–Japanese war (1904–5). If anything, the trend to personalize and popularize the war was even greater in this war as so many more 'ordinary' men were involved and many more died in combat. One result of this loss of manpower, however, was the start of a more critical intellectual reading of the Japanese military. This left-wing criticism of militarism and imperialism started from about 1900 but grew after 1905, in part because of the enormous tax and national debt burden placed on Japan by the war, and also because of the growth in the 1900s of industrialization and a more recognizably militant mix of intellectuals and workers.[38]

More generally, the Western understanding of military history was adopted elsewhere. In the absence, in most countries, of a large popular readership interacting with entrepreneurial publishers and of a buoyant higher education system committed to scholarly debate, the *modus operandi* focused on Western-style military academies.

History and policy

As so often, military history across the world was employed in order to support already-held views, both within the military and in political circles. Thus, during World War One, Field Marshal Haig, critical of the idea of a Supreme War Council War Board that might limit his role as commander of British forces on the Western Front, wrote: 'From the earliest days, history shows that Aulic Councils, Councils of War, and Committees had invariable failed in discharging the executive duties of command. What is required in war, and especially during the course of a battle, is quick decision', which, he argued, was not possible from a committee.[39]

Haig was far from alone in using history to back his ideas. This was also true of the discussion, indeed, doctrine, and ideology of sea power. Sir John Knox Laughton sought to establish the basis for the subject with his article 'The Scientific Study of Naval History' published in the *Journal of the Royal United Services Institute* (1879). The most influential writer on naval power, Alfred Thayer Mahan (1840–1914), who lectured at the new American Naval War College at Newport, Rhode Island, emphasized the importance of command of the sea in his lectures, published as *The Influence of Sea Power upon History, 1660–1783* (1890), a work that focused on the struggle between Britain and France. Mahan saw the destruction of the opponent's battle fleet as the means to achieve his goal, and treated commerce-raiding as less important. In terms of force structure, this led to a stress on battleships, not cruisers. Mahan's influence on American policy owed something to his friendship with Theodore Roosevelt, who was Assistant Naval Secretary during the successful 1898 war with Spain and later President: both Mahan and Roosevelt wrote histories of the naval aspects of the Anglo–American War of 1812.[40] Mahan's views were widely disseminated – both Kaiser Wilhelm II and Tirpitz, the head of the German navy, read his 1890 book, and it was published in German and Japanese in 1896. Mahan himself had been influenced by the German historian Theodor Mommsen (1817–1903), who had presented Roman naval power as playing a crucial role against Carthage in the Second

Punic War; Mahan's wide-ranging historical frame of reference offers an instructive comment on the intellectual life of the period.

In turn, the British writer Julian Corbett (1854–1922), who provided a nuanced account of naval power in *Some Principles of Maritime Strategy* (1911), with an emphasis on combined operations, also demonstrated the historical validity of his approach in his *England in the Seven Years War* (1907). In offering accounts of naval history, Mahan and Corbett were both also writing about present policy and seeking to relate strategy to power. Mahan's focus, seen with his *The Interest of America in Sea Power, Present and Future* (1897), was on how the USA should draw on the example of Britain to best use naval capability in order to become a great power. In contrast, Corbett's stress was on the way in which Britain should employ its naval strength to preserve its global interests. To Corbett, Britain's interests were not best served by a large-scale land commitment in Europe.[41]

The past appeared to offer policy prescriptions, even if the technology was to be very modern. In practice, naval capability and goals were soon to be rapidly rethought in response to developments in submarine and air warfare. The former shifted the nature of commerce-raiding and made blockade more difficult. Submarine warfare also emphasized a major difference between naval and land capability: the former was restricted to a few powers, and thus the options to be considered in terms of goals and doctrine were limited. If naval capability indicated the dynamic relationship between doctrine based on established practice, and thus, in part, historical analysis and example, and the pressures for change stemming from new technology, this tension was to become more pronounced during the twentieth century.

World War One

There is no clarity as to how best to link the nineteenth and twentieth centuries. One way is to suggest that imperialism and decolonization, instead of being separate chronologically-distinct processes, were in part coterminous. This is scarcely the case in the conventional military narrative, but is more pertinent for an approach to conquest that focuses on its dependence on the popular response. Such a view also provides an unconventional way to approach the importance of World War One: while it helped take Western imperialism to unsurpassed heights with the partition of the Ottoman empire, the war also helped foster the dissolution of empires, for it weakened them in both metropole and colonies and also fostered the spread of ideas, both nationalism and Communism, that were to be the cause of major challenge.

While this locates the war in a global context, it does not explain why Germany and its allies lost, a question that has attracted much high-quality work in recent years. The extent to which this has had only a limited impact on popular perception has been ably discussed by Ian Beckett and Brian Bond, who have taken up the resistance to misleading 'instant' history earlier mounted by John Terraine. In an effective chapter, 'Wastelands?', Beckett criticized the very selective reading of a misleading literary legacy,[42] and offered blunt criticisms of error, bias and cliché in the film *Gallipoli*, the play and later film *Oh! What a Lovely War*, the novel *Regeneration*, and the British television series *The Monocled Mutineer* and *Blackadder Goes Forth*. Bond criticized the grave limitations both of the visual medium, in this case the *Blackadder* series, 'truly the representative popular image of the Western Front for the 1990s', and also of much that was, and is, written at the popular level. Bond argued that current popular notions were largely shaped in the 1960s, in part reflecting the concerns and political issues of the period, but also reviving the anti-war beliefs of the 1930s.

Participation in World War Two had made it easier to understand and appreciate Britain's role in the earlier conflict, but the combination of the end of national service, the culture of the 1960s, anti-Vietnam War sentiment, the impact of CND, and the declining national significance of Armistice Day were more potent. Anti-war culture became more insistent and two-dimensional, as visual replaced literary images.[43] The lost generation and the futility of the First World War are myths so deeply imbedded in popular consciousness that they have become irrefutable facts, as well as folk memory passed down through families, and any attempt to disabuse believers is treated with hostility. Belief in the wrongness of killing has made it difficult to understand the values of combatants, including 'chivalry's vision of love, its camaraderie, concern, and self-sacrifice'.[44] The reading of evidence in the light of subsequent interpretations is a problem:

> In 1930, it was possible to read many texts that would later be entirely associated with the disillusioned view of the war as, in fact, positive alternatives to that interpretation. It was only as the controversy simplified and the disenchantment solidified that the lines of debate were shifted and polarised, in ways that modern readers take for granted but which would have surprised many 1930 reviewers.[45]

The dominant popular image for World War One is of the horrors of intractable trench warfare and of a command failure, focused on Haig, to appreciate and overcome the problems it posed. More generally, the stress has been on the inability to achieve success. This perception has been challenged by scholarly work that has emphasized the learning curve seen during the war, particularly the development of effective infantry–artillery co-operation. This development has been especially associated with the victorious British (understood to include Dominion forces) campaign on the Western Front in 1918, and, as such, displaces the earlier emphasis on new technology in the shape of the tank and, to a lesser extent, the aeroplane. The stress on infantry–artillery co-operation serves as an important reminder of the flexibility of established weapons systems and of the possibility of dramatic increases in capability as a result of incremental changes. This raises a point of more general relevance for military history as it can help explain the reluctance to adopt new weapons and weapons systems.

While the German army was indeed frequently effective at the operational and tactical level, although not without serious flaws,[46] it proved far from effective at their strategic counterpart, and this under-mined success at the other levels. Work on the opening campaign on the Western Front has stressed how the German failure to plan adequately for unforeseen developments, let alone the absence of a real Plan B or of preparations for a lengthy conflict, proved to be major deficiencies in German war-making. This underlines the questionable character of both the accustomed praise of the German General Staff, and, indeed, the tendency to treat Germany as the paradigm power.

The focus in the literature on the Western Front is matched by a lack of comparable work on the conflict in Eastern Europe. Here the war was different in two important respects. First, it was more fluid, with major gains of territory, and second, the campaigning led not only to the defeat of armies but also to states being knocked out of the war or, at least, of effective participation in it: Serbia in 1914, Romania in 1916 and Russia in 1917. This suggests that oft-repeated claims about World War One's indecisiveness require reassessment, or, more particularly, a willingness to emphasize the extent of diversity. From that perspective, consideration of World War One provides an opportunity to consider analytical points that are of value for far more obscure periods.

World War One was also to serve as an important subject for both popular and academic/institutional military history, each of which had developed considerably over the previous century. Although the battles of the memoirs and the greater role of the USA helped ensure that

World War Two dominated the popular market for English-language twentieth-century military history after 1945, interest in World War One remained strong, particularly in Britain. It has become even more so in recent years. As a welcome sign, academics have engaged with the topic and with success, the bulk of Hew Strachan's *The First World War. I. To Arms* (Oxford, 2001) not putting off numerous purchasers, while Michael Howard provided an excellent miniature in *The First World War* (Oxford, 2001). The ability of the war, however, to continue to raise partisan hackles was demonstrated by very different accounts of the importance of American intervention.[47] The legacy of the war overlaps with the next chapter, as a determination to try to avoid its attritional character played a major role in postwar thought and planning.

Notes

1 28 Mar. 1842, BL. Add. 49105 fol. 1.
2 I am most grateful for advice from Helen Nicholson.
3 A. Ferrill, *The Origins of War: From the Stone Age to Alexander the Great* (1985).
4 C. Prendergast, *Napoleon and History Painting: Antoine-Jean Gros's 'La Bataille d'Eylau'* (New York, 1997).
5 G. Rothenburg, *Napoleon's Great Adversaries: The Archduke Charles and the Austrian Army, 1792–1814* (1982).
6 A. Forrest, *Conscripts and Deserters: the Army and French Society during the Revolution and Empire* (Oxford, 1989).
7 S.T. Ross, 'The Development of the Combat Division in Eighteenth-century French Armies', *French Historical Studies*, 1 (1965), pp. 84–94.
8 D. Showalter, *Railroads and Rifles: Soldiers, Technology, and the Unification of Germany* (Hamden, Conn., 1975).
9 BL. Add. 54483 fols. 18, 22.
10 C.A. Bayly, *The Birth of the Modern World 1780–1914* (Oxford, 2004), esp. pp. 237–8.
11 M.J. Bastable, 'From Breechloaders to Monster Guns: Sir William Armstrong and the Invention of Modern Artillery, 1854–1880', *Technology and Culture*, 33 (1992), pp. 213–47.
12 M. Gershovich, *French Military Rule in Morocco. Colonialism and its Consequences* (2000).
13 T.S. Abler, *Hinterland Warriors and Military Dress: European Empires and Exotic Uniforms* (Oxford, 1999).
14 C.V. Reed, *The British Naval Mission at Constantinople: An Analysis of Naval Assistance to the Ottoman Empire, 1908–1914* (D.Phil., Oxford, 1995).
15 J.A. Millward, *Beyond The Pass. Economy, Ethnicity, and Empire in Qing Central Asia, 1759–1864* (Stanford, 1998), pp. 211–24.
16 Report by Lieutenant F.A. Fynney, PRO. WO. 33/2749 pp. 157, 163.
17 S.N. Sen, *Anglo–Maratha Relations 1785–96* (Bombay, 1994), pp. 294–5.

18 I.F. Clarke, *Voices Prophesying War: Future Wars, 1763–1984* (Oxford, 1966) and (ed.), *The Tale of the Next Great War, 1871–1914: Fictions of Future Warfare and of Battles Still-to-Come* (Liverpool, 1995).

19 Wood to Maurice, 20 July 1891, LH, Maurice papers 2/3/39.

20 C. Bassford, 'Wellington on Clausewitz', *Consortium on Revolutionary Europe. Proceedings, 1992* (Tallahassee, 1993), pp. 385–9.

21 M. Howard, *Clausewitz* (Oxford, 1983).

22 C. Condren, *The Status and Appraisal of Classic Texts: An Essay on Political Theory, Its Inheritance, and the History of Ideas* (Princeton, 1985).

23 T.R. Brereton, *Educating the U.S. Army. Arthur L. Wagner and Reform, 1875–1905* (Lincoln, Nebraska, 2000).

24 A. Whitaker, 'Flourish of Trumpets. Enter the Military 1930–1943', in J.R. Barager (ed.), *Why Perón Came to Power. The Background to Peronism in Argentina* (New York, 1968), p. 141.

25 G. Wawro, *The Franco–Prussian War. The German Conquest of France in 1870–1871* (Cambridge, 2003), pp. 307–8.

26 R.A. Butlin, 'Historical Geographies of the British Empire, c.1887–1925', in M. Bell, R.A. Butlin and M. Hefferman (eds), *Geography and Imperialism 1820–1940* (Manchester, 1995), pp. 169–70.

27 Clausewitz, Carl von, *On War*, edited by M. Howard and P. Paret (Princeton, 1976, 2nd edn, 1984).

28 A. Herberg-Rothe, *Das Rätsel Clausewitz. Politische Theorie des Krieges im Widerstreit* (Munich, 2001), pp. 201–45.

29 R. Foley (ed.), *Alfred von Schlieffen's Military Writings* (2001).

30 A. Bucholz (ed.), *Delbrück's Modern Military History* (Lincoln, Nebraska, 1997), esp. pp. 12–20.

31 M.P. Gautier, *Captain Frederick Marryat: L'Homme et L'Oeuvre* (Paris, 1973).

32 J. Milner, *Art, War and Revolution in France 1870–1871. Myth, Reportage and Reality* (New Haven, 2000), pp. 139–81, re the Paris Commune.

33 J.W.M. Hichberger, *Images of the Army: The Military in British Art, 1815–1914* (Manchester, 1988).

34 B. Liddell Hart, 'Strategy and the American War', *Quarterly Review* (July 1929), pp. 118, 130, London, King's College, Liddell Hart Archive, Liddell Hart papers 10.5/1929/1; J. Luvaas, *The Military Legacy of the Civil War* (Lawrence, Kansas, 1999).

35 M. Moten, *The Delafield Commission and the American Military Profession* (College Station, Texas, 2000), pp. 86, 209–10.

36 C. Reardon, *Soldiers and Scholars: The U.S. Army and the Uses of Military History, 1865–1920* (Lawrence, Kansas, 1990).

37 S. McConnell, *Glorious Contentment: The Grand Army of the Republic, 1865–1900* (Chapel Hill, 1992); J.T. Glatthaar, *Forged in Battle: The Civil War Alliance of Black Soldiers and White Officers* (1990); N. Trudeau, *Like Men of War* (Boston, 1998); K.P. Wilson, *Campfires of Freedom. The Camp Life of Black Soldiers during the Civil War* (Kent, Ohio, 2002).

38 I am most grateful to Stewart Lone for his advice.

39 Haig, memorandum on operations on the Western Front 1916–18, BL. Add. 52460 pp. 56–7.

40 R.W. Turk, *The Ambiguous Relationship: Theodore Roosevelt and Alfred Thayer Mahan* (Westport, 1987); M.R. Shulman, *Navalism and the Emergence of American Sea Power, 1882–1893* (Annapolis, 1995); J.T. Sumida, *Inventing Grand Strategy and Teaching Command: The Classic Works of Alfred Thayer Mahan Reconsidered* (Baltimore, 1997).

41 D.M. Schurman, *Julian S. Corbett 1854–1922: Historian of British Maritime Policy from Drake to Jellicoe* (1981).

42 These works, largely published in 1928–30, are also criticized in C. Barnett, 'The Western Front Experience as Interpreted Through Literature', *RUSI Journal*, 148, no. 6 (Dec. 2003), pp. 50–6.

43 I.F.W. Beckett, *The Great War 1914–1918* (Harlow, 2001); B. Bond, *The Unquiet Western Front. Britain's Role in Literature and History* (Cambridge, 2002), quote, p. 86; S. Audoin-Rouzeau and A. Becker, *14–18: Understanding the Great War* (New York, 2002); J. Terraine, 'Instant History', *RUSI Journal*, 107 (1962), pp. 140–5, and *The Smoke and the Fire: Myths and Anti-Myths of War 1861–1945* (London, 1980). On Terraine, G. Sheffield, 'John Terraine as a Military Historian', *RUSI Journal*, 149 (2004), pp. 70–5.

44 A.J. Frantzen, *Bloody Good. Chivalry, Sacrifice, and the Great War* (Chicago, 2004), p. 265.

45 J.S.K. Watson, *Fighting Different Wars. Experience, Memory, and the First World War in Britain* (Cambridge, 2004), p. 311.

46 S.D. Jackman, 'Shoulder to Shoulder: Close Control and "Old Prussian Drill" in German Offensive Infantry Tactics, 1871–1914', *Journal of Military History*, 68 (2004), pp. 103–4.

47 K.D. Stubbs, *Race to the Front. The Material Foundations of Coalition Strategy in the Great War* (Westport, 2002) is far bolder than D. Trask, *The A.E.F. and Coalition Warmaking, 1917–1918* (Lawrence, Kansas, 1993).

Chapter 8

1914–today

> The man with the Winchester always beats the man with the revolver.
> *A Fistful of Dollars*, 1964

The period from 1914 to the present offers two main narratives, each of which pose problems for analysis: first, developments in Western and Soviet war-making; and second the world question, the shifting control of much of the world and its people, particularly the fall of the European colonial empires. Traditionally, the focus has been on the first, very much approached in terms of the quality and quantity of resources. Indeed, the boast voiced in Sergio Leone's film *A Fistful of Dollars* that is quoted above – one, in the event, thwarted by the ingenuity of the character played by Clint Eastwood – sums up the dominant impression. As far as the bulk of the world's population is concerned, however, the second narrative is more important.

This period may seem to have a clear-cut development. As a result of World War One, in 1918, with the collapse of the Ottoman Empire, Western societies reached their hitherto maximum power in territorial terms. This territorial extent was to be enhanced further in 1945 when Japan surrendered, and it and its empire, which included Manchuria and Korea, were occupied. In contrast, in 2003–4, despite loose talk of a new age of American empire, the limitations of Western military power were apparently demonstrated, first by the difficulty of achieving control in Iraq after its regular forces had been overcome, and second, by the ability of North Korea and Iran to defy American pressure over their nuclear armament programmes – although Libya proved more accommodating in heeding international pressure for it to abandon the development of weapons of mass destruction. Judgements may be premature and the opportunities for archival research are limited, but the caution that the Americans showed in 2003 in avoiding the commitment of ground troops in Liberia and Congo further underlined the limitations of Western power, as indeed did the difficulties the French encountered in maintaining order in Ivory Coast.

These limitations were not new, although the extent to which there had been a major shift in the global context of military power from the situation in the 1910s was disguised by the degree to which the USA, the dominant world power, did not seek to exercise its influence by formal empire – by spreading territorial control – and thus did not use its military power to that end, with all the defeats that that might have entailed. In light of its experience of the Vietnam War, the USA would probably not have been able to overcome the problems that faced the European colonial empires had it chosen to match them by seeking to retain the Philippines, instead of granting independence, as was done in 1946, or by maintaining its post-World War Two occupation of Japan, which in fact ended in 1952. Thus, rather than a transition within the global power system, which made the European colonial empires less able to maintain their position but the USA still able to do so, a fundamental shift in military capability, especially in terms of the political and ideological responses to foreign rule, had occurred, one that made the maintenance of all Western territorial power far more difficult.

Although the demise of imperial control was the most important development in military history during this period, it would be mistaken to see this in terms of a simple trajectory. Indeed, the difficulties the British faced in Iraq in the early 1920s, which, in some respects prefigured those of 2003, serve as a reminder of parallels across the period. This narrative of military history, however, was largely ignored in favour of a focus on conflict within the West, so that the military history of the twentieth century became a matter of the two World Wars and the Cold War. Indeed, from this perspective, the Iraq crisis of 2003 saw the coming together of the two separate narratives: the Western emphasis on conventional operations and decisive battle, challenged by a non-Western practice of far more porous boundaries between politics and conflict, within a situation in which victory in battle did not bring ready control.

Conflict within the West, however, certainly engaged the bulk of historical attention at both the popular and the official levels. In the latter case, learning the lesson from the most recent war was seen as the most appropriate way to maintain and enhance effectiveness, and this led to a very functional approach to the analysis of campaigns. This was true both of wartime, with learning curves much in evidence during the two World Wars, and also between conflicts. The extent to which lessons were learned, for example by the British in anti-submarine warfare during World War Two, was, however, to be a matter for controversy.[1]

The lessons of World War One

One of the most prominent instances of learning between conflicts was the attempt among military planners and thinkers in the 1920s and 1930s to focus on the supposed lessons of World War One, in large part in order to avoid a repetition of the costly stalemate of much of that conflict on the Western Front. The German army ordered a large number of staff officers to prepare studies of the recent conflict, a methodical instance of a wider process.[2] In Britain, a framework for writing the history of the war was established in 1915. When completed in 1948 this comprised 29 volumes, offering, in total, a mass of information, though with less clarity about responsibility for failures.[3]

Guidance to the future apparently rested on an account of the recent past (in the Japanese case, the Russo–Japanese War of 1904–5)[4] that was sometimes amplified across a longer timespan. As a result, this chapter has an overlap with the previous one in that both include World War One. There are other reasons for this overlap. From some perspectives, the war ushered in the modern age of total warfare but, from others, it did so by developing what had already been anticipated over the previous half-century. The extent to which the war was different in 1918 to what it had been in 1914 also helps in placing it with both earlier and later periods.

In the inter-war period (1918–39), there was an hitherto unprecedented range of experience to consider, as the recent conflict had also seen air and submarine warfare, and thus commentators had to consider their impact, both in isolation and in combined operations. For example, the German air offensive on London was studied by British airmen interested in the strategic potential of air power.[5] There was also considerable speculation about the future role of tanks, and some of this made reference to historical lessons. Colonel Lindsay, the Inspector of the British Royal Tanks Corps, argued in 1926 that cavalry was too vulnerable to modern small arms, also claiming 'All civil evolution is towards the substitution of mechanical power. History shows that the military mind has usually lagged behind in its appreciation of civil evolution and its possibilities'.[6]

The use of gas in World War One also seemed to offer lessons, as well as to require fresh consideration. Charles Foulkes, Director of Gas Services for the British forces in France in 1917–18, toured India in 1919–20 in order to lecture and to consider how best to employ gas against hostile tribesmen on the North-West Frontier, producing a guide, *Gas Warfare on the Indian Frontier.*[7] In 1926, the British Chemical Warfare Research Department proposed the establishment of a small research and experimental organization for India, as it would 'allow a commencement to be made with the investigation of certain offensive aspects of the subject, which can only be done under Indian conditions'.[8] That year, the French used tanks, armoured cars and bombing when they attacked sections of Damascus seen as hostile. The city as a whole was encircled by barbed wire and machine-gun posts.[9]

World War One also attracted the attention of commentators who were not in government service. The most prominent for military historians was Basil Liddell Hart (1895–1970), a British ex-army officer, who had served in the conflict, turned military correspondent and ardent self-publicist. His ideas affected by his reading of World War One, Liddell Hart sought to turn his perspectives into rules given credence by history. Thus, in a 1920 memorandum, 'Explanation of the theory of the application of the essential principles of strategy to infantry tactics', Liddell Hart wrote,

> The improvements in weapons and the wide extensions enforced by them have created new conditions in the infantry fight. It has developed into what may be termed group combats; the defenders realising that a self-contained group based on a tactical point is more effective than a trench line, the breaking of which results in the whole line falling back; the attackers countering this method of defence by endeavouring to penetrate between the centres of resistance and turn their flanks.[10]

Particularly keen to press for advances that did not entail frontal attacks, and advocating an 'indirect approach' that emphasized manoeuvre, not the attrition that he held resulted from a slavish adherence to Clausewitz's ideas, Liddell Hart used history to press his arguments. Thus, in 'Strategy and the American War', an article published in 1929, he argued that the Union campaign of 1861–2, with the focus on an unsuccessful direct advance on the Confederate capital of Richmond, indicated the ineffectiveness of the strategy of direct approach, and that, instead, decision occurred in the West, with the Union capture of New

Orleans and Vicksburg, the latter opening 'the Chattanooga gateway into Georgia'. Again, Grant's 1864 campaign was presented as indecisive in battle, whereas 'the geographical advantage of having worked round close to the rear of Richmond – was gained by the bloodless manoeuvres which had punctuated his advance'. In contrast to Grant, 'Sherman's economy of force by manoeuvre' was praised: 'The indirect approach to the enemy's economic and moral rear had proved as decisive in the ultimate phase as it had been in the successive steps by which that decision was prepared in the West'. That was not the sole lesson, Liddell Hart thought the American Civil War had offered to those preparing for World War One.

More generally, in *The Decisive Wars of History* (1929), Liddell Hart pressed the case for attacking the enemy where they were not expecting it, a theme he returned to in *The British Way of Warfare* (1932) in which, following the naval historian Julian Corbett, he used history to support his argument that Britain was most successful when it placed the emphasis on sea power, and not on large-scale intervention on the Continent. Clausewitz was castigated, in the lectures published as *The Ghost of Napoleon* (1933), for an emphasis on mass and direct attack.[11]

History was also employed by other writers. In *The Defence of Piedmont, 1744–1748* (1927), Spenser Wilkinson, the recently-retired Professor of the History of Warfare at Oxford, pressed the case for the interdependence of generalship and policy, arguing that this had been lacking during World War One. In his *The Rise of General Bonaparte* (Oxford, 1930), Wilkinson attributed Napoleon's success in part to his ability to apply the doctrine 'of the necessity of enveloping movements',[12] at the same time underlining his theme that ideas and an understanding of their role, not least as illustrated by history, were important to success. Wilkinson indicated the eclectic nature of Napoleon's use of the past:

> The lives of Alexander, Hannibal, and Caesar were the best possible sources for all that the Emperor summed up as composing the divine part of war. The campaigns that Bonaparte had closely studied before 1796 were those of the War of the Austrian Succession in Italy [1741–48]. . . . Throughout his career it was Bonaparte's practice when preparing himself for a campaign to study carefully the most recent campaigns in the contemplated theatre of war.[13]

Thus, at the same time that new weaponry such as aircraft and tanks appeared to suggest major changes in the nature of war, history was used to underline the value of an understanding of recent conflict. A commitment to the lessons supposedly taught by it was particularly apparent in France where victory in World War One was presented as demonstrating the value of their military system.[14]

In addition to attempting to learn from the war, there was also a more general process of writing its history. This led to accusations of partiality and prejudice. Major-General Frederick Barton Maurice, who had resigned in 1918 after publicly criticizing the Prime Minister,[15] Lloyd George, for his claims about manpower, was involved in controversy as the result of a number of his works, including *Forty Days in 1914* (1918).[16] Public interest provided a market for books such as that or John North's *Gallipoli: The Fading Vision* (1936). Responsibility for the failure to defeat the Germans at Jutland was another cause of postwar controversy.

Commanders and commentators alike sought to learn not only from World War One but also from subsequent wars, as the impact of new technology suggested that there was no fixed point for the learning of lessons but, instead, a need to focus on the most recent conflicts. Thus, in 1936, when he resigned the post of Chief of the [British] Imperial General Staff, Sir Archibald Montgomery-Massingberd saw the Italian invasion of Abyssinia as demonstrating the inability of a strong air force to ensure an early victory.[17]

Alongside the drawing of lessons from World War One for strategic, operational and tactical purposes, there was also a process of memorialization that itself helped to reframe strategic cultures. Thus, whereas German nationalists felt betrayed and put an emphasis on the need for will and the overcoming of domestic critics in any future struggle, many commentators in the West emphasized the suffering caused by the war and the need to avoid its repetition.[18] In Japan, from the end of the Russo–Japanese war in 1905 until the 1920s, the two conflicting trends in military history were a consequence of rapid industrialization and urbanization. On the one hand, in response to the challenges these posed, the military itself promoted the idea of a unique Japanese military spirit (commonly known as *Bushidō* or *Yamato damashii*). This emphasis on spirit was reflected in official writings and more popular works by sympathetic authors. On the other hand, there was a continuing reaction against the economic costs of the military, and during the 1920s the public mood of Japan was largely anti-militarist. This changed with the Manchurian incident of 1931 and the rising influence of the armed forces in Japanese politics. As a result, it became far more difficult (and dangerous) to be openly critical of the Japanese military either then or in earlier conflicts. Instead, the trend once again was to emphasize the unique spirit both of the Japanese and especially of the Japanese military. The nationalistic character of most scholarship became more pronounced in the 1930s and 1940s, as censorship effectively made it impossible for more liberal scholars to publish anything, for fear of persecution.

Once major war resumed, in Europe in 1939, the extent to which many who had served in World War One took a prominent role encouraged reference to the lessons to be learned from the earlier conflict. In September 1939, Sir John Dill, the commander of the British I Corps in France, claimed, 'we are up against the same problem as faced us in 1914–18, i.e. we cannot afford to take risks on the Western Front because there, almost alone, the war can be lost'.[19] In 1943, when Allied forces were mounting amphibious attacks on Italy, Churchill referred to the Gallipoli operation of 1915 when he stressed to Field Marshal Alexander, GOC 15th Army Group, the need for close control of operations.[20] J.F.C. Fuller's wartime journalism also made reference to the example of Gallipoli,[21] clearly one that meant a lot to his readers, or at least he felt it should, but he ranged more widely in his frame of reference. Thus, while in the *Evening Standard* of 25 October 1941, he located Allied strategy with reference to the 1915 debate over options between Westerners and Easterners, in his article 'Armor and Counter Armor', in the May 1944 issue of the *Infantry Journal*, Fuller described all-round defence against tank attacks in terms of castles and wagon fortresses, and in *Newsweek* on 5 June 1944, condemnation of the Italian campaign led Fuller to press for an amphibious attack on the Ligurian or French coast: 'Why emulate Hannibal when you are the heirs of Nelson?'

Reviewing World War Two

The quest to analyse recent conflict continued after 1945. NATO forces devoted particular attention to analysing the German–Soviet conflict of 1941–5 in order better to understand the difficulties of fighting the Soviet Union. There was also great interest in responding to the Soviet capacity for rapid and wide-ranging armoured advances seen in 1943–5, as well as in understanding Soviet doctrine, not least about the operational level of war and the concept of deep battle. The success of the air war on Japan affected the doctrine of strategic air power, while physicists reaped a large dividend from the atom bomb in the shape of far greater government peacetime support for research. The process of learning continued. In the Middle East, the Egyptian and Syrian military and political leaderships sought to analyse their failure in 1967 in order to ensure that they were best placed to fight Israel when war resumed, and this learning process played an important role in the greater effectiveness they displayed in the 1973 Yom Kippur War.

Aside from this functional approach to learning from recent conflicts, there was also a frequently related attempt to provide an accurate public record of the conflicts. This was seen, in particular, in the publication of official histories.[22] These involved large-scale projects that provided experience and employment in military history, and helped to bridge the worlds of academe and the military. Thus, the *United States Army in World War II* ran to 78 volumes,[23] and its naval and air equivalents to 15 and seven respectively. The British government published an *Official History of the Second World War*, but was less open in other respects. The Naval Staff Histories for military professionals were only published internally, for example the accounts of the evacuation from Dunkirk in 1940 in 1949 and of the naval operations off Norway in 1940 in 1951, and some of them were at first classified (kept confidential) in order to encourage the writers to be forthright. These Histories were partly based on earlier Battle Summaries produced in order to provide rapid evaluations. The Air Historical Branch also produced classified studies.

As far as the British *Official History of the Second World War* was concerned, its editor suggested that he had been appointed 'on the principle that, knowing nothing about the subject, I couldn't be suspected of cherishing false opinions', drawing from Liddell Hart the reply that 'comradeship can be very cramping to the service of history' and that the World War One official history had been affected by this, as well as by official restrictions.[24] Brigadier Molony, a volume editor of the *Official History of the Second World War*, wrote

> In general in military affairs I suppose the fields in which suppression or gloss might usually intrude are
>> Relations between:
>>> Political directors of the war and commanders
>>> Commanders in the same or different services
>>> Allies ditto ditto
>>> Commanders' handling of forces.
> The occasions would be friction (not in Clausewitzian sense), factiousness, blunders, incompetence, etc. etc.[25]

The publication of historical works were often the centrepiece of disputes over the conduct of recent wars. These were seen among the defeated, most obviously the Germans after World War One, where the question of whether the army had been defeated or undermined by disaffection on the home front was politically explosive. There were also serious disputes among the victorious. These related to Allied failures, such as the Japanese assault on Pearl Harbor, not only the lack of American preparation but the follow-up strike controversy,[26] as well as the British loss of Malaya and Singapore, and British defeats in North Africa in 1941–2; but also to controversies over the causes of Allied success and over whether more could have been achieved, for example the dispute over Allied strategy in 1944 in the battle of Normandy and subsequently in the advance across France,[27] or the wisdom of the American decision to invade the Philippines that year as part of the campaign against Japan. In Britain in 1947, there was controversy among former military leaders over how best to present the failure in Malaya and Singapore. Admiral Layton was motivated, at least in part, by a consideration of the historical record. He wrote to the First Sea Lord, providing an insight into the kind of topic a commander felt should be covered:

> The following are typical points on which the future naval and military historian will want to be satisfied and on which I feel there should be some considered naval judgement on record:
>
> i)   The Far Eastern Combined Intelligence Bureau: was it a failure, and if so, why?
> ii) Japanese landings on the West Coast of Malaya: how important were they and how far could or should they have been controlled from the sea (with particular reference to Penang)?
> iii) How far was the general strategical situation re-assessed after the Japanese occupation of southern Indo-China in July 1941? What was done and what ought to have been done?
> iv) How far was the location of aerodromes in Malaya discussed between services with a view to their landward and seaward defence?
> v)   Was the preliminary work on naval aerodromes which was undertaken in 1941 (none of which ever reached completion) an unnecessary and unwise diversion of resources from the requirements of the RAF.

Layton produced a report critical of planning and preparations, but this was turned down for publication by the Secretary of the Admiralty as unhelpful.[28]

Before the issue of how best to offer a public account after the war was faced, there came the post-mortems carried out during the conflict, as combatants sought to rectify their own limitations and to understand how best to profit from their opponents' mistakes. The Germans were able to do so during the battle for France in 1940, but there was a far less coherent British response to their defeat there. Furthermore, the British generals manipulated the reporting of the conflict, releasing, through the press, their version of a 'stab in the back' myth. Failure was blamed on inter-war neglect, the inadequacies of the French high command, and the failure of the French to fight.[29] That April, soon after the end of the Winter War with Finland in which they had initially done very badly, the Soviets held a secret high-level analysis of the conflict that has recently been published as a result of the opening of their archives.[30]

After the war, the devastation of a bombed and defeated state and a discredited ideology created problems in assembling material on how the German state had operated in practice,[31] but much good scholarship has been done. It has revealed that serious deficiencies in German war-making, many of which reflected structural weaknesses of the Nazi state, were also in part a product of a failure to understand the situation. Will was no substitute, and violence was part of a process of hasty improvisation that could not act as a substitute for the rational crisis management required by the Germans. Albert Speer, who became effective head of the war economy, sought to provide the latter, but he faced multiple sources of opposition, some of which were systemic to the regime but part of which were due to the attitudes of the army. Tensions over manpower repeatedly emerged, and they highlight the more general role for military capability of relevant decisions. Thus, in early 1942 Admiral Raeder decided to meet the shortage of shipyard workers for U-boat maintenance by drawing on labour engaged in new U-boat construction. As a consequence, a useful short-term increase in the number of operational U-boats was achieved at the cost of cutting new production.[32]

The scholarly volumes being edited by the Militärgeschichtliches Forschungsamt (Research Institute for Military History) in Potsdam are part of the process by which the Germans are coming to grips with the scholarly issues involved in assessing the conflicts. This is less apparent in Japan. There, the defeat of 1945 was blamed largely on the armed forces, and from its creation in 1954, the Japan Self-Defence Force has rejected any direct link with the imperial military. In historiography, the left-wing scholars silenced by the war years completely occupied the field until the 1970s. Their approach was broadly Marxist in terms of seeing a conspiracy, prior to 1945, between the military and big business, supported by conservative governments and the newly created urban bourgeoisie, both to repress the masses at home and to exploit surrounding nations. The most common terms in this historiography were '*gunkoku-shugi*' (militarism, though taken to mean a mix of fascism and militarism) and '*tennō-sei*' (the emperor-system, that is, a system of repression using the symbol of the monarchy to keep the masses docile).

In the late 1960s, the hundredth anniversary of the Meiji restoration saw major publications and republications of histories and historical documents relating to the Meiji era (1868–1912). This both made much more information easily available to historians and also prompted some rethinking of what had become (or was becoming) a sterile left-wing orthodoxy. The fact that Japan's economy was already by that time producing a mass middle class defined by an affluent consumerist lifestyle may also have assisted this rethinking.

Thus, from the late 1960s to the 1980s, the two broad trends in military history were the now dogmatic Marxist critiques plus the newer emphasis on documents and on policy and decision-making at various levels of the military. Additional trends in the early 1980s were, first, a growing number of personal memoirs by former soldiers wishing to tell the truth (as they saw it), either to expose brutality and atrocities or to rescue the military's reputation from the left-wing scholars; and, second, an increased concern with war crimes, notably the Nanjing Massacre of 1937, but also Japanese use of 'comfort women' and experiments in biological weapons (Unit 731).

The arguments in the 1990s and 2000s continue largely to follow earlier themes, discussing militarism, war crimes, the documentary discussion of policy-making, the role of film in war, etc. There continues to be considerable popular interest in battlefield history, and battlefield tourism in Saipan developed. A multi-volume work from the National Institute of Defence Studies, a research centre within Japan's National Defence Agency, addressed all aspects of the battles of the Pacific war.

The wartime conduct of the Japanese military was actively contested, with nationalist commentators determined to prevent critical comment. The *cause célèbre* was high school textbooks dealing with Japanese conduct in China. Cases brought in the Tokyo District Court in 1965, 1967 and 1984 opposed the Japanese Ministry of Education and the historian Saburo Ienaga, whose descriptions of the Nanjing Massacre in 1937 and of biological warfare experiments in China by the Japanese army had attracted the attention of the ministry's censors. The ministry won the 1965 case in 1993, and the 1967 case in 1989, but in 1997, Ienaga narrowly won a decision from the Supreme Court. The Nanjing Massacre was fiercely contested within Japan with discord over the numbers killed and the extent to which massacre was an aspect of Japanese war-making in China.[33]

Across the world, the dominance by memoirs was a feature of the postwar decades, one that has reduced to the world of reprints as senior combatants have died off. As the writers of post-1945 memoirs were keener than their nineteenth-century predecessors to attribute blame to others, the process frequently led to battles of memoirs, with campaigns fought out before an engaged and partisan readership, many of whom were keen to purchase books about their former commanders. Thus, the view of strategy in 1944 in Eisenhower's *Crusade in Europe* (1948) was different to that in Montgomery's *Memoirs* (1958).

These disputes were particularly apparent in Britain, which, at least in this respect, was singularly undeferential. Thus, there were heated arguments over generalship in North Africa, especially over the respective importance of Auchinleck and Montgomery in causing the Axis defeat, while the combative Dorman-Smith took his differences with Montgomery and Churchill to the legal battlefield, winning, in 1954, a libel case against the latter for statements in his *The Hinge of Fate* (1951).[34] Subsequently, Dorman-Smith had counsel interview Liddell Hart, Michael Howard and Correlli Barnett about the memoirs of Field Marshal Sir Harold Alexander, which were published in 1962.[35] These memoirs were based on a *Sunday Times* series that appeared in 1961, advertised as 'the newspaper event of the year' and supported by 'one of the most widespread newspaper poster campaigns'. Alexander offered a combative defence in the *Western Mail* of 15 February 1961: 'I have every right to put the record straight about it'.[36]

Dorman-Smith also attacked the first volume of the official history of the war in the Mediterranean and the Middle East as a whitewashing job that failed to engage with the flaws of the intervention in Greece in 1941,[37] a decision that had greatly concerned Fuller at the time. The controversies were fuelled by critical scholarly engagement, especially Correlli Barnett's *Desert Generals* (1960), which caused great offence by offering a civilian reading of military competence, and, in refuting what he termed the 'Montgomery Myth', by castigating Montgomery in order to praise Auchinleck, while Liddell Hart who, in the words of one critic, 'spoke as from Sinai', also weighed in with his last book, his *History of the Second World War* (1970).[38] Montgomery, who referred to Dorman-Smith as 'a menace', wrote 'I have never met Sgt Barnett and don't want to'.[39]

The controversies ranged from grand strategy to specific points about weapons. Thus, the relative effectiveness of British and German tank and anti-tank guns in North Africa in 1941–2 was extensively discussed. Liddell Hart made the useful point that impressions on these heads 'are always influenced by the result of a fight, and are far from being scientific evidence'.[40]

It was not only Allied memoirs that were controversial. General Heinz Guderian's *Panzer Leader*, which was published in 1951 with an English translation in 1952, exaggerated the author's role in the development of German tank warfare and also presented Guderian's politics in a favourable light. This influenced Keegan's somewhat naïve biography, *Guderian* (1973), but subsequent scholarship offered a more searching perspective, downplaying the general's role and questioning his politics.[41] Liddell Hart's foreword to the 1952 translation also aroused debate, as it was linked to Guderian's willingness to stress how much he owed to Liddell Hart's ideas, while Liddell Hart himself played a role in the debate on West German rearmament.[42] At the time, Sir James Butler, the editor of the British official history of the war, complained about the foreword on a different basis:

> It doesn't seem to me that there is any comparison, for instance, between reprehensible acts which British and American commanders may have been instructed to carry out in the nineteenth century and the sort of things which Guderian and his fellows put up with on the part of the Nazi government without protest or without effective protest.

Liddell Hart replied by stressing the need to obey orders as an aspect of 'the essential requirements of military discipline',[43] and this view had indeed been clearly expressed at the time of the British postwar trial of Manstein.[44] The War Office was unhappy with Foreign Office pressure for prosecutions. Liddell Hart himself took a critical view of some of the official histories, claiming that they were partisan and glided over awkward incidents, a view also expressed by Dorman-Smith.[45] In turn, Liddell Hart was criticized for his role in the successful 'Rommel industry'.[46]

At the younger level, male interest in the war was inculcated by boys' magazines such as, in Britain, *Lion*, *Valiant* and *Commando*, and by popular fiction, such as, in Britain, the Biggles and Gimlet stories of W.E. Johns (1893–1968), which interacted with films.[47] It is unclear how far this culture contributed to a sustained interest in military history, but it may well have helped ensure reader demand. A shift has since occurred as interest in failure has become more sympathetic. This has been readily apparent in Britain, but is less the case in the USA, not least in response to the unease following the attacks on 11 September 2001. Even in Britain, sensitivity about failure led to a controversy in late 2003 about a forthcoming BBC series on the evacuation from the Dunkirk beaches, specifically whether the BBC was intent on 'debunking the myth of the heroic little ships'.[48]

The 1960s is not generally seen as a period fascinated with war, but on 3 September 1969 the British comic weekly *Punch* put 'The War Industry' on its front cover, showing a book and film, television and theatre shots of war. At that stage, the industry was indeed a major one. Part of it was far-ranging, with Montgomery in 1968 bringing out *A History of Warfare*, to which research assistants had made a major contribution, while in 1966 Madame Tussaud's spent £50,000 on a Trafalgar exhibition, and in 1964 the BBC's series *The Great War* (on World War One) and the film *Zulu* were major successes.

World War Two, however, was the focus, especially thanks to the success of Purnell's *History of the Second World War*, the first issue of which appeared on 7 October 1966. Surviving correspondence indicates the pressures that moulded such a project, with scholarship and commercial appeal at variance, as in the response to the idea of 'featurettes'.[49] The publishers, Purnell, part of the British Printing Company, pressed Liddell Hart, the editor in chief, to increase the number of American, Japanese and Soviet contributions in order to aid the chance of co-publication deals with foreign publishers, and also wanted a book club style. Liddell Hart argued in response that most Japanese and Soviet scholars wrote badly, while 'the basic difficulty about the American ones is that while there are plenty of good academic ones there are few of these who can write readably enough for a popular history such as ours', and that they would want too much money.[50]

The project was a gamble as there was little experience with part-work publishing, and it cost over £800,000 to produce. It benefited, however, from a major promotion campaign. Costing £95,000, and focusing on ABC1 men over forty, this included two forty-five second commercials, newspaper advertisements stressing the direct link with readers: 'If you can whistle Lili Marlene – this is your story', and special issue posters. The magazine-style layout of the weekly and the 3000 illustrations in the 128 weekly issues helped, and by 1967 nearly 300,000 copies were being sold weekly.[51] Foreign language editions followed, including in Italy and France, and in November 1967 over one million copies of the various editions were sold in Europe in one week. The average weekly sales in Britain of the 128 issues were 325,000 and the project made a pre-tax profit of £7 million.

Individual items led to controversy, Liddell Hart privately responding to complaints from two Polish generals, 'It seems to me that the Poles remain just as touchy and as inclined to overrate their importance as they were in 1939'.[52] There were also complaints about omission: Major General Moulton in his review of the first volume in the *Glasgow Herald* of 18 February 1967, took exception to the lack of an adequate account of the British Expeditionary Force in action before the Dunkirk evacuation. Hugo Stafford-Northcote, however, replied to complaints about his article on the invasion of Syria that, as the original piece had been ripped to pieces by sub-editors, he was not fully answerable, but also that

> the relative importance of the Palmyra and Damour battles depends, I suppose, on whether the writer is Australian, British, Indian, Free or Vichy French – or even Syrian or Lebanese! . . . Palmyra – viewed from Iraq, possibly loomed as large in the scheme of things as would Damour to observers at, say, Middle East Command H.Q. in Cairo![53]

Success led the British Printing Company to press on, to consider the idea of a part-work on Arab–Israeli wars, a plan that owed much to the prominence of the Six Days War of 1967, but that collapsed in 1968. Instead, a *History of the First World War*, launched on 24 October 1969, followed. The news release issued the previous day referred to the success of books on the conflict, specifically Barbara Tuchman's *The Guns of August*, Alistair Horne's *Verdun*, Alan Moorehead's *Gallipoli*, Donald Macintyre's *Jutland*, Kenneth Macksey's *The Shadow of Vimy Ridge*, and Correlli Barnett's *The Swordbearers*. Readers of the World War Two part-work who had been consulted had shown, it was claimed, an overwhelming preference for a World War One sequence, rather than for a history of warfare through the ages or one on post-1945 conflicts. The news release added:

It was from material such as this that Homer and Thucydides, Tolstoy and the authors of the Book of Genesis, wrought their immortal tragedies. . . . on our side the names of Ypres and Passchendaele, Gallipoli and the Somme, Jutland, Heligoland Bight and Zeebrugge are even more a part of our national consciousness than El Alamein, Kohima, the Imjin River or Suez.

The advertisements, such as those in the *Daily Express* on 23 October and the *Daily Telegraph* the next day, were focused on dramatic photographs, including the female spy Mata Hari in a seductive pose, and stressed immediacy: 'Everywhere you will stand next to heroes', adding that eye-witness accounts 'give life to the arrows on the maps'. As a reminder of transience, it is no longer the case that battles at Heligoland Bight (1915) or Kohima (1944) are part of the British national consciousness.

Time and political changes, especially the demise of Communist rule in the Soviet Union, has led to the release of far more documentary material about World War Two. This has freed scholars from the shadow of the official histories and encouraged them to re-examine campaigns and issues. For example Bernd Fischer has demonstrated that the official Albanian Communist view of the war was so politicized as to lessen greatly its value, not least because it underrated both the role of the early non-Communist resistance and initial German success.[54] The opening up of Soviet archives helped Krizstián Ungváry produce a detailed account of the struggle for Budapest in 1944–5, while, as is the case with much work on World War Two, he also employed a large number of interviews. Interest in World War Two led to the translation of the book into English and its publication in London in 2003, thus drawing attention to a major battle generally neglected in the West. Equally, most material on Hungarian military history, whether written in Hungarian or not, has not been translated into English because it does not seem commercially viable to do so; and this even for World War One, in which Hungarians played a major role in the forces misleadingly referred to as Austrian. The cost of translation has long been an issue in limiting access to foreign scholarship, leading for example in 1968 to a failure to translate Joachim Wieder's *Stalingrad und die Verantwortung des Soldaten* (Munich, 1962).[55]

Scholarship taking advantage of the opening of archives is not restricted to Eastern European topics. In his first-rate revisionist account of the Malaya campaign, somewhat misleadingly entitled *Singapore 1942. Britain's Greatest Defeat*, Alan Warren notes that 'the case for a reconsideration of the Malayan campaign has been immeasurably increased by the release of new material by the British Public Record Office and the Australian War Memorial during the 1990s'.[56] As with many other studies of generalship, there is a criticism of a lack of rapid responsiveness on the part of the commander, although valuable attention is also drawn to the failure of subordinate commanders, to the wider problems of British military conduct at this stage,[57] and to the Japanese skill in mobile warfare.

Mobility, more generally, has attracted attention and praise, both in writing about this war and in discussion of the operational dimension of war. This is an aspect of the reaction against what was seen as the stasis of World War One, and also, in part, reflects an unwillingness to engage with the attritional character of some of World War Two, especially on the Eastern Front. This reaction and the value placed on mobility are an aspect of the degree to which military history encapsulates current cultural values. A stress on mobility can also be seen in counterfactual discussion about past conflicts. Thus, Fuller refought the American Civil War, arguing that

> the most effective way to protect Richmond was to base a powerful army on Chattanooga, and carry out a defensive-offensive campaign in Tennessee, while a less powerful army covered the capital. A vigorous campaign in Tennessee would almost certainly have drawn Federal [Union] forces out of Virginia to meet it, and simultaneously have directly protected the vital railway hub Chattanooga–Atlanta, as well as indirectly . . . Vicksburg.[58]

Similarly mobility, dominating the tempo of war, operating on the line of least expectation and least resistance, and manoeuvring onto the enemy's rear, have been praised in more recent works on warfare as a whole.[59]

The opening up of Soviet material from 1992 has permitted a re-examination of World War Two on the Eastern Front. Archives such as those of the Soviet Supreme High Command provide an opportunity for re-considering both narrative and explanation.[60] This has not only been a matter of altering details. Thus, Operation Mars, a disastrous Soviet attack in November 1942 on the central front west of Moscow, which failed and was covered up, not least with a wholly inaccurate and incomplete account of the poor planning and execution of the operation, has been rescued from neglect with a study that undermines the Soviet portrayal of a continuous and heroic drive to victory from late 1942.[61]

On the German side, there is still a tendency to regard their defeat as due to being beaten in 'the production battle in the factories'[62] and to minimize or ignore the extent to which they were outfought. Furthermore, the willingness to accept that the Wehrmacht was involved in atrocities is contested, and there is considerable opposition to the idea that military violence against unarmed civilians was integral to the Wehrmacht's conduct during the war. This, in part, is because this argument challenges the sanitization of the Wehrmacht's reputation during the Cold War and as post-war West German society was integrated.[63]

There is also much material on German operations, especially corps- and division-level sources, that requires evaluation. All too much of the work on the German side is based on post-war analyses of their own campaigns by German commanders and staff officers. This places the responsibility for defeat on resource issues, the size and climate of the Soviet Union, and, above all, Hitler's interventions, leading to a situation in which 'the quasimythical level of excellence attributed to German operational and tactical planning' persists in the face of extensive archival evidence that highlights battlefield mistakes by German commanders.[64]

At the popular level, World War Two continues to attract work from the supposed 'righting of wrongs' perspective, but in practice this can be one-sided and lacking in perspective. For example, the recent German focus on civilian losses to Allied bombing and as a result of the Soviet advance is apt to underrate or ignore the extent to which in Europe during World War Two the Germans began and developed anti-societal warfare. Thus Hermann Knell's *To Destroy a City: Strategic Bombing and Its Human Consequences in World War II* (Cambridge, Mass., 2003), which has had a considerable impact in Germany with its account of the British air force's devastation of Wurzburg in March 1945, inaccurately presents German policies in the 1930s and the attack on the Soviet Union as defensive and preventive. However partisan, a lack of subtlety doubtless assists sales. At the popular level, an English-language version of 'righting of wrongs' revisionism is Lynne Olson and Stanley Cloud's *For Your Freedom and Ours. The Kosciuszko Squadron* (2003), which draws attention to the harsh consequences of Soviet policies for Poland, not least for Polish aces who fought in the Battle of Britain.

Strategic bombing was not only an emotive issue for those who suffered it, as was indicated by the controversy over the exhibition planned for 1995 by the Smithsonian Institution's National Air and Space Museum. This was to centre on the *Enola Gay*, the plane that dropped the atomic bomb on Hiroshima. In the event, claims that the exhibit, whose critical script reflected the state of scholarly research, was unpatriotic led to its cancellation: in the end, only a belated and curtailed display was offered.[65] The dispute was related to the more general one of war guilt between the USA and Japan, an issue which, for the USA, focused on the pre-emptive Japanese attack at Pearl Harbor. As an instance of continued sensitivity, a Hawaii'an historian writing about Japanese-Americans who fought for the Japanese has recently received threats.[66]

Military history and politics

Controversy over recent military history has not been limited to debating World War Two. More recent conflicts have also been considered. Again, there has been the effort by the defeated to rewrite history, most obviously with the Vietnam War. This has seen a classic form of reappraisal, with the argument that a deficit in will was responsible for failure. Thus, there has been the claim that a refusal to employ a more robust offensive strategy, by unrestricted air attacks on North Vietnam and/or by ground attacks there and in Laos, robbed the Americans of victory in the Vietnam War, while a lack of sustained domestic support allegedly ensured defeat. This is a classic instance of the refusal to consider campaigns and conflicts in terms of wider commitments. The USA sought a limited war, and there was also, as earlier with the Korean War, a concern about the full range of American strategic interests. The possible consequences elsewhere, particularly in Western Europe and the Middle East (and also, during the Vietnam War, in Korea), of a more robust offensive strategy during the Korean and Vietnam Wars receive insufficient attention. So also does the improved strategic situation for the USA in South East Asia that followed the overthrow of Sukarno, the Indonesian nationalist leader, in 1966, which provided the Americans with greater strategic depth. This overthrow owed much to the CIA and, like the overthrow of Mohammed Musaddiq in Iran in 1953, indicated the extent to which a successful use of power did not have to mean troops storming ashore, or at least landing, on the beaches; indeed the latter was often the sign of a failure of policy, as with the Americans in Vietnam.

The consideration of recent military history also had clear political resonances. Thus, the sinking of the Argentinian warship the *General*

Belgrano in 1982 was presented as the necessary prelude to the British recapture of the Falkland Islands, or as an aggressive step by the Thatcher government that scuppered chances of peace. Debate over the wisdom of the Israeli invasion of Lebanon the same year and, still more, the advance on Beirut was linked to the reputation of Ariel Sharon, then the Defence Minister responsible for ignoring the restraint sought by the Israeli government, and subsequently Prime Minister. Discussion about contentious military episodes in this manner has been most marked in the West. In part, elsewhere there has been a deliberate amnesia about warfare now deemed embarrassing, a situation especially characteristic of post-1945 Japan, although also seen in other countries, for example in post-1945 Italy.

Across part of the world, there has also been an active process of moulding the presentation of military history. The Communist regimes of Eastern Europe, the Soviet Union, China, Cuba, and Mongolia were especially guilty of this. The Academy of Military Service, established in 1958 under the Chinese Central Military Committee, was given responsibility for producing military histories of the conflicts waged by Communist forces; this led to the publication of the three-volume *War History of the Chinese People's Liberation War* (Beijing, 1987), followed by *The Chinese People's Volunteers in the War Against U.S. Aggression and Aid to Korea* (Beijing, 1992). Other works produced by the Academy considered pre-Communist Chinese military history, including *Selected Wars of Ancient China: Case Studies* (Beijing, 1992), and the *War History of Modern China* (Beijing, 1997).[67] Chinese historians in the post-1949 era favoured an interpretation of Chinese history that forced everything into a rather safe and unimaginative Marxist framework in which peasant uprisings were seen as the locomotive of history; this approach affected military history.

In Mongolia, a very partisan account was presented of the warfare that led to the imposition of Communist control after World War One. Across most of the Third World, wars of national liberation were also presented in a tendentious light, with heroism and teleology both securely on the side of the anti-imperialists. Such presentation was entrenched in institutional scholarship, while simplified accounts were propagated through state education and media systems. Censorship and less overt pressures were also significant. Thus, the Arab world had no equivalent to the self-styled 'new historians' who criticized Israeli conduct and what they presented as the overly nationalistic account of the Arab–Israeli wars.[68]

More recent military history was also affected by political shifts. Thus, after the end of Communist rule, Uzbekistan has made Timur (Tamerlaine or Tamburlaine) into a father figure. His statues have replaced those of Lenin and there is considerable pride about his conquests. This is not the limit of the rediscovery of a pre-Communist history. The Uzbek government is now also focusing on Abdullah II (r. 1582–98) because he unified the state and expanded it significantly with successful military campaigns elsewhere.

The paucity of critical work elsewhere ensured that, despite decoloniz-ation, the bulk of military history continued to be produced in the West, and thus to reflect its interests. Indeed, this was abruptly made clear when Western interventions in Third World countries, such as Afghanistan in 2001, led to a sudden flurry of Western publications on their military history. The latter were generally structured in Western terms. Thus, popular works on Afghan military history, for example Stephen Tanner's *Afghanistan: A Military History from Alexander the Great to the Fall of the Taliban* (New York, 2002), focused on Alexander the Great's campaigns, the three Anglo–Afghan Wars, the Soviet invasion, and American intervention. Similarly, Somalia entered Western consciousness when the USA sent troops there in 1992 and left it when they withdrew in 1994, repeating the situation seen with World War Two (when British forces had conquered Italian Somaliland in 1940), while neighbouring Ethiopia appeared largely only to record British and Italian operations between 1868 and 1941. At the same time, crises provided opportunities for the publication of scholarly work. Thus, Western interest in Chechnya, as a result of conflict there between Russia and the Chechnens from 1994, led not only to relatively populist works, such as Robert Seely's *Russo–Chechen Conflict, 1800–2000. A Deadly Embrace* (2001), but also to more scholarly studies, such as Moshe Gammer's *Muslim Resistance to the Tsar. Shamil and the Conquest of Chechnia and Daghestan* (1994), a book paperbacked in 2001.

The established narrative of military history had seemed challenged as the age of Western colonial empires receded and its brevity appeared more apparent. Western territorial control of many colonies, and Russian/Soviet control of much of the Caucasus and Central Asia, both lasted for less than 150 years, in much of Africa and South East Asia for less than seventy years, and in most of the Middle East for less than thirty years. The brutal use of massive force that had worked for the French in Syria in 1926 proved far less successful there in 1945. Indeed, the shelling and bombing of Damascus in 1945 in response to anti-French agitation exacerbated hostility, and this contributed to the withdrawal of French troops the following year.[69] The French were initially more successful when they used force to suppress opposition in Algeria, Indochina and Madagascar, but within two decades each was to be independent. France, its colonies and its military had all been transformed by the experience of World War Two, and this affected the continued viability of colonial rule;[70] although that also affected Britain, which had not suffered defeat, as well as Portugal, which had remained neutral.

The spread of American hegemony across much of the world after 1945, its revival after serious problems in the 1970s and its active expeditionary posture from 1990, however, provided a new demonstration of Western military capability, and therefore a revived motive for the focus on Western military history as an account of the basis for the present situation. Within the military, where the motivation is utilitarian, this can be readily understood. Thus, as the 2002–3 handbook for the Nonresident seminar syllabus of the Strategy and Policy Division of the College of Distance Education of the United States Naval War College noted, 'The overall purpose of the National Security Decision Making Course is to educate military officers and U.S. government civilians in the effective development and command of armed forces within the constraints of national resources' (p.v.). The case-studies that year were Theory and Prototype Studies; The Classical Prototype: Athens vs. Sparta; The American Revolution and Maritime Theory; Policy and Strategy in a Revolutionary Era: Europe 1792–1815; Limited War and Escalation Control: The Wars of German Unification; The Russo–Japanese War and Modern Naval Strategic Thought; World War II: The United States, The Grand Alliance, and Global War; The Cold War, Containment and Korea; Limited War in a Revolutionary Setting: The Vietnam Conflict; Limited War in a Global Setting: The Gulf War; Strategies and Policies of Terrorism; and Retrospect and Prospect: The Terror War. The latter two reflected the rapid response of military educators to the issue of the moment, and the need to make historical courses relevant.

As a sign of the shift in American military culture, this list can be contrasted with the paintings given by the West Point Class of 1920 that hang in room 301 of the Library at West Point and represent various methods of combat. The topics are the 'Roman invasion of Britain', 'French artillery in 1812 under Napoleon', 'Cavalry on the first day of Gettysburg', a 'Scene from the Franco–Prussian War', and 'Panzer attack at Perrone, 1940'.

More generally, the need to make historical courses relevant can be seen with a stress on the history of joint warfare. Such operations, and associated doctrine, planning, command structures, and procurement, became more important from the 1980s and, even more, 1990s, leading to a more integrated sense of military power, as well as to a questioning of former boundaries between tactical, operational and strategic perspectives and activities. This reconceptualization of military power has had scant impact on the world of popular military history, although it helped lead to a recovery of interest in past episodes of naval power projection, as in *Seapower Ashore. 200 Years of Royal Navy Operations on Land* (2001) edited by Peter Hore; but it was more important within the military educational world. For example, the shift in the strategic nuclear role from air power to submarines led to a reconsideration of the doctrine and history of air power in terms of a greater emphasis on joint operations. As far as historical work was concerned, the emphasis on joint operations led to a positive re-evaluation of Corbett's views on naval power.[71]

The reconceptualization of military power indicates the interplay of 'real world' experience in the reformulation of doctrine.[72] Thus, American interest in co-operating with local forces, seen in Afghanistan in 2001, led the Army Command and General Staff College Press to publish a collection produced by its Combat Studies Institute on 'compound warfare': regulars and irregulars fighting in concert. The preface declared: 'knowing how the dynamics of compound warfare have affected the outcome of past conflicts will better prepare us to meet both present crises and future challenges of a similar nature'.[73]

Within the West, navies and air forces in particular are relatively uninterested in non-Western military history, while land forces that may come into contact with non-Western forces should be more so. Military studies are not motivated by abstract criteria. Nor, as indicated in Chapter two, are publishers. The combined effect is to ensure insufficient attention to a whole range of military activity outside the West. This can be amplified if the internal military history of non-Western states is also considered, although there are important exceptions. For example, interest in the issue of modernization ensured that the role of the military in the transformation of states, both Western, especially Germany, and Third-World, attracted considerable scholarly attention.[74]

Alongside public interest in military history has come a degree of ambivalence about its study within the military, which reflected, in particular, developments in weaponry that appeared to transform the nature of war. The first of these, from 1945, was atomic weaponry, and the impact of this capability was enhanced by the extent to which it was discussed in terms of distinctly ahistorical theoretical models. This approach continued to predominate thereafter more generally with warfare, despite the strengthening of the institutional framework of military history as part of the expansion of military education, which saw, for example, the establishment of the Department of History at West Point in 1968. In 1994, the French Ministry of Defence was responsible for the foundation of a Centre d'études d'histoire de la Défense, based at Vincennes from 1995. This centre has organized numerous conferences, helped fund research and published more than fifty works. In December 2000, Alain Richard, the French Minister of Defence, declared 'the place of history is fundamental in the formation of officers, in order to illuminate their actions and their role in society'.[75]

However, the importance in military thought, especially in the USA, of notions of future war, such as Rapid Dominance[76] and the American idea of a '36-hour war', and the rejection of incremental notions of change,[77] did not encourage a historical perspective, and there were complaints about its neglect.[78] Instead, as futuristic concepts and vocabulary dominated doctrine and procurement, there was pressure on established attitudes and structures. From the early 1990s, military historians have had to contest claims that, as a consequence of recent developments in military technology, summarized as a Revolution in Military Affairs, and of the post-Cold War strategic environment, there has been a change that is so abrupt that a historical perspective appears irrelevant. Although these claims have been pushed hard from the 1990s, they did not begin then, but were related to a longer-standing confidence in increasingly sophisticated technology. This was also related to a determination to lessen casualties by removing the soldier from the battlefield, a goal that helped direct doctrine, force procurement and a quest for ever more sophisticated technology. The question that needs to be asked is how far the resulting weaponry and command systems makes a significant difference to the outcome of combat, or whether the outcome is determined by other factors that may or may not be influenced by the technology.

Claims that a historical perspective on war is irrelevant are misguided, although they reflect a powerful impulse within modern American military culture that draws on a wider practice in the West. For at least a quarter-millennium, it has been customary to emphasize the importance of an approach, insight or development by stressing its novel character and consequences, and the search for them has been an important aspect of Western intellectual culture. Advantages, indeed, have flowed from this emphasis on innovation, but in military history, a subject dominated by the West, this stress on the novel and transforming also has a symbolic quality. This cultural point appears particularly important in light of modern interest in the symbolic character of military systems.

To argue that military history should abandon its focus on the new and the revolutionary might seem counter-intuitive, especially if cutting-edge technology is regarded as the great force multiplier. Military realities, however, are both too complex and too dependent on previous experiences to make the search for military revolutions helpful. An emphasis on continuities captures the role of limitations, especially of Western tactical, operational and strategic military effectiveness with regard to non-Western environments, although continuity does not imply an absence of change. Such an understanding, of both continuity and change, underlines the value of an historical approach, provided it is free from the ahistorical teleological quest for military revolution. To turn to present Western security concerns, it is readily apparent that strategic cultures have, or draw on, very different historical imaginations, and this seems to have policy implications, and to repay consideration.

The shrinking of distance

There is an instructive parallel with the question of whether developments in technology have overcome traditional, or indeed all, geographical constraints by shrinking distance. This is an instance of the role of technology in military change, namely the central importance not of technological developments intended primarily for military purposes, but rather the application of innovations from non-military technology. Thus, in the case of communications, advances in civil aviation and in motor transport proved of considerable military importance. The same has also been true of other spheres, such as medicine. Western force projection became more effective in the late nineteenth century and, even more, the early twentieth century, as troop losses to disease fell because of the application of advances in medical knowledge and public health practice – although, in addition, advances made during war, such as triage and helivac, subsequently changed civilian medicine.

In practice, however, the shrinking of distance that more rapid and more far-flung Western force deployment permitted in the twentieth century, if anything, accentuated the need to consider constraints, as units are brought into new environments without lengthy, if any, prior acculturation. As the secret British War Office publication *Warfare in Undeveloped Countries. Part 1. Desert Warfare* (1954) by General Sir Frank Messervy noted, 'The enemy is often, by force of circumstances, highly experienced in operations in the peculiar type of country and climates. . . . The belief must not be allowed to spread that the enemy is superior in any way.'[79] The issue was reflected in military history, with books offering illustrative case studies such as Harold Winters' *Battling the Elements* (Baltimore, 1998), which provided the 'overarching message . . . that, despite the evolving technology in warfare, physical geography has a continuous, powerful and profound effect on the nature and course of combat'.[80] Winters' study suffered, however, from the extent to which the problems posed by alien environments were considered in terms of Western forces.

The shrinking of distance was not only a matter of the deployment and support of forces, and of the reduced time-distance between sensor and shooter, but also of the extent to which the activities of forces were covered at home (see Chapter four). This extended the role of military history at the simplest level, as it provided the frame of reference within which news could be presented and assessed. This creation and discussion of a frame of reference, however, was very much a case of history only within the experience of many of those alive. Thus, the frame of reference offered for American military activities in Iraq in 2003 moved from being the rapid success of the Gulf War of 1991 to the intractable commitment of the Vietnam War, a negative comparison that was contested by supporters of the intervention. What was striking was the limited reference to scholars or scholarship. Instead, ahistorical comparisons were offered with alacrity by public figures and media pundits. History served as a box from which words and images could be pulled for citation.[81] Anything more appeared to be only of minority interest.

The definition of the frame of reference in American terms for American readers was understandable, but also part of an isolation of the American military experience and imagination that can be more generally misleading. In specific historical terms, this leads to mistaken assessments, such as that the Americans were largely responsible for the German defeat in 1918,[82] but there is a more general problem of the conflation of 'an American mythology of military prowess'[83] with an exaggerated sense of exceptionalism in American military history.[84] Both draw on the presentation of the American past by Hollywood.

Conclusions

Irrespective of the shrinking of real-time and imaginative distances, with all this can entail about the greater apparent proximity of threats, the strategic cultures of modern Western societies have been affected by social changes, including the individualism and collapse of deference that sapped support for conscription as a form, rationale, and ideology for the organization of the military resources of society. These changes have been linked to a reconceptualism of modernity that has important implications for military history. The critiques that have eroded the earlier triumphalist Western view of modernity, as the rise of mass participatory democracy, secular or at least tolerant cultures, nation-states, and an international order based on restraint, have implications for the assessment, at least in the West, of the legitimacy of war and military service. Most conflict, however, is not waged in the West, and, in part, this situation is linked to the inapplicability, if not, with the end of colonial empires, collapse, of the traditional Western concept of war as being essentially conflict between sovereign states. As the protocols of war, the conditions of engagement and the aftermaths of conflict become more diverse, if not nebulous, so do the complexities of assessing military history.

Notes

1 Commander Saunders to Liddell Hart, 4 Sept. 1964, LH, Liddell Hart papers, 4/35.
2 H.R. Winton and D.R. Mets (eds), *The Challenge of Change. Military Institutions and New Realities, 1918–1941* (Lawrence, Nebraska, 2000); D. French, *Raising Churchill's Army. The British Army and the War against Germany 1919–1945* (Oxford, 2000); R. Chickering and S. Förster (eds), *The Shadows of Total War: Europe, East Asia, and the United States, 1919–1939* (Cambridge, 2003).
3 A. Green, *Writing the Great War: Sir James Edmonds and the Official Histories, 1915–1948* (2003).
4 A.D. Harvey, 'The Russo–Japanese War 1904–5. Curtain Raiser for the Twentieth Century World Wars', *RUSI Journal*, 148 no. 6 (Dec. 2003), pp. 58–61.
5 D. Juniper, 'Gothas Over London', *RUSI Journal*, 148 no. 4 (Aug. 2003), p. 79.
6 LH, Montgomery-Massingberd papers, 9/5/7, p. 9.
7 LH, Foulkes papers, 2/18, 6/102–8, 112.
8 Sixth Annual Report of the Department, PRO. WO. 33/1128, p. 19.
9 P.S. Khoury, *Syria and the French Mandate. The Politics of Arab Nationalism 1920–1945* (Princeton, 1987), pp. 191–6.

10 LH, Liddell Hart papers, 7/1920/167.
11 *Quarterly Review* (July, 1929), quotes pp. 125–8, LH, Liddell Hart papers, 10.5/1929/1; A. Danchev, *Alchemist of War: The Life of Basil Liddell Hart* (1998); B.H. Reid, *Studies in British Military Thought: Debates with Fuller and Liddell Hart* (Lincoln, Nebraska, 1998).
12 S. Wilkinson, *The Rise of General Bonaparte* (Oxford, 1930), p. 146.
13 Ibid., p. 149.
14 E.C. Kiesling, *Arming Against Hitler: France and the Limits of Military Planning* (Lawrence, Kansas, 1996).
15 N. Maurice, *The Maurice Case* (1972).
16 LH, Maurice papers, 3/2/7, 3/5/95–101, 117.
17 LH, Montgomery-Massingberd papers, 10/6.
18 I. Ousby, *The Road to Verdun. France, Nationalism and the First World War* (2003).
19 Dill to Montgomery-Massingberd, 25 Sept. 1939, LH. Montgomery-Massingberd papers 10/14.
20 Churchill to Alexander, 14 Sept. 1943, LH, Alanbrooke papers, 6/2/18.
21 *Newsweek*, 13 Mar. 1944.
22 R. Higham (ed.), *The Writing of Official Military History* (Westport, Conn., 1999); J. Grey (ed.), *The Last Word? Essays on Official History in the United States and British Commonwealth* (Westport, 2003).
23 R.D. Adamcyzk and M.J. MacGregor (eds), *United States Army in World War II: Reader's Guide* (Washington, 1992).
24 J. Butler to Liddell Hart, 29 Aug., reply 5 Sept., 1947, LH, Liddell Hart papers, 4/28.
25 Molony to Liddell Hart, 19 Oct. 1966, LH, Liddell Hart papers, 4/30.
26 H.P. Willmott, *Pearl Harbor* (2001), pp. 142–57.
27 M. Blumenson, *The Battle of the Generals: The Untold Story of the Falaise Pocket: The Campaign that Should Have Won World War II* (New York, 1993).
28 BL. Add. 74806.
29 B. Bond and M. Taylor (eds), *The Battle of France and Flanders. Sixty Years On* (Barnsley, 2001), especially, S. Badsey, 'British High Command and the Reporting of the Campaign', pp. 139–60.
30 H. Shukman (ed.), *Stalin and the Soviet–Finnish War, 1939–1940* (2001).
31 K. Garside, 'An Intelligence Library in Germany', *Journal of Documentation*, 3 (1947), pp. 99–106.
32 B.R. Kroener, R.-D. Müller and H. Umbreit, *Germany and the Second World War. Volume V. Organisation and Mobilization of the German Sphere of Power. Part 2. Wartime administration, Economy, and Manpower Resources, 1942–1944–5* (Oxford, 2003).
33 I. Chang, *The Rape of Nanking: The Forgotten Holocaust of World War II* (1997); K. Honda, *The Nanjing Massacre: A Japanese Journalist Confronts Japan's National Shame* (Armonk, New York, 1999); S. Richter and W. Höpken, *Vergangenheit im Gesellschaftskonflikt: ein Historikerstreit in Japan* (Cologne, 2003).
34 John Rylands University Library, Manchester, papers of Major-General Eric Edward Dorman O'Gowan (formerly Dorman-Smith), GOW/1/2–3, 5–7, 11, 16–18, 20–3, 25–9, 36.

35 Liddell Hart to Howard, 20 Jan. 1964 and reply, LH, Liddell Hart papers, 4/27; legal correspondence, LH, North papers, III/2/5 a–h.
36 LH, North papers, III/3/1.
37 Dorman-Smith to Liddell Hart, no date, received 6 Apr. 1954, LH, Liddell Hart papers, 4/32.
38 North to David Hunt, 1 Mar. 1963, LH, North papers III/2/10b; J. Connell, *Auchinleck* (1959); R. Parkinson, *The Auk: Auchinleck, Victor at Alamein* (St Albans, 1977); P. Warner, *Auchinleck: The Lonely Soldier* (1981); J. Strawson, *El Alamein: Desert Victory* (1981); M. Carver, *Dilemmas of the Desert War: A New Look at the Libyan Campaign 1940–42* (1986); L. Graecen, *Chink: a Biography* (1989); N. Smart, 'Living in the Past: British Generals and the Second World War', *Archives*, 28 (2003), pp. 97–116.
39 Montgomery to John North, 9 Dec. 1962, LH, North papers, III/2/Mon. 3.
40 Playfair to Liddell Hart, 10 Feb., 11 Mar. 1954, Liddell Hart to Playfair, 12 Feb. 1954, LH, Liddell Hart papers, 4/32.
41 K. Macksey, *Guderian: Panzer General* (1975); R.L. Di Nardo, *Germany's Panzer Arm* (Westport, 1997).
42 B. Bond, 'Liddell Hart and the German Generals', *Military Affairs*, 41 no. 1 (1977), pp. 16–22; A. Searle, 'A Very Special Relationship: Basil Liddell Hart, Wehrmacht Generals and the Debate on West German Rearmament, 1945–1953', *War in History*, 5 (1998), pp. 327–57.
43 Butler to Liddell Hart, 28 Jan. 1952, and reply 29 Jan., LH, Liddell Hart papers, 4/28.
44 R.T. Paget, *Manstein: His Campaigns and His Trial* (1951).
45 Liddell Hart review in *Manchester Guardian* 26 Jan. 1954, Liddell Hart to Butler, 3 Nov. 1966, [Dorman-Smith], 'Further Comments on the Official History of the Mediterranean and Middle East, Vol I', 24 Aug. 1954, LH, Liddell Hart papers, 4/28, 4/32.
46 David Hunt to North, 15 Apr. 1963, LH, North papers, III/2/11a.
47 See section 'The Making of a British Legend' in P. Addison and J. Crang (eds), *The Burning Blue: A New History of the Battle of Britain* (2000).
48 *The Times*, 5, 8 Dec. 2003.
49 Director of the Imperial War Museum to the editor, Barrie Pitt, 26 Apr. 1966, LH, Liddell Hart papers, 3/183.
50 Patrick Cavendish to Liddell Hart, 13 Oct., reply 19 Oct., Norman Marshall to Liddell Hart, 24 Oct. 1966, LH, Liddell Hart papers, 3/183.
51 'History Makes History (and Money)', [no author], *Advertisers Weekly*, 7 Apr. 1967, pp. 32–4.
52 Liddell Hart to Barrie Pitt, 14 May 1967, LH, Liddell Hart papers, 3/183.
53 Stafford-Northcote, 28 June 1967, LH, Liddell Hart papers, 3/183.
54 B. Fischer, *Albania at War, 1939–1945* (1999), pp. 186–7.
55 Kenneth Garside to Liddell Hart, 19 June, Kenneth Parker (of Cassell and Co.) to Liddell Hart, 29 Aug. 1968, LH, Liddell Hart papers, 4/27.
56 A. Warren, *Singapore 1942*, p. xii. For conclusions, pp. 291–3.
57 See also W.F. Buckingham, *Arnhem 1944, A Reappraisal* (Stroud, 2002).
58 J.F.C. Fuller, *The Conduct of War 1789–1961* (1961), p. 102.
59 B. Alexander, *How Great Generals Win* (1993).

60 See, for example, D.M. Glantz, *Kharkov 1942: Anatomy of a Military Disaster Through Soviet Eyes* (Rockville, New York, 1998), *Barbarossa. Hitler's Invasion of Russia 1941* (Stroud, 2001), *The Battle for Leningrad, 1941–1944* (Lawrence, Kansas, 2002); Glantz and J.M. House, *The Battle of Kursk* (1999), and Glantz and H.S. Orenstein (eds), *The Battle of Kursk 1943. The Soviet General Staff Study* (1999) and *Belorussia 1944. The Soviet General Staff Study* (2001).

61 Glantz, *Zhukov's Greatest Disaster: The Red Army's Epic Disaster in Operation Mars* (Lawrence, Kansas, 1999).

62 K.-H. Frieser, 'Kursk – Turning Point of the War?', *RUSI Journal*, Vol. 148, no. 5 (Oct. 2003), p. 80.

63 H. Herr and K. Naumann (eds), *War of Extermination. The German Military in World War II 1941–1944* (2000); A. Searle, *Wehrmacht Generals, West German Society, and the Debate on Rearmament, 1949–1959* (Westport, 2003), p. 283; O. Bartov, *Germany's War and the Holocaust: Disputed Histories* (2003).

64 S.H. Newton (ed.), *Kursk. The German View. Eyewitness Reports of Operation Citadel by the German Commanders* (Cambridge, Mass., 2002), esp. pp. 405–6, 441.

65 P. Nobile (ed.), *Judgment at the Smithsonian* (New York, 1995); E.T. Linenthal and T. Engelhardt (eds), *History Wars: The 'Enola Gay' and Other Battles for the American Past* (New York, 1996); K. Bird and L. Lifschultz (eds), *Hiroshima's Shadow: Writings on the Denial of History and the Smithsonian Controversy* (Stony Creek, Conn., 1997).

66 E.S. Rosenberg, *A Date Which Will Live: Pearl Harbor in American Memory* (Durham, 2003); J.J. Stephan, *Hawaii Under the Rising Sun: Japan's Plans for Conquest After Pearl Harbor* (Honolulu, 2003).

67 I have benefited greatly from reading a paper by Wu Chunqiu, 'AMS and Chinese Official Military History: A Brief Introduction'.

68 See, for example, B. Morris, *Righteous Victims: A History of the Zionist–Arab Conflict, 1881–2001* (New York, 2001). For a critique of these revisionists, E. Karsh, *Fabricating Israeli History. The 'New Historians'* (2nd edn, 2000).

69 P.S. Khoury, *Syria and the French Mandate. The Politics of Arab Nationalism 1920–1945* (Princeton, 1987), pp. 616–17.

70 M. Albord, *L'Armée française et les Etats du Levant, 1936–1946* (Paris, 2000).

71 J. Goldrick and J.B. Hattendorf (eds), *Mahan is Not Enough: The Proceedings of a Conference on the Works of Sir Julian Corbett and Sir Herbert Richmond* (Newport, 1993); K. Neilson and E.J. Errington, *Navies and Global Defense: Theories and Strategy* (Westport, 1995); A. Dorman *et al.* (eds), *The Changing Face of Maritime Power* (1999).

72 R.F. Futrell, *Ideas, Concepts, Doctrine: A History of Basic Thinking in the United States Air Force, 1907–1964* (2nd edn, Maxwell Air Force Base, Alabama, 1989).

73 Anon. preface to T. Huber (ed.), *Compound Warfare. That Fatal Knot* (Fort Leavenworth, 2002), p. x.

74 V.R. Berghahn, *Militarism. The History of an International Debate 1861–1979* (Cambridge, 1984).

75 A. Richard, speech, *La Lettre*, 12 (Dec. 2000), p. 12; G.C. Kennedy and K. Neilson (eds), *Military Education: Past, Present, and Future* (Westport, Conn., 2002).

76 H.K. Ullman and J.P. Wade, *Rapid Dominance – A Force for All Seasons: Technologies and Systems for Achieving Shock and Awe* (1998).

77 W.A. Owens, 'Creating a U.S. Military Revolution', in T. Farrell and T. Terriff (eds), *The Sources of Military Change. Culture, Politics, Technology* (Boulder, 2002), pp. 205–19.

78 J.B. Hattendorf, 'The Uses of Maritime History in and for the Navy', *Naval War College Review*, 66 (2), spring (2003), pp. 13–14, 35.

79 *Warfare in Undeveloped Countries 1. Desert Warfare* (1954), p. iii.

80 H.A. Winters, *Battling the Elements. Weather and Terrain in the Conduct of War* (Baltimore, 1998), p. 4.

81 For a better-quality piece, M. Boot, 'The Lessons of a Quagmire', *New York Times*, 16 Nov. 2003.

82 J. Mosier, *The Myth of the Great War* (2001).

83 G. Chet, *Conquering the American Wilderness. The Triumph of European Warfare in the Colonial Northeast* (Amherst, 2003), p. 146.

84 J.M. Black, *America as a Military Power. From the American Revolution to the Civil War* (Westport, Conn., 2002).

Chapter 9

Conclusions

Perhaps only an absolute ruler, firmly in the saddle, can hope to maintain unswervingly the military ideal of the 'armed forces' objective, although even he will be wise to adjust it to the realities of the situation and to weigh well the prospects of fulfilling it. But the strategist who is the servant of a democratic government has less rein. Dependent on the support and confidence of his employers, he has to work within a narrower margin of time and cost than the 'absolute' strategist, and is more pressed for quick profits. Whatever the ultimate prospects he cannot afford to postpone dividends too long. Hence it may be necessary for him to swerve aside temporarily from his objective or at least to give it a new guise by changing his line of operations. Faced with these inevitable handicaps it is apt for us to ask whether military theory should not be more ready to reconcile its ideals with the inconvenient reality that its military effort rests on a popular foundation – that for the supply of men and munitions, and even for the chance of continuing the fight at all, it depends on the consent of the 'man in the street'. He who pays the piper calls the tune, and strategists might be better paid in kind if they attuned their strategy, so far as is rightly possible, to the popular ear.

Liddell Hart, 1929[1]

It is perfectly acceptable to look for modern parallels – I do it myself – but one must not get into the habit of thinking that the recent conflict in Iraq, for example, is the same as the Athenian invasion of Sicily with guns and aircraft.

John Lazenby, 2004[2]

The emphasis in this book has been on a cultural approach, but considering military history in this light is understood as a far from simple or easy process. 'Culture' is used somewhat loosely as an analytical term, but it provides a way to bring together organization and tasking, 'war and society', and the 'face of battle'. An emphasis on culture offers a more relativist mode of explanation in military history – by comparing the strategic and organizational cultures of competing states and their militaries, rather than by measuring them against an absolute or universal scale of technological capacity or proficiency. This approach needs to be open to the variety of military cultures across the world, past and present (and, planners note, future as well), and this openness means not only an interest in non-Western military history, but also an understanding of its variety and complexity – as well as the avoidance of misleading approaches to the respective capability of West and 'non-West', and to warfare between them.

This openness challenges model-based approaches that emphasize apparently scientific analysis, designed to demonstrate universal laws, and thus a limited and readily-defined group of subjects; and this challenge is made in a context in which the Western defence community is becoming more dependent on combat models.[3] Such an openness is also at variance with the pronounced dominance of Western assumptions, paradigms and examples in military history, and if this dominance is most obviously pronounced in popular military history, it can also be seen in its academic and military-educational counterparts. The net effect is seriously misleading, and this has become a greater problem with the projection of Western power elsewhere.

A cultural emphasis also ranges across time, and thus poses new questions for the explanation of change because the changes that have to be explained increase in number and complexity. Across both time and space, the cultural specificity of particular types of warfare emerges as a building block for analysis, displacing attention from a crudely functionalist account of capability, effectiveness and success, based on the appropriate use of resources and on the maximization of the latter. Culture, instead, focuses on perception and expectations, especially the perception of opportunities, of problems, of options, and of success. This poses more serious analytical problems than those of establishing the cause of victory, and also involves addressing issues and using sources that are more usually considered by scholars who do not specialize in military history. That, however, is a comment on the need to move beyond the established assumptions and methods of tactical and operational history in order to understand the reasons for success, and thus to evaluate capability.

The widespread failure to do so reflects a mismatch in the assessment of means and ends. Although military history is unique in that it deals with the organization and execution of violence in terms of the deliberate killing and wounding of numbers of human beings, that killing is intended as a means to an end rather than an end in itself. The assumptions that relate killing to the pursuit of ends vary, and these, again, are best understood in a cultural perspective.

The cultural approach also relates to the practice of military history: its content and themes. The history of military history is similarly focused on tactical and operational topics and methods, with a particular emphasis on material culture in the shape of weaponry. This provides an apparently global approach, and one that seemingly either overcomes cultural distinctions or defines them, in terms of clearly established rates of adaptation, in a readily-grasped fashion. The adaptation of weaponry was not, however, the key cultural element, but rather only seems so from the perspective of a modern Western approach that is focused on weaponry. Instead, it is necessary to consider less precisely defined cultural issues relating to goals, social contexts, and organizational ethos and practice. These do not so readily lend themselves, as the use of weaponry does, to cross-cultural analysis, but provide an appropriate background for understanding this usage.

A perception, if not ideology, of modern warfare in terms of a Revolution in Military Affairs based on futuristic weaponry and control systems lends itself to an approach to military history that encourages a focus on past shifts in capability and their consideration in terms of weaponry. This is an aspect of contemporary Western perceptions, although it is not new. In 1806, Robert Fulton, the American pioneer of submarine warfare, placed past, present and future change in a continuum driven by scientific progress: 'It does not require much depth of thought to trace that science by discovering gunpowder changed the whole art of war by land and sea; and by future combination may sweep military marines from the ocean',[4] a chilling challenge to the British naval position the year after the sweeping victory over a Franco–Spanish fleet at Trafalgar.

It is possible to adopt a functionalist approach toward Western confidence in advanced weaponry, one related to economic engagement with technology, the interest of the public in machines, and a socio-cultural, political and economic unwillingness to consider heavy casualties. There is also an apparently paradoxical contrast between a decline in bellicosity in Western (and Eastern) societies, as far as participation through military service is concerned, and a rise in the volume of work published on military history. The latter is very much for the spectator, and is not produced from societies in which a large percentage of the male population serves. Indeed, the volume of military history published can, at least in part at present, be seen as a counter-culture to dominant critical norms about war, although the character of these norms are themselves contentious. The notion that war was anachronistic led to a measure of optimism in the late 1980s and early 1990s, which owed much also to the ending of the Cold War and to talk of a 'new world order'. Even while Cold War tensions were still high, Volker Berghahn could write,

> the militarism discussed in the first four chapters of this volume is functional only to the type of transitional society with which historians and social scientists have, implicitly or explicitly associated it. It is dysfunctional to the high-technology societies of East and West after 1945, which are publicly committed to an improvement of living standards and possess total weapons.[5]

The apparently changing nature of norms about war indicates the extent to which war, and responses to it, are culturally constructed, both in terms of societies as a whole and with regard to particular militaries or, indeed, even units. The meanings of victory, defeat, loss, and suffering vary considerably, and so, with that, does the willingness to accept casualties. Indeed, there has been a major shift from the willingness to take heavy casualties, seen in the two World Wars, to the far greater sensitivity to casualties seen over the last three decades, at least in so far as Western societies and militaries are concerned: Iranian attitudes and tactics in the Iran–Iraq War of 1980–8 serve as a ready contrast, while the practice of suicide bombing and fighting, as seen with the Tamil Tigers and with Arab terrorists, is also very different to Western military doctrine and practice. The Western unwillingness to accept heavy casualties in part stems from the military's increasing tendency to make claims about how new technology will make weapons more precise and minimize both friendly and civilian casualties, as well as collateral damage. The public believes the claims and expects war to be less bloody, and is consequently less willing to accept casualties, which become someone's fault and failure. A presumption of Western superiority reinforces this.

Western sensitivity to casualties in the 1980s and 1990s did not prevent offensive operations. Although, in 1982, the British War Cabinet believed that domestic public opinion would not accept a thousand (British) fatalities, that did not prevent them from launching a successful reconquest of the Falkland Islands from the Argentinian invaders.

Similarly, in 1991 and 2003, despite the emphasis at all levels on force protection,[6] American-led coalitions dominated by American forces defeated Iraq, and American casualties after the conquest of Iraq in 2003–04 did not lead to the rapid end of the occupation, although they did sap public support for it.

In response to the claim that there has been a major shift in Western culture away from conflict, has come the rejoinder, very strongly in the USA after the terrorist attacks on September 2001, that people will respond to a crisis. Rather, however, than arguing that civic militarism can (or cannot) revive, or, indeed, as Victor Davis Hanson has done, that it is the defining characteristic of Western military culture,[7] it is more appropriate to note that the evidence for such militarism is limited and, even more, that its military effectiveness is likely to be problematic. The notion of fighting to the end in defence of home and hearth, as brilliantly portrayed by Winston Churchill in response to the threat of a German invasion of Britain in 1940, is not one that is helpful in light of the likely character of modern attacks on the West. Furthermore, modern Western states rely on a professionalized military. Their characteristics include not only an ability to use complex weaponry, but also a willingness to take orders, accept risk (and remain physically fit) that separates them from the bulk of civilian society. This contrast is increasing, and the rising rates of obesity today among the young in the USA, Britain and elsewhere are a good indication of a growing separation.

Underlining a major theme of this book, that military history serves a variety of purposes, including institutional education, academic scholarship, popular interest, commercial opportunity, and collective myth-making, and that these need to be considered when the subject is evaluated, the notion of civic militarism today plays a role in both analytical constructs and social heroics. The latter should be a target for academics, for myth-making in the field entails a falsification of war that is inaccurate, if not immoral.

All societies have sought to disseminate a benign account of their war-making in terms of purposes, methods, and results, but it is no accident that this is particularly pronounced in autocratic states. Thus, Napoleonic propaganda, such as the *Bulletins of the Grande Armée* published in the *Moniteur* newspaper, whose distortions led to the phrase 'to lie like a bulletin',[8] was employed to sustain a sense of military greatness that, in turn, encouraged fresh aggression; while the Nazis disseminated extraordinarily misleading accounts of campaigns.[9]

Propaganda responded both to social shifts and to new technology. The former, in the shape of a mass, educated public, whose consent, if not enthusiasm, appeared necessary to the war effort, created demands for an attractive presentation of conflicts, while new technology, in the form of newsreels, provided both opportunities for the dissemination of a particular impression and the problem of producing sufficient images. The latter focused on the impression of successful attack, and this very much influenced the visual sense, and thus collective memory, of World War Two, with a stress on advancing tanks and screaming dive-bombers. It is in terms of these Nazi images that the early campaigns of the war are recalled, not least because of the capture of Nazi newsreels by the Western allies. Had Germany won the war, then they would have been even more present as its historical record.

Even for the successful opening campaigns of the conflict, however, these images are misleading not least because they put a premium on tactical strength and not on the extent to which German victory was, at least in part, dependent on the mistaken operational decisions of their opponents. These included the over-extended Polish defensive perimeter, the British failure to use sea power effectively against the German forces invading Norway, and the French commitment of their reserve to active service on the extreme left of their front in 1940. More generally, newsreels foreshortened the process of war, making the strategic dimension operational, and the latter tactical, and focused overwhelmingly on images of attacking weapons. It thus made potent, for a new generation, traditional methods in the presentation of war, with all the problems they posed for those striving for an accurate account.

The destruction of the Nazi regime ensured that its accounts did not enter the historical mainstream, but the role of victors in manipulating the historical record was abundantly demonstrated with the Soviet Union. Success in the 'Great Patriotic War' served to validate the role of the Soviet state and the Communist Party, was also used to justify Soviet control over Eastern Europe, and provided a frame of reference for presenting the Cold War. The particular account of the 'Great Patriotic War' in terms of national endurance against aggression, leading, through great, centrally-directed effort, to victory, was a social myth of great potency. It also subordinated the individual or the group, in the shape of military leadership or unit fighting quality, to the collective. Military history of this type remains very important, both in states where the legitimacy of the current system rests on success in particular conflicts, for example China, and in those where the military continues prominent in the current political situation, such as Pakistan, Turkey and Myanmar. Most Latin-American and African states provide instances of both.

To switch from how dictatorial (and other) regimes controlled the reporting of past and current wars, to the way in which publication strategies mould our current perception of military history is, at once, to run together two very different situations, and yet also to be reminded of the extent to which the information presented is manufactured. The commercial reasons that dominate the concern of publishers are not abstract concepts or excuses for the publishers' own intellectual agenda, but products of a situation in which non-Western or lesser-known battles and wars sell badly. Thus publishers are affected by the role of television programmers, the press, and those who set school syllabuses and design degree courses. These non-Western subjects sell less well, as readers do not like to venture into the unknown, and through education and the media, they have not had exposure to this material in the same way that they have had to Western warfare. Publishers can be criticized as an aspect of this situation, or for not being adventurous enough in pushing the boundaries of their markets, but it would be unreasonable to suggest they could create markets on their own without some appetite to purchase being there in the first place, and there seems to be a wide-spread lack of interest in non-Western approaches.

The public, however, can only buy what publishers choose to publish. What sells is as much to do with how the books are marketed by publishers as it is to do with the subject and author; a best seller is made so by the marketing department telling the public that it is a best seller, and there is no doubt that many book buyers are influenced in this way. Some book buyers buy books simply because they are best sellers. It becomes a circular process that is aided when the author is perceived as being a celebrity. Publishers are disingenuous about publishability which is largely governed by perceived potential sales in the short term.

To give a personal view – and the historian is best advised not to shy away from this, nor to hide away as an oracular figure – I played a role in the *Cambridge Illustrated Atlas of Warfare* series. The first volume, *The Middle Ages 768–1487* (Cambridge, 1996), edited by Matthew Bennett and Nicholas Hooper, was misleadingly titled as it was in fact restricted to Europe, with an excursion into the Middle East for the Crusades: the New World, the Orient and Africa were all neglected. As author of the sequel, *Renaissance to Revolution 1492–1792* (Cambridge, 1996), I found it difficult to persuade the packager, Calmann and King, to include a spread on the Orient, as, for commercial reasons, the emphasis was to be on Britain and the USA.

Intervention by the packager could be more direct. For example, I produced a draft map of India in the eighteenth century designed to show the peripheral nature of the European impact in the first six decades of the century. The standard north–south map places a premium on European penetration, making the relationship between India and the surrounding seas apparently central: India appears primarily as a peninsula and eye-lines focus on Delhi from European coastal positions, such as Bombay, Calcutta, Goa, Madras and Pondicherry. The customary maps also indicate only European victories, such as those of forces of the British East India Company under Robert Clive at the battles of Arcot (1750) and Plassey (1757), and also organize space and time in terms of British annexations. In contrast, the major theme of my draft map was the contested succession to the Mughal empire by a number of expansionist powers: Britain, but also the Maratha Confederation, the Nizam of Hyderabad, the Nawabs of Bengal and the Carnatic, and the Sultan of Mysore. To do so, and to show the impact of invasions by Nadir Shah of Persia and the Afghans, I wanted a perspective in which India opens up from the Khyber Pass, with a central alignment thence via Delhi. As a result, the coastlines would appear more peripheral. I also wanted to include British defeats, for example at the hands of the Marathas in 1779 and of Mysore in 1780 and 1782, or the unsuccessful advance on Mysore in 1791. Again, however, marketing consideration militated against this map.

Another instructive instance comes from the discussions surrounding a book I was asked to edit by Thames and Hudson on 'the seventy great battles in history'. My first proposal for the seventy battles sought, I suggested, to 'avoid the standard hackneyed list', tried 'to avoid a Eurocentric approach' and attempted to give 'due weight to the different parts of the world'. It included, for example, Nehavend, Atlakh/Talas River, Ain Jalus, Nicopolis, Varna, Tunu, Chaldiran, Alcazarquivir, Tondibi, Jao Modo, Gulnabad, Karnal, Cesmé, Nezib, Nanjing (1853), and Gundet,[10] all of which, alas, fell by the wayside as the publisher, cogently, courteously and firmly, pushed forward commercial considerations, although the availability of information was also a factor in some other cases. For example, as David Graff pointed out with reference to the battle of Gaixia (Kai-Hsia in the Wade–Giles), 'Beyond the basics of who fought whom, where, and when, our main source (Ssu-ma Ch'ien's *Shih-chi*) offers little more than historical fiction: more a romance than a battle narrative'.[11] As a reminder of the crucial issue of author availability, Third Panipat was left out because the scholar approached was unwilling to tackle the subject. A similar problem in finding scholars willing to write on Asian naval history has affected the projected *Oxford Encyclopedia of Maritime History*, which has sought to address the problem of Eurocentricity in naval history.[12]

It would be instructive for readers to consider what they know about each, if not any, of the battles just named, all of which were important. Instead of these battles, a more familiar list of seventy was selected, although that raised issues of significance, for example in the case of Omdurman (1898). Fortunately, the publisher was far more enlightened than most: thus, for example, Liegnitz, the major Mongol victory in their invasion of Europe, was kept in, and an effort by one of the contributors to replace it by Bouvines rejected, with the publisher accepting my advice that it was instructive to include this clash between Western and non-Western forces. There would be no reason to believe that the same process of publisher choice did not affect other projects; for most, indeed, there is scant evidence that any efforts are even made to contest the dominance of Western concerns.[13]

More generally, aside from 'great battles', there is the problem of judging what is worthy of discussion in military history. For example, is it more important to emphasize Portuguese failures in Africa in the late seventeenth century – in the Zambezi Valley and at Mombasa – or Austrian successes in Hungary; if the latter, how much weight should then be put on Austrian reverses in the Austro–Ottoman war of 1737–9? How far are European gains in North America in the same period to be counterpointed by Dutch failure on Formosa (Taiwan), or Russian in the Amur Valley?

The lack of any obvious agenda for discussion is even more apparent prior to the period of Western power projection that began in the late fifteenth century. This projection, at least, provides a reason justifying focusing attention on the military history of states representing less than a quarter of the world's population; although, as Chapter six indicates, the effectiveness of this power projection is generally exaggerated. Prior to the late fifteenth century, however, it is unclear why medieval European (and it tends to be Western European) warfare deserves the relative attention it receives. Its impact on warfare elsewhere was limited, and, in scale, conflict in East and South Asia was more important. Even in the case of the Middle East, the focus on the Crusades is misleading, not least because the extent of their success in part rested on the more long-lasting struggles between Islamic powers that competed for dominance of the region. Furthermore, in terms of the dissemination of military technique, the impact of the Seljuk Turks and subsequently the Mongols was more significant than that of the Crusaders.

Similar points could be made about the Classical period: although the geographical span of Hellenistic and later Roman power was wider than that of medieval Western Europe, their consequence for the rest of the world was limited. As a result, their relative role in standard military histories is excessive: more a question of retelling what is readily synthesized than critically thinking about real significance.

What is discussed by military historians is important not only from the perspective of avoiding Eurocentricity but also because, from the cultural approach, comes the conclusion that not only the forms of war but even its fundamental principles were subject to variety and change. This challenges the basic assumption of sameness or at least similarity, hitherto underlying military history, an assumption that permitted the ready reading from both general arguments and particular case-studies to other periods and episodes; an intellectually lazy inference that encouraged a focus on what was well-known and on the global 'lessons' it was supposed to teach. This assumption also condoned the lack of any treatment of large periods of time (especially the Middle Ages) and of much of the world, particularly sub-Saharan Africa, and East and South East Asia.[14] Remove, however, the sense that military history is a matter of finding common themes or 'lessons' between Salamis and Trafalgar, or Alexander the Great and Wellington, and you are left with a more challenging subject, one, indeed, that may tell you something about war.

The contested role of the past in military history is not an abstract issue, particularly in crises when supposed lessons from the past are deployed in support of particular policy options, not least in order to elicit and encourage public support. The role of analysis was not restricted to military history. Thus, Munich and appeasement played a role in the mental furniture of American and British policy-makers: in the Vietnam War, the Suez crisis and at the time of the Falkland crisis.[15] Equally, the politics of the present have affected military historians. Saburo Ienaga's opposition to American policy in the Vietnam War and, specifically, to Japanese support for America, played its role in his hostile portrayal of Japanese policy in the 1930s in *The Pacific War, 1931–1945: A Critical Perspective on Japan's Role in World War II* (1968, English translation 1978).

The military aspects of past lessons often played a lesser role than their political dimension, but were abundantly seen during the build-up to the attack on Iraq in 2003, as the merits of expeditionary warfare were widely canvassed and historians took public positions. In Britain, for example, John Keegan was an active supporter of action, while Correlli Barnett was not: the controversy entailed the use of historical examples.

Thus, in a letter in the *Daily Telegraph* on 29 January 2003, Barnett included the following:

> I am sorry that Sir John Keegan has joined those who rubbish as an 'appeaser' anyone who believes that an American-led war on Iraq would be unjustified and potentially disastrous in its wider political consequences . . . I am on record as a harsh critic of Chamberlain's attempt to 'appease' Hitler in the 1930s and as a convinced supporter of the campaign to re-take the Falkland Islands.

The same issue contained a letter from Nigel Nicolson criticizing Keegan's analogy and declaring 'the true comparison is with the Suez crisis of 1956 and the Cold War'. In *The Times* of 29 July 2002, retired Field Marshal Lord Bramall drew attention to the contrast between achieving military objectives and securing outcomes, citing a

> remark by a notably 'hawkish' General Gerald Templar who when, during the Suez crisis (1956) Britain was planning a massive invasion of Egypt through Alexandria, said something to the effect of: 'Of course we can get to Cairo but what I want to know is, what the bloody hell do we do when we get there?'.

The direct applicability of past examples is unclear: in 1798 the uprising in Cairo against the policies of the French occupying force was quickly suppressed by the ruthless use of artillery,[16] as was that in Damascus in 1926, but the relevance of that to policy in Baghdad in 2003–4 was uncertain, not least because, to be understood, each instance needs to be considered in its context – which makes comparison difficult.

The use of the past in 2003, in the shape of both comment pieces and correspondence, was instructive, although it is far from clear that there was any influence on policy in either Britain or the USA. When Blair or Bush offered Churchillian echoes, it was presumably not the Churchill of Gallipoli and the Russian Civil War that they had in mind. They were providing history as answers, not the history as questions offered by scholars alive to the difficulties and dangers of predicting outcomes.[17]

Far from military historians influencing policies and responses, it was rather the crisis that affected military history, both in providing opportunities for the expression of views and in encouraging a particular focus on Western–Islamic relations. The Afghanistan conflict in 2001 had already introduced much of the newspaper-reading public to the concepts of asymmetrical warfare and the Revolution in Military

Affairs. This public context of discussion is also important to the memorialization of military events, not least because it ensures that academic voices are but some among many, and far from the most heeded. Military history is only an aspect of the discussion of war, and is demotic to an extent that is unusual among branches of history.

The wider significance of wars and warfare is rarely considered in such works. A great master of the subject, Napoleon, offered an instructive context when, in 1816, he told Lieutenant-Colonel Wilks, Governor of the island of St Helena where he was being held prisoner,

> your [British] coal gives you an advantage we cannot possess in France. But the high price of all articles of prime necessity is a great disadvantage in the export of your manufactures . . . your manu-facturers are emigrating fast to America . . . In a century or perhaps half a century more: it will give a new character to the affairs of the world. It has thriven upon our follies.

Napoleon claimed that, whatever Britain had done, the American colonies would have become independent, and he asked Wilks, who had served there, if India would follow.[18] Just as the nature of military activity was shaped by political goals, cultural pressures and socio-economic developments, so they were challenged and affected by the requirements of effective military action. In drawing links between the stirrup and the feudal system, small arms and the emergence of the nation-state, and the emergence of terrorism as a major military challenge and the future relationship of the individual to the state, it is necessary, however, to avoid offering mechanistic causal relationships. War had an enormous impact on the historical process, but as Napoleon noted, it was not alone at work. Throughout, an understanding of war requires contextualization. Military history exists in a context of other histories.

The 'pattern syndrome' is seductive when considering impact, contextualization and development. There is always a desire to seek patterns in order to explain the world. Unfortunately such patterns are often illusory, but there is resistance to the idea that chaos and disorder are more prevalent than order. As far as military historians are concerned, it is a question of imposing orders as well as order on the chaos. As far as participants in the events in question were concerned, it was about trying to impose order on the events as they unfolded, irrespective of planning or desired outcome. Whether the emphasis is on chaos or on the variety stressed throughout this book, it is clear that

244 Rethinking military history

there are fundamental challenges to mono-causal, synoptic accounts. It is also readily apparent that there are many topics still to tackle and much room for debate. Far from military history being 'done', anachronistic or undesirable, it is an important and varied subject, one also worthy of study as a branch of intellectual history.

Notes

1 *Quarterly Review* (July, 1929), p. 127, LH, Liddell Hart papers, 10.5/1929/1.
2 J.F. Lazenby, *The Pelopennesian War. A Military Study* (2004), pp. xiii–xiv.
3 H. Löfstedt, 'Duels of Systems and Forces' in B. Boob-Bavnbek and J. Høyrup (eds), *Mathematics and War* (Basel, 2003), p. 252.
4 Fulton to Lord Grenville, 2 Sept. 1806, BL. Add. 71593 fol. 134.
5 V. Berghahn, *Militarism: the History of an International Debate, 1861–1979* (Cambridge, 1984), p. 117. The book was published in 1981. The fifth chapter was on the military–industrial complex.
6 M. Codner, 'An Initial Assessment of the Combat Phase', in J. Eyal (ed.), *War in Iraq. Combat and Consequence* (2003), p. 20.
7 V.D. Hanson, *Carnage and Culture: Landmark Battles in the Rise of Western Power* (New York, 2002).
8 J.D. Markham, *Imperial Glory. The Bulletins of Napoleon's Grande Armée* (2002); R.B. Holtman, *Napoleonic Propaganda* (Baton Rouge, 1950).
9 J.W. Baird, 'The Myth of Stalingrad', *Journal of Contemporary History*, 4 (1969), pp. 187–204.
10 J. Black to Colin Ridler, 10 Feb. 2003, Black mss.
11 Graff to Ridler, 9 Apr. 2003, e-mail, printed copy in Black mss.
12 J. Hattendorf to J. Black, 6 Jan. 2004, Black mss.
13 See P.K. Davis, *100 Decisive Battles. From Ancient Times to the Present* (Santa Barbara, 1999); S. Förster, M. Pöhlmann and D. Walter (eds), *Schlachten der Weltgeschichte. Von Salamis bis Sinai* (Munich, 2001).
14 For a different approach, see J. Black, *War. An Illustrated World History* (Stroud, 2003).
15 J. Record, *Making War, Thinking History. Munich, Vietnam and Presidential Uses of Force from Korea to Kosovo* (Annapolis, 2002).
16 R.L. Tignor (ed.), *Napoleon in Egypt* (Princeton, 1993), p. 9.
17 See for example T. Dodge, 'Cake Walk, Coup or Urban Warfare: the Battle for Iraq', and F.A. Jabar 'The Iraqi Army and Anti-Army: Some Reflections on the Role of the Military', in Dodge and S. Simon (eds), *Iraq at the Crossroads: State and Society in the Shadow of Regime Change* (Oxford, Jan. 2003), pp. 59–75, 127.
18 BL. Add. 57315 fol. 39.

Selected bibliography

All books cited are published in London unless otherwise indicated.

As the very essence of any work on rethinking military history is that it has to stay abreast of recent work, it is important to draw attention to the specialist journals, both for their articles and for the debate contained in their review articles and reviews. The *Journal of Military History* is particularly important for the American dimension, and *War in History* and the *RUSI* [Royal United Services Institute] *Journal* for British work. Among encyclopedias, the *Reader's Guide to Military History* (2001) edited by Charles Messenger is the most useful. In offering a brief list of books here, there is no point reprinting the titles of the works cited in the Notes to each chapter of this book. Work on the history of war can be approached via J.M. Black, *War and the World 1450–2000* (New Haven, 1998), Black (ed.), *War in the Modern World Since 1815* (2003), and H.P. Willmott, *When Men Lost Faith in Reason. Reflections on War and Society in the Twentieth Century* (Westport, 2002). On technology see W.H. McNeill, *The Pursuit of Power: Technology, Armed Force and Society since AD 1000* (1983) and A. Crosby, *Throwing Fire: Projectile Technology through History* (Cambridge, 2002). For more theoretical discussions of military change, Theo Farrell and Terry Terriff (eds), *The Sources of Military Change. Culture, Politics, Technology* (2002) and Colin Gray, *Strategy for Chaos. Revolutions in Military Affairs and The Evidence of History* (2002). One of the best books on the presentation of war is Brian Bond's *The Unquiet Western Front. Britain's Role in Literature and History* (Cambridge, 2002).

Classic texts of military history include Sun Tzu *The Art of War*, edited by Ralph Sawyer (Boulder, 1994), Carl von Clausewitz, *On War*, edited by Michael Howard and Peter Paret (Princeton, 1976), Alfred Thayer Mahan, *The Influence of Sea Power upon History, 1660–1783* (1890), and Julian Corbett, *Some Principles of Maritime Strategy*, edited by Eric Grove (1986). For the cultural turn, C. Cameron, *American Samurai: Myth, Imagination, and the Conduct of Battle in the First Marine Division, 1941–1951* (New York, 1994) and L. Smith, *Between Mutiny and Obedience: The Case of the French Fifth Infantry Division During World War I* (Princeton, 1994). On the naval dimension

J.B. Hattendorf (ed.), *Ubi Sumus? The State of Naval and Maritime History* (Newport, 1994), and (ed.), *Doing Naval History. Essays Toward Improvement* (Newport, 1995), J. Goldrick and Hattendorf (eds), *Mahan is Not Enough* (Newport, 1993), S. Rose, *Medieval Naval Warfare, 1000–1500* (2001), J. Glete, *Warfare at Sea, 1500–1650* (1999), R. Harding, *Seapower and Naval Warfare, 1650–1830* (1999), L. Sondhaus, *Naval Warfare, 1815–1914* (2000), G.W. Baer, *One Hundred Years of Sea Power. The U.S. Navy, 1890–1990* (1993), and R. Spector, *At War, At Sea. Sailors and Naval Warfare in the Twentieth Century* (2001). On air warfare, M.S. Sherry, *The Rise of American Air Power: the Creation of Armageddon* (New Haven, 1987) and J. Buckley, *Air Power in the Age of Total War* (1998).

Warfare in Asia can be approached through T.J. Barfield, *The Perilous Frontier: Nomadic Empires and China* (Oxford, 1989), N. Di Cosmo (ed.), *Warfare in Inner Asian History, 500–1800* (Leiden, 2002), B.A. Elleman, *Modern Chinese Warfare, 1795–1989* (2001), J. Gommans, *Mughal Warfare* (2002), D.A. Graff, *Medieval Chinese Warfare, 300–900* (2001), and Graff and R. Higham (eds), *A Military History of China* (2002). Valuable introductory works on Africa include J.K. Thornton, *Warfare in Atlantic Africa, 1500–1800* (1999), B. Vandervort, *Wars of Imperial Conquest in Africa, 1830–1914* (1998), and A. Clayton, *Frontiersmen. Warfare in Africa Since 1950* (1998). Important work on medieval warfare can be approached through J. France, *Western Warfare in the Age of the Crusades, 1000–1300* (1999), J. Haldon, *Warfare, State and Society in the Byzantine World 560–1204* (1999) and H. Kennedy, *The Armies of the Caliphs. Military and Society in the Early Islamic State* (2001); and, for the early modern period, J. Glete, *War and the State in Early Modern Europe* (2001), R. Murphey, *Ottoman Warfare, 1815–1914* (2000), A. Starkey, *European and Native American Warfare 1675–1815* (1998) and H.M. Ward, *The War of Independence and the Transformation of American Society* (1999). For the last two hundred years, I.F. Beckett, *Modern Insurgencies and Counter-Insurgencies* (2001), B. Bond, *The Pursuit of Victory: From Napoleon to Saddam Hussein* (Oxford, 1996), A. Bregman, *Israel's Wars, 1947–1993* (2000), M. Howard, *The First World War* (Oxford, 2002), R. Reese, *The Soviet Military Experience* (1999), G. Rothenberg, *The Napoleonic Wars* (1999), S. Sandler, *The Korean War* (1999), S. Tucker, *Vietnam* (1998), and G. Wawro, *Warfare and Society in Europe, 1792–1914* (2000).

Index